Entrepreneurs and Democracy

T0328785

What legitimizes power within a corporation? This question is of concern to the millions of citizens whose lives depend upon the fate of business corporations. The rules, institutions, and practices of corporate governance define the limits of the power to direct, and determine under what conditions this power is acceptable.

Effective corporate governance has long been defined in terms of economic performance. More recent studies have focused on philosophical, political, and historical analyses. *Entrepreneurs and Democracy* unites these strands of inquiry – the legitimacy of power, the evolution of multiple forms of governance, and the economics of performance – and proposes a framework for future study. It explores the opposing tensions of entrepreneurial force and social fragmentation that form the basis of legitimate corporate governance in modern societies. In doing so, it identifies a common logic that links both the democratization of corporate governance and the growth of economic performance.

PIERRE-YVES GOMEZ is Full Professor of Strategic Management at EM Lyon and Director of the French Corporate Governance Institute (IFGE, Lyon). He has published several award-winning books in French and English, including *Trust, Firm and Society* (1997) and, with Harry Korine, *The Leap to Globalization* (2002).

HARRY KORINE is Teaching Fellow in Strategic and International Management at the London Business School and Senior Research Fellow at the French Corporate Governance Institute (IFGE, Lyon). In addition to his academic and consulting activities, he is the Chairman of the Board of Forma Futura Invest AG, an independent asset management firm based in Zurich.

Business, Value Creation, and Society

Series editors
R. Edward Freeman, *University of Virginia*
Stuart L. Hart, *Cornell University* and *University of North Carolina*
David Wheeler, *Dalhousie University, Halifax*

The purpose of this innovative series is to examine, from an international standpoint, the interaction of business and capitalism with society. In the 21st Century it is more important than ever that business and capitalism come to be seen as social institutions that have a great impact on the welfare of human society around the world. Issues such as globalization, environmentalism, information technology, the triumph of liberalism, corporate governance, and business ethics all have the potential to have major effects on our current models of the corporation and the methods by which value is created, distributed, and sustained among all stakeholders – customers, suppliers, employees, communities, and financiers.

Published titles:

Fort *Business, Integrity & Peace*

Forthcoming titles:

Crane, Moon & Matten *Corporations and Citizenship*
Painter-Morland *Business Ethics as Practice*
Rivera *Business and Public Policy*
Doh & Yaziji *Corporate Governance, NGOs and Corporations*

Entrepreneurs and Democracy

A Political Theory of Corporate Governance

PIERRE-YVES GOMEZ
and
HARRY KORINE

CAMBRIDGE
UNIVERSITY PRESS

CAMBRIDGE UNIVERSITY PRESS
Cambridge, New York, Melbourne, Madrid, Cape Town, Singapore,
São Paulo, Delhi, Dubai, Tokyo, Mexico City

Cambridge University Press
The Edinburgh Building, Cambridge CB2 8RU, UK

Published in the United States of America by Cambridge University Press, New York

www.cambridge.org
Information on this title: www.cambridge.org/9780521169608

First published 2008
Reprinted 2009
First paperback edition 2010

A catalogue record for this publication is available from the British Library

Library of Congress Cataloguing in Publication data
Gomez, Pierre-Yves.
Entrepreneurs and democracy: a political theory of corporate governance /
Pierre-Yves Gomez, Harry Korine.
  p. cm.
ISBN 978-0-521-85638-6
1. Corporate governance. 2. Entrepreneurship. 3. Industrial policy.
1. Korine, Harry, 1962– 11. Title.
HD2741.G657 2008
338´.04–dc22
2007052889

ISBN 978-0-521-85638-6 Hardback
ISBN 978-0-521-16960-8 Paperback

Contents

Figures and tables

Figures

Tables

Foreword

Entrepreneurs and Democracy is an important and timely book. For scholars of corporate governance, the book establishes a truly comprehensive political and social context for current debates on the roles and responsibilities of investors and owners in the modern corporation. And for practitioners, *Entrepreneurs and Democracy* is a highly readable guide to the historical and philosophical antecedents of some of the dilemmas they face in reconciling the demands of diverse and increasingly fragmented groups of shareholders. For example: what duty is owed to investors who do not care about the long-term prospects of the firm and wish merely to profit from the short-term upsides (or downsides) available to them through rapid changes in stock market valuations?

Authors Gomez and Korine are suitably modest in asserting their purpose as simply to create a common space for historians, economists and political philosophers 'to talk to each other'. In fact they embrace a breathtaking array of sources, ranging from Hobbes, Locke and Smith to Tocqueville, Schumpeter and Keynes, to create a strong theoretical basis for their central assertion that democracy is vital to the effective functioning of the capitalist enterprise because 'democracy imposes the competition of markets on the entrepreneur'.

With their arguments firmly rooted in the domain of liberal political philosophy, Gomez and Korine advance an elegant critique of the contradictions inherent in purely economic approaches to corporate governance. Interestingly they do this without recourse to the well-established arguments of stakeholder theorists who note that the assertion of shareholder versus stakeholder rights is a distraction and a false dichotomy, if not simply redundant. Instead Gomez and Korine argue that the rights of disparate and fragmented investors and owners have never been especially important to strategic decision-making in firms – especially compared with the hegemonic influence of the family owner-entrepreneurs and technocrats who dominated corporate boardrooms and executive suites for the first two hundred years of industrial capitalism.

The authors describe the legitimacy and credibility of the entrepreneur as a vital force in establishing the confidence of investors. And they note the historic importance of the establishment of property rights and the ability to pursue profit to the notion of liberty. But Gomez and Korine describe the emergence of shareholder activism – the attempt to assert the rights of large numbers of small investors and their fund managers – as essentially a late twentieth-century phenomenon, accelerated by the somewhat ideological arguments of neoliberal economists.

Of course any attempt to assert the supremacy of the rights of non-homogeneous shareholders of the firm as though they were a uniform entity is ultimately doomed to failure because not all investors or owners want the same thing. We have only to think about the radically different interests of mutual funds, hedge funds and social investors to understand the point. Depending on orientation, shareowners may hope for short-term gains *or losses* in share price; dividend policy may be vital or irrelevant to them; and mode of engagement of the owners (regardless of size of shareholding) may range from abject failure even to vote on resolutions to physical disruption of the annual general meeting.

Add to these observations the breaking down of traditional barriers between owners, investors, managers and workers, the emergence of civil society groups and the declining relevance of labour unions (historically the main counter to the wilder excesses of industrial capitalism) and we see that simplistic advocacy of shareholder rights in a world of global capital markets is highly problematic. In the last section of the book the authors update the conclusions of Berle and Means' systematic economic analysis in *The Modern Corporation* to take account of these institutional phenomena and the growing democratization of capital. They follow this with a very respectful *coup de grâce* to the 'Pure Economic Model' of corporate governance: 'Paradoxically, the clarity of PEM allows us to see that all of the critiques of the model have a common route: what is underestimated is the degree to which property ownership is fragmented.'

Clearly, liberal democracy demands an effective response to the problem of disenfranchizement of investors and owners, whether that phenomenon is associated with agency issues or the absence of effective information exchange, exacerbated by technological or transaction cost issues. As Gomez and Korine explain, we are too early in the game of shareholder democracy and indeed theories of corporate governance to predict exactly how things will evolve. But surely corporate governance practices will need to change to embrace the increasingly powerful democratic influences that now permeate the capitalist project.

David Wheeler
Dean of Management
Dalhousie University
Halifax
Nova Scotia

Introduction

'*What* gives the right to direct a corporation?' This question is at the heart of corporate governance. It is also of central concern to the millions of citizens whose lives depend upon the fate of business corporations. The rules, institutions, and practices of corporate governance define the limits of the power to direct and determine under what conditions this power is acceptable. In our sense, to direct means to exercise an entrepreneurial force that impacts the entire corporation, giving it an orientation and laying the foundations for its long-term survival. The legitimacy of exercising this force in the name of the corporation is not automatically assured, but is rather a subject of rules and limits. Corporate governance is the definition of these constraints.

As befits a subject with implications for many spheres of human activity, the study of corporate governance draws on a wide variety of disciplines. In spite of, or perhaps precisely because of its broad grounding, the field, in our view, lacks a coherent, holistic vision that would make it possible to pull together the different strands of inquiry. The more research is done, the stronger this impression becomes, because the three principal disciplinary axes along which research is moving – economics, history, and political philosophy – do not speak to each other and are not compatible in terms of approach and methodology.

However erroneously, the primary voice in the study of corporate governance is often considered, today, to be economics, more particularly financial economics. The contemporary articulation of the 'governance problem' in economics emerges in the 1970s, with the reactivation of agency theory and renewed attention to property rights. Neo-liberal scholars[1] refocus research on the right to direct from the

---

[1] In this book, the terms 'liberal' and its corollaries (neo-liberal; anti-liberal) refer to a definition that is consistent with how the terms are understood in the history of thought: 'liberalism is distinguished by the importance it attaches to the civil and political rights of individuals. Liberals demand a substantial realm of personal freedom ... which the state should not intrude upon, except to protect

point of view of the divergence of individual economic interests, point-ing out that the interests of management are naturally opposed to the interests of shareholders. After decades of very widespread faith in managerialism, that is to say an a priori faith in management as disin-terested, technocratic experts in the service of the corporation, this represents a complete reversal of point of view; now, management is also considered to be made up of rational, self-interested individuals, and it is recognized that management self-interest can conflict with the interests of the shareholders. The theory which is inspired by neo-liberalism defines corporate governance as a game of opposing forces to orient the corporation, between those who hold power and those who hold information, an agency problem which needs to be regulated by the institutions of the corporation and, more generally, by the financial markets. This is why financial economics reduces corporate governance to the financial dimension and economic calculation plays such a critical role. If financial markets are efficient and the price of the share accurately reflects the *performance* of the corporation, then shareholders are effectively in control. In order to answer the question 'What gives the right to direct a corporation?' contemporary econom-ics focuses on financial performance, as verified and acted upon by the shareholders.

Agency theory holds pride of place in corporate governance. Thousands of articles and books have been published on this theore-tical basis, demonstrating in considerable detail how the study of the relationship between principal and agent sheds light on and can, in some but not all cases, resolve the conflict of forces between manage-ment and shareholders. Since agency relationships can be found almost everywhere, this focus has led to an ever greater array of different, partial solutions, with no end in sight. Nonetheless, the lack of realism that arises from the dogmatic insistence on efficient financial markets upon which the entire theoretical edifice is based has led to vigorous questioning, both from inside and from outside of economics. Criticism

others from harm; today, particularly after the decline of communism, it is the dominant ideology in many parts of the world' (Ted Honderich (ed.), *Oxford Companion to Philosophy*, Oxford: Oxford University Press, 1995, p. 483). As we will show, economic liberalism is a dimension of the liberal ideology (see also M. Blaug, *The History of Economic Thought*, Aldershot: Edward Elgar, 1990). We will not, in this book, distinguish between the different branches of liberal thought – liberalism, libertarianism, etc. For our purposes liberalism is to be considered as the ideological reference of modern Western society and capitalism.

has also arisen based on the fact that the vast majority of corporations are not quoted on the financial markets and are of necessity ignored by agency theory. Other theoretical currents have been thrown into the breach more recently to address these concerns – for example, stakeholder theory[2] that proposes a redefinition of the function of management, or resource based assessments that seek to understand corporate governance in terms of an optimal allocation of competence.[3] These well-articulated criticisms aside, there is no way around acknowledging that agency theory is the basis for economic reflection on corporate governance – including critical reflection – and that this approach has produced an important and sophisticated corpus of analysis that influences the whole range of contemporary thought in corporate governance.

In parallel with economics, the field of history has also built up a body of research in corporate governance. Work in business history and economic history focuses on understanding how the governance of the corporation has evolved over time. More often than not, the research is built around the detailed analysis of a single country or the comparison of national singularities.[4] National studies of this type show how specific cultural, economic, and political characteristics have shaped the path followed in the development of corporate governance. Static analyses typically based on the shareholding structure have helped consolidate the partial results of country specific longitudinal work, providing evidence of several major governance types: the Anglo-Saxon, the Rhine River (France/Germany), or the Japanese, etc. Historical research has sought to show how, since the origins of capitalism, each country has produced its own institutions and rules, creating systems of corporate governance that are in line with systems of political

---

[2] See E. Freeman, *Strategic Management: A Stakeholder Approach*, Marshfield, MA: Pitman Press, 1983; E. Freeman and D. Reed, 'Stockholders and stakeholders: a new perspective on corporate governance', *California Management Review* 25 (3) (1983), 88–106; T. Donaldson and L. Preston, 'A stakeholder theory of the corporation: concepts, evidence, and implications', *Academy of Management Review* 20 (1) (1995), 65–91.

[3] For a recent and complete overview, M. Huse, *Boards, Governance and Value Creation: The Human Side of Corporate Governance*, Cambridge: Cambridge University Press, 2006.

[4] For examples, M. J. Roe, *Strong Managers, Weak Owners: The Political Roots of American Corporate Finance*, Princeton, NJ: Princeton University Press, 1994; M. Levy-Leboyer, 'Le patronat a-t-il échappé à la loi des trois générations?', *Le Mouvement Social* 132 (1985), 3–7; A. Chandler, *Scale and Scope: The Dynamics of Industrial Capitalism*, Cambridge, MA: Harvard University Press, 1990.

governance in each country: laws of incorporation, rules and rights of business, stock market and trading regulation, etc.[5] The great question faced by historical research concerns the influence of globalization – does globalization lead to the convergence of all the different national types towards one global interpretation of corporate governance, or, on the contrary, is globalization compatible with multiple types of governance, either region or ownership specific (i.e. for family owned, for cooperatives, for public companies, etc.)? Without a more general theory to understand whether or not all societies are converging – after all, corporate governance is just one dimension of society – the questions posed by globalization cannot be definitely answered. Such a general theory of societal convergence does not yet exist.

The historical approach to the study of corporate governance contrasts distinctively with the austere purity of financial economic theory. Whereas economics reduces corporate governance to rational calculation and a principal agent problem, history describes a multiplicity of particular cases, almost as many as there are different national cultures. Each country, even each region, if it is of sufficient cultural differentiation, can give rise to its own type of governance. Of course, at the highest level of analysis, all of these different interpretations revolve around shareholders, management, and entrepreneurs. However, local history has such a determining influence on how the institutions of corporate governance are understood and interpreted, that each case seems special. In contrast to the extreme homogenization proposed by economic theory, the historical approach offers extreme heterogeneity. The historical approach has the great advantage of being able to demonstrate that corporate governance is closely tied to the *evolution* of mentalities and interpretations, indeed that corporate governance is anchored in the societies in which it is exercised and therefore cannot be studied in isolation. For the historian, corporate governance is often idiosyncratic and in continuous evolution. In answer to the question 'What gives the right to direct?', history points to the multiple paths whereby different interpretations of corporate governance become locally established.

---

[5] D. North, *Institutions, Institutional Change, and Economic Performance*, Cambridge: Cambridge University Press, 1990; M. Aoki, *Towards a Comparative Institutional Analysis*, Cambridge, MA: MIT Press, 2001; P. Frentrop, *A History of Corporate Governance*, Amsterdam: Deminor, 2003.

From its vantage point, and since the beginnings of capitalism, political philosophy has also been interested in the question 'What gives the right to direct?' Liberal political philosophy, in particular, has sought to establish the principles upon which a society composed of free individuals can be based: at its core, liberal thought has asked how it is possible to build a stable political organization on the autonomy of its constituent members. The corporation and its governance were not left out of this inquiry; rather the corporation has itself been the subject of extensive liberal reflection, in the specific context of the productive organization. It was not necessary to wait until the term 'corporate governance' was coined, for philosophers interested in politics and law to discuss the nature of power exercised in the corporation and inquire about the source of the authority to direct. The preoccupation of philosophers in the field of corporate governance was and is the *legitimacy* of power. From the earliest days of liberal thinking, philosophy had to develop a theory of legitimate private entrepreneurial action that was legally and politically compatible with the acceptable exercise of power over others. The notion of private property was advanced as the basis for sovereignty over things and hence for the freedom to act. This foundational principle of the modern liberal society was then extended to the corporation, which, when looked at in terms of the social capital it represents, could be considered to be an object of private property.

Of course, the extension of the notion of private property ownership to an *organization* has given rise to great deal of criticism and debate. It is one thing to own the physical objects, such as machines or buildings, quite another to affirm that the person who owns the objects *therefore* has the authority to direct the organization, a social space made up of free individuals. Basing corporate governance on private property ownership has met two principal objections, vigorously articulated over the last two centuries. The first objection concerns the relationship between the individual interest of property owners and the collective interest of society. The corporation concentrates the means of production, often at a very large scale, and the effects of this concentration are felt, more generally, far beyond the sphere of the owner: how to make sure that society does not suffer from self-interested profit seeking on the part of owners. The second major objection to basing corporate governance on private property has focused on the nature of this property. What, really, is the owner the owner of? If a corporation concentrates machines and tools under one (legal) roof, it also mobilizes the competences, experiences, and networks of people; it relies on collective infrastructure (education, justice, etc.) and consumes resources that may or may not be renewable and thus diminishes the potential for action of future generations. These important criticisms have given rise to a great deal of debate, but they have not managed to break the ideological dominance of the liberal political project upon which modern Western societies are based. Still today – perhaps even more so than in the past – reflections on corporate governance start with the liberal model.

In sum, the question '*What* gives the right to direct a corporation?' is answered by economics from the point of view of *performance*, by history from the point of view of the *evolution* of governance, and by liberal political philosophy from the point of view of the foundations of *legitimacy*. However, the lack of bridges between the different disciplines, a state of affairs encouraged by narrow specialization, makes it difficult to keep the essential question(s) of corporate governance in focus.[6] What with corporate governance also being the subject of a considerable amount of descriptive work detailing its institutions (boards, board committees, general meetings, etc.) and its practices (selection of board members, remuneration of management, role of employee shareholders, etc.), the field is starting to look like a giant puzzle, with the pieces in clear view, but the whole only vaguely discernible. And yet, both the researcher and the practitioner sense that there must be a way of pulling together the different approaches. Indeed, how can one deny that the performance, the evolution, and the legitimacy of corporate governance are interlinked and that the economic, historical, and political approaches provide complementary responses to the same question?

This book is motivated by our conviction that the time is now ripe to present a holistic vision of corporate governance. We insist that ours is a vision of the whole and not a synthesis of everything and everyone that has gone before us. It is not our intention to embark upon the unrealistic task of building a general theory of corporate governance

---

[6] Comments along these same lines can be found in R. Monks and N. Minow, *Corporate Governance* (2nd edition), Oxford: Blackwell, 2001, in Freeman, *Strategic Management*, and also, in a more partial manner, in Frentrop, *History of Corporate Governance*, or M. Roe, *Political Determinants of Corporate Governance*, Oxford: Oxford University Press, 2003.

that would replace all existing theories: the diversity of motivations and methods of research makes such a task not only humanly impossible to carry out, but also intellectually flawed. More modestly, we would like to take up the challenge posed by the giant puzzle of ideas that today constitute corporate governance and offer a meta-analysis that shows how research on the performance, the evolution, and the legitimacy of different forms of corporate governance can be rendered coherent. In other words, we would like to propose a framework for interpretation that allows economists, historians, and political philosophers to *talk to each other*.

In order to establish such a dialogue, we propose to work with the liberal political model as a basis. We do not pretend to judge the validity of this model, but simply take it as the ideological and political context in which the corporation is situated and to which questions of corporate governance necessarily refer. This remark is important, for we will not cover alternative forms of governance such as cooperatives or mutuals in this book; nor will we provide any detailed discussion of political alternatives such as those Marxism has long argued for. We focus on understanding corporate governance within the liberal context, and our interpretation is based on an assessment of the historical evidence. Since the origins of modern liberal society, two forces have opposed each other in corporate governance: on the one hand, the *entrepreneurial force*, whose role it is to *provide direction to collective activity*. Like any force, the entrepreneurial force is balanced by a *counterweight* that limits its scope and defines its content. The entrepreneurial force is *legitimate*, if it leads to *performance*. However, in providing direction to collective activity, the entrepreneurial force invariably impinges upon the autonomy of the individual, either inside the corporation or through the actions of the corporation. In effect, the existence of an entrepreneurial force contradicts the principle of individual freedom, the principle upon which modern liberal society has been built. This is why the liberal political project gave birth to a second constitutive force of governance: *social fragmentation*. The institutions, the rules, and the practices of governance that are considered legitimate in modern society are those that prevent power from being concentrated, because the concentration of power bears the seeds of oppression for all. The power to govern therefore has to be fragmented to ensure the freedom of the individual. While the entrepreneurial power tends to prevent the dispersion of energies, social fragmentation tends to prevent their concentration. Too much entrepreneurial force can be highly performing, but also oppressive; too much fragmentation ensures individual freedom, but also reduces efficiency. From the unstable equilibrium between entrepreneurial force and social fragmentation emerges corporate governance that is both legitimate and performing.

In the first part of this book, we show that the opposition between the entrepreneurial force of direction and social fragmentation is a central concern in *liberal political philosophy*. In working with the principal philosophical texts, we demonstrate that, ever since liberalism's foundational debate between Hobbes and Locke, this dialectical opposition of forces forms the basis of all models of legitimate governance in modern society. A fortiori, it also constitutes the basis of legitimate corporate governance. Two of the defining characteristics of capitalism – the function of the entrepreneur and the system of corporate governance – are thus shown to be linked by the same question: how to direct the productive action of people who want to stay autonomous and free.

In the second, historical part of the book, we review the three principal models that ensure such an equilibrium of forces: the familial model, the managerial model, and the public model of corporate governance. The entrepreneurial force of direction and the social fragmentation of this force oppose each other, but they also complement each other, and their interactions give rise to the institutions and the rules that ensure an equilibrium between them. This is why there exist not just one possible model of governance, but as many models as there are equilibria between the *performance* demanded by the entrepreneurial force and the *legitimacy* assured by social fragmentation. Historical observation reveals that the large corporations that dominate their markets have moved, over time, from the familial model, to the managerial model, and on to the public model. We describe the characteristics of each model, defining who holds the entrepreneurial force (successively, over time: the single entrepreneur, the managerial technocracy, and shareholders) and what counterweight limits this force (successively, over time: the family, the trade union, and public opinion). We will show how, at each stage in history, the entrepreneurial force is confronted by social fragmentation, a confrontation that results in corporate governance institutions that are specific to each model and era. One can discern a process of transformation in corporate governance that accompanies economic development over time. We show that this process can be understood as the *democratization* of corporate governance. Our reflection is based upon the observation that, in modern liberal society, the governance of human beings tends, over time, to democratize: the more the entrepreneurial force becomes concentrated in ever larger corporations, the greater the need for social fragmentation to maintain the legitimacy of governance – so as to ensure that corporations are governed according to the liberal spirit. This tendency is of general import, but becomes especially clear when one takes a long-term, historical view.

We do not wish to make an evaluative judgement of this evolution. In our reading, democracy is a technique of government *à la* Foucault that, by means of its institutions and procedures (which we will rigorously define), provides an effective means of orienting collective activity as the fragmentation of interests becomes more and more pronounced. In much the same way as we do not consider liberalism in terms of its virtues and ideals but recognize it as the ideological system that has imposed itself upon our societies over the last two centuries, we do not pronounce judgement on democracy, but note that it is the technique of government that is best suited to liberalism. In the heritage of Tocqueville and Schumpeter, we argue that democracy, as a technique, has the tendency to extend its reach in line with the extension of modern liberal society. Democracy has spread from the political sphere, to the civic and economic spheres: the history of corporate governance does not escape this movement.

The observed tendency of corporate governance to democratize over time begs the question of economic efficiency. Can one explain the continuing evolution of corporate governance models in terms of improvements in performance? Conversely, if different models of governance co-exist during the same period of time, are they equally performing? Even more generally, the democratization observed over the long term – does it serve economic performance or is it imposed by political attitudes against the economic interests of society? In order to answer these questions, in the third part of the book we subject our framework to a confrontation with economic analysis and an explicit consideration of *performance*. We show that, following the pioneering study of Berle and Means,[7] corporate governance was stated as an

---

[7] A. Berle and G. Means, *The Modern Corporation and Private Property,* New York: Macmillan, 1932.

economic question, a new way of addressing the fundamental problem of liberal society, namely the problem of balancing the entrepreneurial force of direction and social fragmentation so as to ensure corporate governance that is both legitimate and performing. Agency theory represents a relatively recent, but brilliantly succinct economic reformulation of this problem in the spirit of liberal political philosophy. If we reflect upon agency theory from this point of view, its analytic strengths, but also its limitations manifest themselves very clearly. Paradoxically, we find that agency theory is not liberal enough, because it underestimates the degree to which interests are fragmented today. Division occurs not only between shareholders and management, but also, in increasing measure, among shareholders who differ in terms of their size, motivation, time horizon, and willingness to exert influence and within management itself, according to hierarchical position. The current state of affairs leads to agency problems that are so general as to appear insoluble. To counter this generalized agency problem, we show how the economic theory of the *guarantee* can be invoked to overcome these difficulties and form a new basis for analysing the relationship between corporate governance and economic performance in the liberal context. Consequently, we are able to conclude that the democratization of corporate governance does not represent a political evolution that is unrelated to economic performance, but, on the contrary, that there are good economic reasons to think that the democratization of corporate governance and the growth of economic performance go hand in hand.

Our work might appear overambitious, if it were not for the fact that, as we have already pointed out, our intent is not to do the work of philosophers, historians, and economists, but rather to propose a common ground for dialogue between these disciplines on the subject of corporate governance. We wish to acknowledge explicitly the debt we owe to past research in these fields. By offering a meta-analysis that makes the links between the political *legitimacy* of power in the corporation, the historical *evolution* of corporate governance forms, and economic *performance*, our framework for analysis attempts to provide a bridge between the different approaches. We believe that the dialectic opposition between the entrepreneurial force of direction and social fragmentation provides the principle upon which such a bridge can be built: it stands as the basis of modern political philosophy, develops over time in the history of the institutions of governance, and plays a determining role in the economic performance of the corporation.

In order to provide more general support to our analyses and hypotheses, we have sought to avoid the cultural bias of basing everything we say on the experience of one country or one region. The information used to illustrate our work systematically draws on data from four countries: the United States, the United Kingdom, Germany, and France, countries that are considered to have very different, if not radically opposed, traditions of corporate governance. Having said that, we cannot pretend to have applied our framework to these countries in every detail; this would have required far more research and more space than a single book allows. We only seek to verify that our ideas can be supported by facts from different countries and different eras of history, without any particular cultural idiosyncrasy.

This book will have met its objective if the reader comes away with the conviction that, over and above necessary disciplinary differences, corporate governance can be understood in its own right: the subject can be looked at from different angles, but these are compatible with one other. We would hope that the reader feels stimulated in his/her own understanding, because, whatever the discipline, there exists a common base of knowledge to draw upon. Finally, we hope that this book motivates further reflection on the future of corporate governance, as social fragmentation continues and giant corporations concentrate more and more of the entrepreneurial force. In the epilogue, we sketch out some of our own ideas on the future of corporate governance; these, like the entire content presented here, are offered as an invitation for further debate.

Establishing the ideological foundations: the contribution of liberal political philosophy

Introduction to Part I

Corporate governance can be understood as a set of explicit or implicit contracts (or social contracts) that defines the relationships among the three principal actors in the corporation: the *sovereign*, who in the vast majority of modern legal systems is the shareholder; the *governed*, namely all stakeholders, including holders of shares; and the *governing*, who direct and/or control the corporation, that is to say orient its activity. Analogously based on the voluntary contractual triad of sovereign, governed, and governing, and equally embedded in a society of natural law, corporate governance shares with modern political governance a common root in consent by the governed. From political and historical points of view, consent by the governed in corporate governance cannot be assumed or taken for granted. In our analysis, consent by the governed and its obverse, the right to govern, therefore serves as the starting point.

In everyday life, human beings evolve in social structures in which they either govern or are governed: the state, the town, the church, the family, clubs, associations, and also business corporations. Each of these social structures has its own institutions and rules determining, on the one hand, the extent of the power wielded by those who exercise authority, and, on the other hand, the counterweights defining the scope of the power exercised and keeping it in check. The existence of limitations on the power of authority is the price that has to be paid to ensure that the governed accept the authority of the governing as legitimate.

Without the consent of the governed, no governance is possible. What is the basis of consent by the governed? Without a doubt, force has played a historical role and continues to play a role in ensuring consent. However, even force is only effective if the governed are convinced that the power exercised over them is necessary and legitimate. If governance is not considered necessary and legitimate, and history has provided a great many examples of this process, the governed eventually revolt. As Hume pointed out in his great political treatise,

NOTHING appears more surprising to those, who consider human affairs with a philosophical eye, than the easiness with which the many are governed by the few; and the implicit submission, with which men resign their own sentiments and passions to those of their rulers. When we enquire by what means this wonder is effected, we shall find, that, as FORCE is always on the side of the governed, the governors have nothing to support them but opinion. It is therefore, on opinion only that government is founded; and this maxim extends to the most despotic and most military governments, as well as to the most free and most popular.[1]

What makes some forms of governance natural and easily acceptable, while others are considered odious and unacceptable? We will argue that consent by the governed is closely tied to the norms of time and place, the mentality and the education of the population concerned. Thus, the exercise of authority on the basis purely of force or of social status appears arbitrary and despotic to our modern eyes, but it was not considered thus in the Middle Ages. On the contrary, our long ago ancestors would likely have found it very difficult to accept authority based on the quality of education or on the number of shares owned, such as we generally accept it today.

Every form of governance can be interpreted as a political system that implicates the governed and the governing in a relationship of reciprocal dependence and acceptance of rules which establish the extent and the limits of power. In order to understand how societies are governed, it is essential first to inquire about shared beliefs concerning what is and what is not considered acceptable governance. Although the question of what constitutes acceptable governance in society is the point of departure for historians and political scientists, it receives surprisingly little attention in corporate governance.[2] Much of

---

[1] D. Hume, *Of the First Principles of Government*, 1752, Part I, Essay IV, 1.

[2] It is worth noting several important exceptions in the legal tradition. See, amongst others, J. Charkham and A. Simpson, *Fair Shares: The Future of Shareholder Power and Responsibility*, Oxford: Oxford University Press, 1999; B. Cheffins, 'Putting Britain on the Roe map: the emergence of the Berle-Means Corporation in the United Kingdom', in J. A. McCahery *et al.* (eds.), *Corporate Governance Regimes: Convergence and Diversity*, Oxford: Oxford University Press, 2002, pp. 147–72; J. Coffee, 'The future as history: the prospects for global convergence in corporate governance and its implications', *Northwestern University Law Review* 93 (1999), 641–720; J. Coffee, 'The rise of dispersed ownership: the role of law and state in the separation of ownership and control', *Yale Law Review* 111, Oct. (2001), 1–82.

corporate governance research appears to be based on the premise that corporate governance can be understood without making any reference to the modern society in which it has taken shape. In other words, the corporation is supposed to represent a unique kind of social structure that is not affected by the mentality and shared beliefs of the societies in which it evolves, a kind of political no man's land.

Is corporate governance really so different? In modern corporate governance, the stakeholders are the 'governed'. They voluntarily restrict their individual liberty in order to participate in the corporation under the authority of directors. Would the governed accept to live by the rules of the corporation unless they consider the governance exercised over them to be necessary and just? We will argue that what is considered just governance in the particular case of the corporation cannot be defined independently of the general social rules (or the *episteme* of society, in Foucault's terms) that determine what constitutes the just exercise of power. In order to analyse corporate governance seriously, both its evolution as a set of institutional arrangements and its effects on economic performance, it is necessary first to determine its essence, that is to say its intellectual underpinnings and the shared beliefs that make the exercise of authority acceptable and, indeed, the normal state of affairs in the corporation.

Of course, there are important differences between corporate governance and other forms of social governance, such as political governance or governance in a family; the corporation is an organization that is oriented towards economic performance, and this orientation towards performance is what underlies, at least in part, the legitimacy of those in power. But there also exists a point of convergence for *all* the institutions of modern Western society – including corporate governance. All of the institutions build upon the same way of conceiving the modern human being, his/her liberty and rights. The modern individual may be governed in many different places, by many different institutions, but there exists a common denominator that defines the acceptable rules of legitimate power to be compatible with the mentality of a given society. Thus, the question '*What* gives the right to direct a corporation?' cannot be separated from the larger question of determining on what basis the individual *consents* to be governed in society.

In the modern conception of power such as it has developed in Western society, liberal political thought represents the pivotal ideology either as a reference or as a motivating force for political action.

Since the corporation is typical in many ways of modern society, the acceptance of legitimate governance of the corporation must be understood in terms of the general political framework elaborated by liberal thought. This is particularly crucial to clarify the basis of corporate law and the legitimacy of entrepreneurs in modern society. Our approach does not imply that corporate governance can only be intellectually legitimated in the context of liberal framework, nor indeed that we share (or challenge) this ideology. We do not wish to take sides: other ideological references for corporate governance, such as socialism or cooperative associational thought, for example, also merit consideration and study. Recognizing the domination of the theoretical and political framework established by liberal philosophy in the intellectual structuration of modern society, we propose to examine in this book how the question of corporate governance has been developed within this framework.

The objective of this first part of the book consists of laying out the foundations. In so doing, we will describe the two fundamental dimensions of modern governance: first the figure of the entrepreneur, who incarnates the concentration of creative power in our societies and ensures that the particular interests of individuals are transformed into the general interest (Chapter 1); and, second, the procedures of democracy that establish and institutionalize the social fragmentation that is necessary to protect individual liberty and ensure that every individual can pursue his/her own interests. We will show that the dialectic opposition between the entrepreneurial concentration of force and social fragmentation institutionalizes the technique of democracy as a template for acceptable governance (Chapter 2). It is in the context of this dialectic opposition and the resulting political liberal framework that corporate governance has taken shape and reached its present state of evolution.

1 | The invisible crown: political foundations of the legitimate entrepreneur

The question 'What gives the right to direct a corporation?' cannot be answered without careful consideration of its corollary, 'Who has the right to direct a corporation?' In other words, who has the right to commit the corporation to a strategy, to choose its growth path and thereby have a decisive hand in determining both the corporation's future and that of its stakeholders? The question of *who* has the right to direct a corporation has a widely accepted general answer: direction is legitimately vested in the founder of the corporation and his/her descendants, or in the management designated by the founders. Intuitively, we draw a connecting line between those who exercise legitimate authority and the person or persons who have started the corporation. The founders and their descendants, but also the people who recreate the corporation by contributing to its development or the people who save the corporation from bankruptcy, are all considered to have an original or *genetic* tie with the corporation, and their legitimacy to direct derives from this bond.

Where does our shared belief in the legitimacy of the founding entrepreneur come from? Why is this belief so strong that the entrepreneur is often considered to be a general model of good governance, not only for business, but for all modern institutions, including even, sometimes, the nation state? The strength of our shared belief in the legitimacy of the entrepreneur is all the more astounding in light of the fact that the large, managerial enterprise has been the motor of economic progress and technological innovation for the last hundred years – after all, in the managerial enterprise, the *genetic* link between the founding entrepreneur and the manager has, in many if not all cases, become very tenuous. This model of legitimacy is so strong that it persists and carries over as an invisible crown to the founding entrepreneur's successors, *whether or not* they have a direct connection to the founder. Nonetheless, direction by an entrepreneur is still thought of as an ideal type for governance. So much so, that the entrepreneur in business is accorded a degree of power that would be considered unacceptable if it were held by a politician, a bureaucrat, or just about any other societal actor.

While many corporations, in particular smaller ones, operate under the direction of their founders, many others, including some of the very largest, do not, and yet reference is made to entrepreneurial direction as a model in these cases *as well*. In fact, it is very common for the leaders of large, managerial corporations to refer to 'entrepreneurship', to 'entrepreneurial spirit', and to their own role as 'entrepreneurs' to justify their power, although these leaders are simply well-paid employees. Why do professional managers prefer to justify their power by virtue of their role as entrepreneurs, rather than by their personal wisdom, their beliefs, their experiences, their strengths, or even divine unction, as leaders were wont to do in past centuries?

Understanding the legitimacy of entrepreneurial direction and the source of that legitimacy is central to understanding corporate governance and its evolution. In modern society, the 'entrepreneurial spirit', handed down, as it were, from the creator of the business, appears to be the natural reference for exercising authority over the corporation. It is not possible to understand why the entrepreneur is considered to be *the* locus of legitimate power in the corporation, if one does not place the question of corporate governance in the context of modern society and its definition of the extent and the limits of acceptable governance. Consideration of corporate governance in the context of modern society leads us to ask how the exercise of power is legitimized in general, beyond the confines of the corporation. To get to the bottom of this question, it is necessary to go back to the origins of modern thought and reflect upon what gives one individual the legitimate right to exercise power over other individuals in our society (1). We will proceed to show that private property is a fundamental building block of governance in the liberal system, the basis for authorizing an individual – the entrepreneur – to exercise authority over other individuals (2). The chapter will conclude on the coherence of the power of the entrepreneur with a liberal society composed of free individuals and anticipate some contradictions inherent in the juxtaposition of power and freedom that are to be discussed in the following chapter (3).

1 Governance by entrepreneurial direction: the dilemma of liberty in the foundational texts of liberalism[1]

Governance of the modern individual

The idea that individuals are autonomous and should be free to decide upon their own destiny, according to their personal preferences and independent choices, emerged and took centre stage in political thought in the Western world (Europe) at the beginning of the age of modernity (seventeenth and eighteenth centuries). This new conception of liberty and indeed of the person took a long time to form fully. Its roots are in the ancient Greek and Judeo-Christian traditions of the European and American societies, and it is a defining characteristic of the specific Western conception of humanism, based on the person.[2] Its immediate antecedents can be traced to the thirteenth century, and it developed slowly, in opposition to the medieval social order founded on political harmony.[3] The great events in this development are well known: the Protestant Reformation and the ensuing reform of the Catholic Church in the sixteenth century that both insisted, although with different nuances, on individual liberty of conscience and consequently introduced a degree of relativity in the common beliefs; the crisis of absolute monarchies in Great Britain (seventeenth century) and France (eighteenth century); and, especially, the founding of the United States of America by Europeans fleeing persecution who wanted to create a radically new society based on the principles of political (and religious) liberty. This long period of doubts and maturation finally led to the articulation, in the West, of the modern definition of liberty, as presented so succinctly by the French philosopher Benjamin Constant,

---

[1] For this section, see David A. Schultz, *Property, Power and American Democracy*, New Brunswick, NJ: Transaction, 1992; Carl D. Becker, *The Heavenly City of the Eighteenth-Century Philosophers*, New Haven, CT: Yale University Press, 1959 [1932]; P. Manent, *An Intellectual History of Liberalism*, Princeton, NJ: Princeton University Press, 1992 [1987].

[2] See Becker, *Heavenly City*.

[3] The greatest theoretician of medieval political harmony is no doubt Thomas Aquinas; his writing marked its apogee and anticipated its decline. See especially, on the role of the law, as 'ordinance of reason for the common good, made by him who has care of the community' (*Summa Theologica*, I IIae question 90, article 4, conclusion). On the political order, see *Summa Theologica*, I IIae, questions 94–6.

in his famous comparison of the Ancient and the Modern:[4] for the ancient Greeks and Christians, liberty consisted of the right to do good and participate in public affairs, liberty being defined in terms of the extent to which one individual could direct *others to the common good*, the power of control marking the essential difference between citizens and slaves; for the modern individual, on the contrary, liberty meant not being subject to anyone's control. The modern free man was *his own master*, because he did not allow anyone to dictate his behavior or belief. The age of modernity brought about an inversion of the traditional relationship between liberty and power: not power as the basis for liberty anymore, but liberty as power. Thus, in his lengthy discussion of liberty and necessity, Hume was led to conclude, 'by liberty, then, we can only mean a power of acting or not acting, according to the determinations of the will'.[5] Or, as it was put more abruptly in article 4 of the 1789 French Declaration of Human Rights: 'Liberty consists in the freedom to do everything which injures no one else.'

The modern conception of liberty contains a dilemma. How to assure social cohesion in a society based on individual autonomy? In other words, how can societies continue to exist if the very definition of liberty means that individuals are not subject to anyone's control? The dilemma appears impossible to resolve, since the modern conception of liberty requires that a harmonious society be built upon independent actors seeking to satisfy their own interests. Can individual liberty be limited in order to allow for governance, without fundamentally changing the nature of liberty? This political dilemma was discussed from the early days of modernity and found its clearest expression in England, in a foundational debate between two philosophers, Thomas Hobbes (1588–1679) and John Locke (1632–1704),

---

[4] B. Constant, 'De la liberté des anciens comparée à celle des modernes', speech given at the Athénée Royal, Paris, 1819; English text 'The liberty of the Ancient compared with that of the Modern', in Benjamin Constant, *Political Writings*, Cambridge: Cambridge University Press, 1986, pp. 304–6.

[5] D. Hume, *An Enquiry Concerning Human Understanding* (1751), Section 8, Part I, from the Harvard Classics edition, Vol. 37, New York and Toronto: P. F. Collier and Son, 1910. This was already the Hobbesian definition: 'according to this proper and generally received meaning of the word, a freeman is he that, in those things which by his strength and wit he is able to do, is not hindered to do what he has a will to' (*Leviathan* Part II, Ch. 21).

that came to serve as a canonical reference for all subsequent treatments of this question.

Hobbes versus Locke

Although the two philosophers start from the same point of reflection – modern liberty implies individual autonomy – they draw opposite conclusions. For Hobbes, liberty leads man to seek exclusively to satisfy his own personal interests. This makes it impossible to satisfy naturally the general interest, and human beings therefore exist in a condition of '*war of every man against every man*' (Hobbes, *Leviathan*, Book 1, Chs. 13, 14; our italics). The only way to prevent this chaos or 'law of the jungle', in Hobbes' view, is to call upon a 'super-authority', a Leviathan, to determine the rules of socially acceptable conduct and to limit the excesses of individual liberty. The Leviathan might be the absolute monarch (at the time of Hobbes' writing, in the middle of the seventeenth century), the system of public regulation, the state itself, or the republic considered as a set of institutions whose rules apply in absolute fashion to all. Whatever its form, a Leviathan is free of material contingencies and conflicts of interest and is therefore able to dictate the common behaviours that are necessary for society's survival. Hobbes' model of governance is based upon the *imposition* of social obligations on private interests by a body or institution that has absolute superiority, over and above the actual society.

For Locke, governance by a Leviathan is not acceptable. Hobbes' model requires that a Leviathan be possessed of qualities which the other individuals in society do not have. Can one credibly expect a king or leader to think of the general interest when all the other individuals are supposed to be motivated only by personal interests? In Locke's eyes, this argument is contradictory. For him, it is necessary to base the governance of modern society on generalized individualism and on absolute autonomy. Locke proposes that the human capacity to reason offers the key to overcoming the destructive free-for-all envisioned by Hobbes. Provided that governance is not imposed, but rather freely decided upon, man *will understand* that personal liberty needs to be limited, to the extent that personal liberty encroaches upon the liberty of others. Locke suggests that political institutions permit discussion and lead people to cooperate, to control each other, and, as a consequence, to limit their personal excesses. The role of contracts in this view is to limit personal liberty, starting with the social contract upon which society is based. By contract, man voluntarily limits personal liberty, and the problem of *'war of every man against every man'* naturally disappears.

Like Locke, Hobbes starts with individualism and reasons that it necessarily leads to excesses and the self-destruction of the social system. A pessimist, Hobbes concludes that the destructive consequences of individualism require a super-institution of governance to limit individual liberties; more optimistic, Locke argues that political institutions will emerge to encourage individuals to collaborate. And yet, the two conceptualizations establish a common vision of modern society, a vision justly called *liberal*, since it is based on individual liberty in the modern sense of the term.[6] Hobbes' vision supposes that individual liberty requires coercive superior institutions (for example, the power of the state or the 'Law' of the markets), whereas Locke's vision supposes that institutions of deliberation are sufficient (assemblies or contracts). The century of Enlightenment and its successors, political and economic liberalism, have developed and established the principle of individual liberty, limited either by rules of institutional constraint (Republicanism *à la* Hobbes[7]) or by procedures of cooperation (liberalism *à la* Locke) in all of the institutions of modern governance, including corporate governance, as we will show below.

The questions and answers provided by Hobbes and Locke can also be applied to the corporation, the modern organization par excellence. In the corporation, it is necessary to provide governance for a very diverse set of free individuals – employees, shareholders, clients, etc. How is it possible to prevent these free individuals from exclusively seeking to satisfy their personal interests and indeed breaking or changing contracts to their advantage? How to prevent the corporation from degenerating into a 'war of every man against every man'? For Hobbes as well as for Locke and the liberal thinkers who follow in their footsteps, an individual's right to govern must be justified in three ways: the right to private

---

[6] As already noted in the introduction, in this book we use the word 'liberal' in a way that is consistent with its meaning in political philosophy. A liberal is someone who explains the functioning of society on the basis of the principles of modernity – individualism, rational legitimacy, and political democracy.

[7] This tradition is represented through a large spectrum of nuances from Harrington's 1656 *Oceana* to Rousseau's 1762 *On Social Contract*. A part of socialist thought is influenced by this liberal republicanist stream.

property, the capacity to grow and fructify the entity governed, and the service to the general interest. Hume puts forth the same notion in different words: 'upon these three opinions, therefore, of public interest, of right to power, and of right to property, are all governments founded, and all authority of the few over the many'.[8]

Property, capacity, and obligation: the right to private property is the source of power, the capacity to grow is based on superior knowledge, and the obligation is defined in reference to the general interest – without this emphasis on the general interest, other individuals would not accept the limitations to their own freedom that come from submitting to the governance of another. Hobbes would nevertheless say that an absolute leader is necessary to overcome self-interested behaviour and achieve social order. Who would accept a Leviathan as leader? For the liberals in the tradition of Locke, the exercise of power cannot be based on social rank, class, or ethnic origin. Individual liberty presupposes that everyone is equal – equally free. The exercise of power cannot contradict individual liberty and must therefore be based on the legitimacy of the leader, all the while avoiding the genesis of Hobbes' Leviathan. From this dilemma the entrepreneur emerges as the legitimate director of the corporation.

2 The role of the entrepreneur in the liberal logic

Private property at the origins of the right to direct the corporation

In liberal thought, individual liberty is assured by *private* property. The right to private property prevents all others from using the assets held by an individual – it *deprives* them of these assets and their use. In this way, the right to private property assures the liberty of the individual who possesses the assets: only the individual holding the right to a property can use, benefit from, and dispose of the property. To exemplify this line of thought, we can quote Jean-Baptiste Say (1762–1832), who conceives of property as the 'owner's assured right to dispose according to his whim without consideration of any other'.[9]

---

[8] David Hume, *Of the First Principles of Government*, 1752, Part I, Essay IV, 5.
[9] J.-B. Say, *Catéchisme d'économie politique*, Ch. 17, Paris: Mame, 1972 [1815] (our translation).

The genesis of the right to private property coincides with the rise of the modern mentality. The stronger the drive for individualism develops, the more established the doctrine of private property becomes. This development is consistent with the definition of modern liberty provided by Benjamin Constant: the free individual is someone who is not subject to anyone's control, because private property guarantees his/her liberty.[10] It is not the notion of personal property itself which is new – this notion must have existed since the beginning of human societies. What is radically new is the role played by private property in society as the *definition* of individual liberty. Thus, the fundamental institution of modern society is private property. As Marx and also Veblen have remarked, the economic system of capitalism grows on the fertile ground of this institution.[11]

In a significant departure from the norms of the past, liberalism affirms that private property is as natural as life itself. A person cannot be truly free and hence truly a person unless the right to private property is guaranteed: a person is an owner. The right of 'acquiring, possessing and protecting property' appears in the first article of the Pennsylvania Declaration of Rights (1776), and in the French Declaration of Human Rights of 1789, property is solemnly established as sacred (Article 2). Some years later Bastiat, one of the most ardent defenders of the new liberal order, would write:

Economists believe that *property* is a providential fact, like the human *person*. The law does not bring the one into existence any more than it does the other. Property is a necessary consequence of the nature of man. In the full sense of the word, man *is born a proprietor*, because he is born with wants whose satisfaction is necessary to life, and with organs and faculties whose exercise is indispensable to the satisfaction of these wants. Faculties

---

[10] It is important not to confuse private property with personal property. Personal property has always existed, in the Western world. The serf, for example, owned his farming utensils, just like the artisan. However, as long as property was associated with a person, that person had to account to society for its use: king, peers, family, etc. For example, if lands belonged to a nobleman, the nobleman could not sell these lands without jeopardizing his title, his social status, or his family ties. In legal terms, the right of *abusus* was limited by social norms and customs. Private property, in the modern sense, conveys to the owner complete rights on the property in question, and deprives all others of these rights. Absent particular legal restrictions, every person can do what he/she wants with their property. See Chapter 3.

[11] See Marx, *Capital*, Vol. I, Part VIII.

are only an extension of the person; and property is nothing but an extension of the faculties. To separate a man from his faculties is to cause him to die; to separate a man from the product of his faculties is likewise to cause him to die.[12]

Might private property not contradict the individual liberty of others? Would not the accumulation of property by a few make it impossible for others to become owners and hence be free? The problem of liberal political thought consists of proposing a theory of just private property, that is to say a theory of property that does not constrain individual liberty. In order for private property to be considered just, liberals consider property to be the result of human labour; labour, in turn, is made possible by the freedom to act in the liberal conceptualization. In the *Second Treatise of Civil Government* (1690), Locke shows that the person who works is the legitimate owner of the fruit of his/her labour:

Though the earth, and all inferior creatures, be common to all men, yet every man has a property in his own person: this no body has any right to but himself. The labour of his body, and the work of his hands, we may say, are properly his. Whatsoever then he removes out of the state that nature hath provided, and left it in, he hath mixed his labour with, and joined to it something that is his own, and thereby makes it his property. It being by him removed from the common state nature hath placed it in, it hath by this labour something annexed to it, that excludes the common right of other men: for this labour being the unquestionable property of the labourer, no man but he can have a right to what that is once joined to, at least where there is enough, and as good, left in common for others.[13]

In a famous illustration of the principle, Locke describes how work turns into private property, depriving others of profit for the benefit of its exclusive owner:

He that is nourished by the acorns he picked up under an oak, or the apples he gathered from the trees in the wood, has certainly appropriated them to himself. No body can deny but the nourishment is his. I ask then, when did they begin to be his? when he digested? or when he eat? or when he boiled? or

---

[12] Frederic Bastiat, *Selected Essays on Political Economy*, Chapter 3, Property and Law, Paragraphs 11 and 12, trans. Seymour Cain, ed. George B. de Huszar. Irvington-on-Hudson, NY: The Foundation for Economic Education, Inc., 1995: first published: *Propriété et loi*, 15 mai 1848, *Journal des Économistes*.

[13] J. Locke *The Second Treatise of Civil Government*, 1690, Ch. V, Section 27.

when he brought them home? or when he picked them up? and it is plain, if the first gathering made them not his, nothing else could. That labour put a distinction between them and common: that added something to them more than nature, the common mother of all, had done; and so they became his private right. And will any one say, he had no right to those acorns or apples, he thus appropriated, because he had not the consent of all mankind to make them his? Was it a robbery thus to assume to himself what belonged to all in common? If such a consent as that was necessary, man had starved, notwithstanding the plenty God had given him.[14]

The writings of Locke and like-minded philosophers establish the place of private property in the modern mentality. Private property is just, because it is the product of work, the effort that an individual has put in to add 'something to them more than nature'. There is a genetic bond between work and private property. This bond is all the more strongly justified because anyone is supposed to be able to do as much: with the advent of individual liberty, poverty ceases to be seen as a misfortune and comes to be considered as a choice.[15] This is why even the poor have an interest in defending private property – work and property represent the only way out of poverty. In Say's words:

the poor man, that can call nothing his own, is equally interested with the rich in upholding the inviolability of property. His personal services would not be available, without the aid of accumulations previously made and protected. Every obstruction to, or dissipation of these accumulations, is a material injury to his means of gaining a livelihood; and the ruin and spoliation of the higher is as certainly followed by the misery and degradation of the lower classes.[16]

In this logic, the person who directs the corporation does so with legitimacy because he/she is the owner of an entity that has grown from his/her own work. At the end of the nineteenth century, at the time when the large, managerial corporation in which the executive was no longer the owner was starting to spread, Marshall would write:

[14] Locke, *Second Treatise*, Ch. V, Section 28.
[15] A consistent body of literature and policy documents this point – from nineteenth-century laws designed to force the poor to work, to contemporary theories on voluntary unemployment that consider unemployment to be an economic choice for those who refuse to work at low salaries.
[16] J.-B. Say, *A Treatise on Political Economy*, Book I, Ch. 14, Para. 10, Philadelphia: Lippincott, Grambo and Co., 4th/5th edition, 1855; first published 1803, in French.

But in the greater part of the business of the modern world the task of so directing production that a given effort may be most effective in supplying human wants has to be broken up and given into the hands of a specialized body of employers, or to use a more general term, of business men. They 'adventure' or 'undertake' its risks; they bring together *the capital and the labour* required for the work; they arrange or 'engineer' its general plan, and superintend its minor details.[17]

We see that, over a considerable amount of time, the image of the legitimate entrepreneur took shape and became firmly established in Western society. In this picture, the link between the liberty to do business and the ownership of private property is a person's work: liberty permits work, work leads to the accumulation of property, and property assures liberty – in a phrase, the virtuous circle of the entrepreneur.

The exemplary figure of the entrepreneur

Why aren't *all* individuals entrepreneurs? Putting the question more precisely, if the liberty to do business is an essential characteristic of modern liberty, then why does not everyone make use of the liberty to do business with the same intensity and the same success? These questions are important in formulating a justification for the authority of the entrepreneur and in making the distinction between employer and employees. This distinction forms one of the foundations of the corporation, but it creates an apparent inequality between free individuals: some individuals (the employees) contractually submit to the governance of others (the employers). How does the liberal model justify this voluntary surrender of individual autonomy?

The model's justification is built on two criteria that are perfectly compatible with the modern mentality, based as it is on the liberty to do business: the quantity and the quality of work. These two criteria distinguish the employer from the employee and help clarify the exemplary nature of the entrepreneur. First, let us consider the quantity of work. In contrast to the old, indolent aristocracies, the entrepreneur is primarily characterized by the nature of the work performed. In the words of Tocqueville:

[17] A. Marshall, 1890. *Principles of Economics*, 1890, Book IV, Ch. XII, Section 2 (our italics).

Not only is work not held in dishonor among these peoples, but it is held in honor; the prejudice is not against it but for it. In the United States, a rich man believes that he owes it to public opinion to devote his leisure to some operation of industry or commerce or to some public duty. He would deem himself disreputable if he used his life only for living. It is to escape this obligation of work that so many rich Americans come to Europe: there they found debris of aristocratic societies among which idleness is still honored. Equality not only rehabilitates the idea of work, it uplifts the idea of working to procure lucre.[18]

As we have already indicated above, the person who works, accumulates; the person who works less, by sloth or by choice, ultimately owns less. Locke writes, 'He [God] gave it [the world] to the use of the industrious and rational, (and labour was to be his title to it;) not to the fancy or covetousness of the quarrelsome and contentious. He that had as good left for his improvement, as was already taken up, needed not complain.'[19] Fairness is maintained: the entrepreneur is the person who works more than others to accumulate the means of production. It is therefore considered just that the entrepreneur proposes to others who do not possess the means of production that they work for him/her. This first justification of the employer–employee relationship is consistent with the liberal theory of ownership as the result of work. The employees or those who are governed by the entrepreneur freely accept to pay the price of their limited effort by surrendering part of their autonomy to the entrepreneur.

The second justification of the employer–employee relationship is found in the quality of work. Individuals may be granted equal rights, but nature has provided them with different levels of individual ability and talent. This is why the work of different individuals can lead to different results. In the eyes of the great liberal economic thinker Say, this social capital is more important than technical capital and of course also more important than financial capital:

---

[18] Tocqueville, *Democracy in America*, 1830, II, 2, 18 p. 535. Here and throughout the book, citations are taken from the H. C. Mansfield and D. Winthrop edition of *Democracy in America*, Chicago: University of Chicago Press, 2000. *DA* stands for *Democracy in America*, followed by the book in roman numerals, the part, the chapter, and the page number.

[19] Locke, *Second Treatise*, Ch. V, Section 34.

The industrious faculties are, of all kinds of property, the least questionable; being derived directly either from nature, or from personal assiduity. The property in them is of higher pretensions than that of the land, which may generally be traced up to an act of spoliation; for it is hardly possible to show an instance, in which its ownership has been legitimately transmitted from the first occupancy. It ranks higher than the right of the capitalist also; for even taking it for granted, that this latter has been acquired without any spoliation whatever, and by the gradual accumulations of ages, yet the succession to it could not have been established without the aid of legislation, which aid may have been granted on conditions. Yet, sacred as the property in the faculties of industry is, it is constantly infringed upon, not only in the flagrant abuse of personal slavery, but in many other points of more frequent occurrence.[20]

During the early years of capitalism, the terms 'industrialist' and 'industry' take on a positive connotation that they did not originally have, and are used to praise the 'intelligent work' of entrepreneurs.[21] In the liberal literature of the early nineteenth century, many of the greatest human virtues are ascribed to the entrepreneur. According to Say, 'In the second place, this kind of labour requires a combination of moral qualities, that are not often found together. Judgment, perseverance, and a knowledge of the world, as well as of business.'[22] Or, in the words of Sombart (1863–1941), ironically an outspoken critic of the entrepreneurial bourgeoisie, 'in order to efficiently discharge his duties, the capitalist entrepreneur needs to possess three moral qualities that, taking different predispositions into account, I would designate by the following terms: liveliness of spirit, perspicacity, and intelligence'.[23]

---

[20] Say, *Treatise on Political Economy*, Book I, Ch. 14, note 30.

[21] Say, *Catéchisme*, Tome I, p. 28. This term bore a negative connotation for a long time and was originally used as a synonym for fraud or deception (see P. Fontaine, 'Le concept d'industrie au XVIIIe siècle', in *Histoire de l'Économie Industrielle, Economies et Sociétés*, Grenoble: Presse Universitaires de Grenoble; 3 (1992), 7–33). The author notes that the *Dictionnaire royal, françois – anglois et anglois – françois* of 1727 translates the French word 'industrie' by the English 'industry, ingenuity, to use cunning and to live upon one's wits'. The qualities of the industrialist were popularly thought to include both cleverness and deception. Slowly, the positive characteristics of the entrepreneur began to be emphasized, and the social role of entrepreneurial direction was articulated, leading to the eventual disappearance of the original negative connotation.

[22] Say, *Treatise on Political Economy*, Book II, Ch. 7, Para. 29.

[23] W. Sombart, *Le bourgeois: contribution à l'histoire morale et intellectuelle de l'homme économique moderne*, 1913, Livre 1, translated from German to French by S. Jankélévitch in 1928, Paris (our translation to English).

As capitalism develops, liberal thought is further refined. Not only is the entrepreneur considered to have superior personal qualities; the entrepreneur is seen to possess also a special talent for combining different means of production. More than an inventor, the entrepreneur is an organizer. At the end of the nineteenth century, Marshall was to describe the entrepreneur in very appreciative tones:

> To return to a class of considerations already noticed (IV. XI. 4 and 5), the manufacturer who makes goods not to meet special orders but for the general market, must, in his first role as merchant and organizer of production, have a thorough knowledge of things in his own trade. He must have the power of forecasting the broad movements of production and consumption, of seeing where there is an opportunity for supplying a new commodity that will meet a real want or improving the plan of producing an old commodity. He must be able to judge cautiously and undertake risks boldly; and he must of course understand the materials and machinery used in his trade. But secondly in this role of employer he must be a natural leader of *men*. He must have a power of first choosing his assistants rightly and then trusting them fully; of interesting them in the business and of getting them to trust him, so as to bring out whatever enterprise and power of origination there is in them; while he himself exercises a general control over everything, and preserves order and unity in the main plan of the business. The abilities required to make an ideal employer are so great and so numerous that very few persons can exhibit them all in a very high degree.[24]

In the liberal society built on individual liberty and equality, the liberty to do business leads to acceptable inequality because it is justified by exceptional abilities. This second justification for the superiority of the entrepreneur over those who become employees permits thinkers to draw a very particular link between authority and organizing competences. The entrepreneur has succeeded because he/she has developed and *proven* his/her abilities by the level of results achieved. In other words, the existence of the corporation proves the entrepreneur's capacity to direct. From a liberal point of view, the capitalist system is thus able to select the best: those who are in authority are necessarily those who have done best. Conversely, those who are governed, those who surrender some of their individual autonomy to the corporation, can be assured that the person who is in authority

---

[24] Marshall, *Principles of Economics*, Book IV, Ch. XII, Section 5.

possesses extraordinary qualities that they do not have and has made successful use of them in starting a business and being able to offer employment or products. The double justification of the entrepreneur's power to direct – quantity and quality of work – does not contradict modern liberty. For a free person, the entrepreneur is a rationally acceptable and even rationally desirable master.

Private vice, public virtue

We have described how the legitimacy of ownership is built on the quantity and the quality of the work of the entrepreneur, but we have not yet addressed the question of how the entrepreneur's contribution to the general interest makes the power to direct acceptable. In the liberal society, it is necessary to hypothesize that entrepreneurs do not act to maximize their wealth *at the expense* of the general interest. Morally and politically, this is an essential part of the liberal vision of the world.

In the pre-modern order, participation in public affairs such as, for example, direction of a business, was legitimized on the basis of wisdom or natural authority and the motivation to serve the general good; in this way of thinking, man achieved liberty by serving society. By contrast, in the modern, liberal order, governance of others is only an unintended by-product of the quest to fulfil the individual self-interest. Situated as it is at the opposite end of the theoretical spectrum from ancient thought and indeed the Judeo-Christian tradition, the liberal vision has to show that pursuit of individual self-interest not only does not harm the general interest, but actually advances it. This reversal of assumptions constitutes the most radical moral revolution in Western thought since the advent of Christianity, and the entrepreneur incarnates a new morality.

It is not from the benevolence of the butcher, the brewer, or the baker that we expect our dinner, but from their regard to their own interest. We address ourselves, not to their humanity but to their self-love, and never talk to them of our own necessities but of their advantages. Nobody but a beggar chooses to depend chiefly upon the benevolence of his fellow-citizens.[25]

---

[25] A. Smith, *Wealth of Nations*, 1776, Book 1, Ch. 2. This famous sentence does not summarize the subtlety of Smithian thought on social regulation. Nevertheless

The argument that has become the credo of modern economics is well known: when each person pursues his/her own self-interest, each maximizes personal utility, and, by aggregation, collective utility is maximized. Over the years, the conceptual leap from the micro of the individual to the macro of society has been the subject of countless controversies and analytical refinements, but the fundamental argument remains the same. The greater the profit obtained by each individual entrepreneur, the greater the wealth of society. Note that the positive outcome for society is not due to any particular moral disposition on the part of the entrepreneur, but is only dependent on the entrepreneur's desire to enhance his/her personal wealth and on the condition that the fruit of the entrepreneur's labours belongs to him/her so that he/she is motivated to exercise individual liberty. As the scholars of economic property rights have shown and the neo-institutionalists of the 1980s have confirmed,[26] better protection for private property rights encourages individual profit maximization, and, by addition, contributes to the economic development of society as a whole.

And yet, acceptance of the argument that the individual pursuit of self-interest leads to the maximization of collective utility necessitated a profound ideological and moral break with the thinking of the time. Thus, in Bernard Mandeville's famous *Fable of the Bees* (1705), the positive effect of private vices turning into public virtues is still considered to be a paradox. That general enrichment would result from unnecessary spending by a few surprises Mandeville and represents an unexpected effect of economic relationships. Based on reason and faith in human progress, the liberal political model could not accept that such a critical result is merely a surprising corollary to economic activity. This is why liberal thinkers such as Adam Smith were very eager to demonstrate that the entrepreneur is naturally compelled to work in a way that furthers the general interest.

The person who employs his stock in maintaining labor, necessarily wishes to employ it in such a manner as to produce as great a quantity of work as possible. He endeavors, therefore, both to make among his workmen the most proper distribution of employment, and to furnish them with the best

its popularity underlines one of the most recurrent themes of modern liberalism. For a recent discussion on the reality of Smith's liberalism see Elias L. Khalil, 'Is Adam Smith Liberal?' *Journal of Institutional and Theoretical Economics* 158 (4) (2002), 664–94.

[26] See Chapter 5.

machines which he can either invent or afford to purchase. His abilities in both these respects are generally in proportion to the extent of his stock, or to the number of people whom it can employ. The quantity of industry, therefore, not only increases in every country with the increase of the stock which employs it, but, in consequence of that increase, the same quantity of industry produces a much greater quantity of work.[27]

In other words, private wealth and the general well-being are not mutually exclusive opposites. For Bastiat, *richesse*, or wealth, does not imply the 'opulence of a few, but rather the ease, well-being, security, independence, instruction, and dignity of all';[28] similarly, to Schumpeter, the entrepreneur is the engine of economic progress:

we have seen that the function of entrepreneurs is to reform or revolutionize the pattern of production by exploiting an invention or, more generally, un untried technological possibility for producing a new commodity or producing an old one in a new way, by opening up a new source of supply of materials or a new outlet for products, by reorganizing an industry and so on. Railroad construction in its earlier stages, electrical power production before the First World War, steam and steel, the motorcar, colonial ventures afford spectacular instances of a large genus which comprises innumerable humbler ones – down to such things as making a success of a particular kind of sausage or toothbrush. This kind of activity is primarily responsible for the recurrent 'prosperities' that revolutionize the economic organism and the recurrent 'recessions' that are due to the disequilibrating of the new products or methods.'[29]

The progress of society is seen to be inextricably linked to the entrepreneur and entrepreneurial direction.[30] The individual who seeks to maximize personal profit contributes to the improvement of society. In this sense, governance by the entrepreneur can be called progressive governance.

---

[27] Smith, *Wealth of Nations*, Book 2, Chapter 1, Introduction.

[28] F. Bastiat, *Sophismes économiques*, 1848, Ch. 1, Physiologie de la spoliation (our translation).

[29] J. Schumpeter, *Capitalism, Socialism, and Democracy*, 1942, II, XII, Crumbling walls, p. 132. (*CSD*; London: George Allen and Unwin Ltd, 1976. In the following all citations refer to this edition.)

[30] See P. F. Drucker, *Innovation and Entrepreneurship*, Englewood Cliffs, NJ: Prentice Hall, 1985. For a recent summary discussion of this question, see P. Davidsson, F. Delmar, and J. Wilklund, *Entrepreneurship and the Growth of Firms*, Cheltenham and Northhampton: Edward Elgar, 2006.

3 The entrepreneur crowned: a modern Leviathan?

The entrepreneur exercises personal freedom in the name of private property and gains in legitimacy with the ability to amass wealth. Corporate governance by the entrepreneur is entirely consistent with the principles of modern society: liberty, reason, and progress. The entrepreneur acts in the name of liberty, uses reason to make business prosper, and, in so doing, also contributes to the progress of humanity. Therefore, it is entirely acceptable (and desirable) that the entrepreneur should direct corporations (and the people working in them) – in other words, that the entrepreneur should exercise the sole force of constraint compatible with modern liberty. If we agree with Locke, people should be actively interested in submitting to the governance of good entrepreneurs: 'The great and chief end, therefore, of men's uniting into commonwealths, and putting themselves under government, is the preservation of their property. To which in the state of nature there are many things wanting.'[31] The entrepreneur does more than just conserve property: the entrepreneur helps increase the property of everyone.

The entrepreneur thus emerges as the central political figure of capitalism. In a divided society that is threatened by chaos at its seams, the entrepreneur is a positive force for social cohesion.

With Schumpeter, it can be said that the entrepreneur takes the place in modern society held in ancient society by the warrior.

His role (that of the entrepreneur), though less glamorous than that of medieval warlords, great or small, also is or was just another form of individual leadership acting by virtue of personal force and personal responsibility for success. His position, like that of warrior classes, is threatened as soon as this function in the social process loses its importance, and no less if this is due to the cessation of the social needs it served than if those needs are being served by other, more impersonal, methods.[32]

The same point is made more directly by Sombart, 'The entrepreneur, although with fewer subordinates, resembles the chief of the army and the head of state who, in the final analysis and this is particularly true for the head of state, are organizers and negotiators.'[33]

---

[31] Locke, *Second Treatise*, Ch. IX, Section 124.
[32] Schumpeter, *CSD*, II, XII, 133.   [33] Sombart, *Le bourgeois*, Book 1.

More than a warrior, the entrepreneur also has the qualities of a prophet, someone who is able to see what others cannot see: business opportunities, technological inventions, and general chances for progress. Like the prophets of old, the entrepreneur is able to recognize and give life to what does not yet exist. A prophet who acts upon what he/ she sees – this is the essence of the way the entrepreneur is described in the classical writings of Penrose or Kirzner[34] and the model for how we think of the entrepreneur today in economics and management studies. Penrose, the great theorist of economic growth by innovation, refers to this logic in order to give the exercise of the entrepreneurial force a systematic rational definition:

[Entrepreneur refers to] individuals or groups within the firm [who are responsible for] the introduction and acceptance on behalf of the firm of new ideas, particulary with respect to products, location, and significant changes in technology, [for] the acquisition of new managerial personnel, fundamental changes in the administrative organisation of the firm ... the raising of capital, and the matching of plans for expansion, including the choice of methods of expansion.[35]

In this view, the entrepreneur is not personified as the creator of the corporation, but represents an active force composed of individuals whose 'spirit' permeates society and orients it.

Both warrior and prophet, imbued with the virtues of a modern hero, the entrepreneur is held up as a positive example for broader society, to the point that many influential people have argued that entrepreneurs should take on broader responsibilities in government. Direction by the entrepreneur is deeply embedded in the modern mentality, as a reference for the just exercise of power: the entrepreneur renders corporate governance compatible with modern liberty.

We have seen how the entrepreneur is referred to in the legitimization of corporate governance: the entrepreneur is an exceptional human being, distinguished from the average by work, abilities, and a sense of economic progress. The abilities required to make an ideal employer are so great and so numerous that very few persons can exhibit them all in a very high degree. This seems to us a singularly

---

[34] E. Penrose, *The Theory of the Growth of the Firm*, Oxford: Basil Blackwell, 1959; I. Kirzner, *Competition and Entrepreneurship*, Chicago: University of Chicago Press, 1973.

[35] Penrose, *Theory*, p. 30.

paradoxical conclusion for a system of political thought based on equality and individual liberty. At the end of the analysis it becomes apparent that acceptable governance requires exceptional human beings. The entrepreneur appears to be a new type of Leviathan, rather fittingly described by Hobbes when referring to the absolute monarch, 'where the public and private interest are most closely united, there is the public most advanced. Now in monarchy the private interest is the same with the public.'[36] Should we conclude that Hobbes finally won out over Locke? It would appear that the liberal, individualist society requires a Leviathan – the entrepreneur. Has the liberal effort to refute political absolutism not led us to accept *economic absolutism* instead? In our view, the question cannot be resolved so easily. The power of the Hobbesian monarch is based on divine unction. The legitimate power of the entrepreneur, by contrast, is based on work, ability, and results. The question that has to be asked is whether or not corporate govern-ance can be entrusted to human beings whose abilities may be excep-tional, but could also be overestimated, whose abilities may be great at one moment, but may also decline over time. Who attests to the entrepreneur's abilities? Who exercises control? Most importantly, who constrains the entrepreneur if his/her errors lead to the oppression of other individuals?

Debates over corporate governance, whether of yesterday or of today, cannot be fully understood without taking a stand on these questions. There is indeed a basic tension between the notion of liberty for every individual and the notion of power for one individual, how-ever legitimate. The entrepreneur alone is not enough to build a system of governance on. If liberal society is to work as intended by its founders, it is necessary to limit the power of the entrepreneur, so that corporate governance stays compatible with modern liberty.

[36] Hobbes, *Leviathan*, II, XIX, p. 16.

2 | Society fragmented and the role of democracy

The entrepreneur also has a dark side. Indeed, what is to prevent entrepreneurs from appropriating all the means of production, denying all others the opportunity of entrepreneurship, and thereby taking away their liberty? If the entrepreneur legitimately, in other words thanks to his/her superior abilities, amasses power based on private property, will he/she not deprive all other potential entrepreneurs of the means to be an entrepreneur? From the beginning of capitalism, this question has dogged the entrepreneur, providing the political basis of a variety of different critiques. Marx makes the notion of 'primitive accumulation' a centrepiece of the socialist critique: by initially accumulating the means of production, certain individuals acquire unilateral power and can organize the productive system to impose their own conditions of exploitation on others.

The capitalist system presupposes the complete separation of the labourers from all property in the means by which they can realize their labour. As soon as capitalist production is once on its own legs, it not only maintains this separation, but reproduces it on a continually extending scale. The process, therefore, that clears the way for the capitalist system, can be none other than the process which takes away from the labourer the possession of his means of production; a process that transforms, on the one hand, the social means of subsistence and of production into capital, on the other, the immediate producers into wage-labourers. The so-called *primitive accumulation*, therefore, is nothing else than the historical process of divorcing the producer from the means of production. It appears as *primitive*, because it forms the pre-historic stage of capital and of the mode of production corresponding with it.[1]

One person's property has implications for the property of others and can lead to their expropriation. Socialists have used this point to

---

[1] Marx, *Capital*, Vol. I, Part VIII, Ch. 26 (1st English edition, Moscow: Progress Publishers, 1887).

condemn liberalism as unjust, but the point is of central concern not only to critics of the capitalist system.

Indeed, understanding the impact of existing property on all new property has also been a constant preoccupation of those who have defended modern liberal society and the economic system built on the legitimacy of the entrepreneur. Because of the impact of existing property, the argument that many individuals do not become entrepreneurs merely by lack of work or lack of talent is not satisfactory. On the contrary, individuals may not become entrepreneurs, because they are *prevented* from doing so by existing entrepreneurs who are trying to maintain a hold on all available wealth. In other words, some individuals may be *forced* to submit to the governance of existing entrepreneurs, and this conclusion contradicts the principles of modern liberal society. How to reconcile the possible excesses of entrepreneurial direction and individual liberty?

The danger posed by entrepreneurial direction for individual liberty engenders a radical and constant stream of critique from within modern liberalism. Unlike the socialist critique, the modern liberal critique is directed not at private ownership of the means of production, but at the irreversible accumulation of property. This is why monopoly is condemned: monopoly prevents the appearance of *new entrepreneurs*. As a necessary complement to the exaltation of the figure of the entrepreneur, liberalism had to develop a systematic doctrine of the freedom to become an entrepreneur. This doctrine is based on the following premise: in order to ensure individual liberty against the possible threat of the entrepreneur, modern society must always be fragmented into a sufficiently large number of actors so that no single one of these can exercise a power of constraint over the others (1). How does this fragmented society function, in spite of its divisions – how does it avoid a 'war of all against all'? It is necessary to build it upon a political order that assures each individual liberty while at the same time maintaining balance and furthering common progress. In the logic of liberalism, it is the political order of democracy that can reconcile the directive force of the entrepreneur and the fragmentation of society by the application of appropriate governance techniques (2).

1 The freedom to become an entrepreneur

Since the modern person is free, he/she has to be free to become an entrepreneur and hence, provided that he/she has the requisite abilities, to exercise the power of entrepreneurial direction over a business venture. Markets, that is to say the possibility freely to enter into and exit from business and to develop offerings without having the price fixed by a higher authority, are an essential characteristic of the freedom of entrepreneurship. Markets extend the fiction of the 'state of nature': on the one hand, the freedom to start a business means that the frontiers of society are not set and that new opportunities will always arise; on the other hand, competition for resources assures all individuals the chance to sell their skills freely. If markets work and continuously extend the economic frontiers of society, then one person's property need not deprive others of property. Such is the economic credo of liberalism, a complement to its political credo of individual liberty.[2]

Of course, the freedom to become an entrepreneur and enter into business is fraught with many concrete difficulties linked to the path dependency of innovation, the necessary initial stock of capital, and the number of competitors present in market equilibrium. All these concrete aspects of the theoretical problem have been extensively researched in microeconomics and industrial organization, and we will not enter into a summary of this work here. Suffice it to say that the power accorded to the entrepreneur is consistent with modern

[2] As long as the economic space is sufficiently large to permit any individual desiring to do so to find a place to work and accumulate private property, modern liberty as defined by Constant does not give rise to the problem of expropriation: with enough space, no one person will deprive another. This is why the philosophers of the Enlightenment always reason on the basis of the 'state of nature', a primitive society or a deserted island imagined along the lines of Daniel Defoe's *Robinson Crusoe* (1704). This convention among philosophers permits them to make the implicit hypothesis that individuals may acquire an unlimited amount of property without worrying about the expropriation of others or the spoliation of the economy. Marx commented ironically on the lack of realism in these Robinsonian worlds (see *Capital*, Vol. I, Part I, Ch. 1). The cultural divorce over the justification of capitalism between Europe and the United States also can be traced to this position. In the United States of the nineteenth century, the frontier moved continually westward, and this allowed every individual to claim new land. Except for the special cases of the Native American whose lands were taken away and the African American who was held as a slave, the question of whether or not private property is just did not need to be asked: all an individual had to do was to move West, and he/she would find new sources of wealth to appropriate. In Europe, by contrast, where the population was dense and the economic space already limited, appropriation of property by one individual always appeared to come at the expense of others, and this created a more fertile ground for the criticism of private property.

liberal society, *if* this power is ideologically and politically circumscribed by the freedom of entrepreneurship available to *all*. This last
liberty has to be defended against the tendency of the entrepreneur to
keep new entrepreneurs out.

The entrepreneur contra the liberty to become an entrepreneur

The problem of acceptable limits to the accumulation of private property was considered from the earliest days of liberal thought.[3] Scholars
realized that the entrepreneur may suffer from hubris: the person who
possesses all the positive qualities necessary to become a successful
entrepreneur may use these qualities to accumulate property in a way
that makes other people dependent and hence less than free. This is also
the essence of the Marxist critique of the accumulation of wealth.

To ensure political acceptability, Locke insists on moderation as an
essential quality in the entrepreneur. In Locke's view, the capacity to
work which permits the entrepreneur to accumulate private property
does not exclude the capacity to be discerning about the meaning and
the extent of this accumulation.

But how far has he [God] given it us? To enjoy. As much as any one can make
use of to any advantage of life before it spoils, so much he may by his labour
fix a property in: whatever is beyond this, is more than his share, and belongs
to others. Nothing was made by God for man to spoil or destroy. And thus . . .
especially keeping within the bounds, set by reason, of what might serve for
his use; there could be then little room for quarrels or contentions about
property so established.[4]

In addition to moral arguments, Locke also postulates technical limitations to the excesses of entrepreneurs. Since work legitimates private
property, the limited amount of work any one individual can possibly
accomplish serves as a natural cap to the growth of personal property.
One person cannot acquire more than his/her work allows the person
to acquire.

---

[3] See Jean-Jacques Rousseau, *Discours sur l'origine et les fondements de l'inégalité
entre les hommes*, 1755; English edition, *Discourse on the Origin of Inequality*,
Indianapolis: Hackett Publishing Company, 1992. Sully Proudhon, *Qu'est ce que
la propriété?*, 1840; English edition by D. Kelley and B. Smith, *What Is Property*,
Cambridge: Cambridge University Press, 1994.

[4] Locke, *The Second Treatise of Civil Government*, 1690, Ch. V, Section 31.

The measure of property nature has well set by the extent of men's labour and the conveniencies of life: no man's labour could subdue, or appropriate all; nor could his enjoyment consume more than a small part; so that it was impossible for any man, this way, to intrench upon the right of another, or acquire to himself a property, to the prejudice of his neighbour, who would still have room for as good, and as large a possession (after the other had taken out his) as before it was appropriated. This measure did confine every man's possession to a very moderate proportion, and such as he might appropriate to himself, without injury to any body.[5]

While this reasoning may have been adequate at the very beginning of capitalism, in the spirit of the ideal-typical society of the early eighteenth century, it does not account for the accumulation of property over time through inheritance and does not address the asymmetries thus generated. Writing over a century after Locke, Marx could see the irony in the initial propositions:

In actual history it is notorious that conquest, enslavement, robbery, murder, briefly force, play the great part. In the tender annals of Political Economy, the idyllic reigns from all time immemorial. Right and 'labour' were from all time the sole means of enrichment, the present year of course always excepted. As a matter of fact, the methods of primitive accumulation are anything but idyllic.[6]

With the growth and development of large corporations, large-scale migration from the countryside to towns, and the profound political and social modifications wrought by capitalism in the nineteenth century, the 'moderation of entrepreneurs' came to be seen as an increasingly shaky foundation for liberalism. It was clearly not possible to rely only on moral forces for organizing a society which is just and remains true to the ideals of modern liberty. In this context, it is important to recall that liberalism had established itself as a new order, in opposition to the traditional Judeo-Christian moral values, and hence could not draw on these for support. Since it was not possible to rely only on the virtue of the entrepreneur and traditional values had been superseded, there was a need for new institutions to limit the hubris of the entrepreneur.

[5] Locke, *Second Treatise*, Ch. V, Section 36.
[6] Marx, *Capital*, Part VIII, Ch. 26.

Whatever these institutions were to be, they could not jeopardize the principle of individual liberty: this would have simply meant replacing one Leviathan by another. Instead, the new institutions needed to be built on the same basic principle of individual liberty, and it was therefore imperative for liberalism to be able to show that the excesses of some entrepreneurs need not be incompatible with liberty for all. Rather, these new institutions had to prevent individual entrepreneurs from controlling markets and thereby establishing excessive power. From a liberal point of view, the best way to limit the power of the entrepreneur is to ensure the fragmentation of society into its component elements: the practically endless number and variety of individual human interests.

Social fragmentation to counter the Leviathan

Greater fragmentation of society implies more confrontation of different interests and hence stronger competition among individuals. As long as the interests of each individual are defended and society stays fragmented, no single individual can capture all of society's wealth. This is why the freedom to enter into business and become an entrepreneur is a cornerstone of the liberal political ideology. This freedom guarantees that existing entrepreneurs will not grab all the wealth of society at the expense of others, preventing monopolies and the emergence of Leviathan-like entrepreneurs. The competition over property which results from the freedom to enter into business safeguards individual liberty, in the sense that liberty means the freedom not to be controlled by anyone. Markets effectively permit the individual to become an entrepreneur, as soon as the individual senses that personal liberty is at risk. In effect, the 'American Dream' translates this political credo into modern myth.

Liberal thought since Locke calls for modern society to be systematically fragmented. Whereas political harmony in traditional societies is built on complementarity and cooperation among individuals, modern liberal society strives to create social agreement on the basis of or despite autonomy and competition. The fragmentation of individual interests is counted upon to ensure competition and the maintenance of individual liberty. This argument is conceptually watertight under the condition that no one individual can prevent another from entering into competition against him. This is, for example, the main objection of Rousseau, father of the 'European republicanism' against 'Lockean liberalism': 'regardless of how they painted their usurpations, [leaders] realized well enough that they were only based on a precarious and abusive right, and that since they had been acquired solely by force, force could deprive them of them without their having any reason for complaint'.[7] The conclusion of Hobbes is turned on its head: far from wishing to avoid the 'war of every man against every man', modern liberal society encourages this state, because competition guarantees individual liberty.

Modern liberal capitalism does not seek to create a peaceful society, but rather wishes to build a society in which the potential for conflict between entrepreneurs forces them to adjust their ambitions to their talents and means, under threat of losing out to their competitors. In this way, the power of one entrepreneur is limited by the fact that another entrepreneur with superior abilities may enter the market. It is thus not surprising that the seminal book of modern political economy, Adam Smith's *Wealth of Nations* (1776), starts with a description of the advantages of fragmentation – the division of labour in a factory. In much the same way as the efficient division of labour stimulates economic development, the social fragmentation of interests is supposed to maintain the political coherence of the liberal capitalist system. Based on the principle of individual liberty, the liberal society considers fragmentation, whether achieved by the market or by the organization of work, to be the basic condition of fairness and efficiency. In effect, the danger posed by the great power accorded to the entrepreneur is reversed: the excesses of entrepreneurs do not limit individual liberties, but, on the contrary, the freedom to enter into business prevents the excesses of entrepreneurs.

The modern entrepreneur is legitimate, as long as those who accept his/her authority can themselves become entrepreneurs and freely choose not to do so. However the realism of this hypothesis might be judged, it is important to recognize that it is postulated as an ideal, indispensable for understanding modern governance in general and hence also corporate governance in particular. From a liberal point of view, one argues that where the freedom to enter into business is not given, the legitimacy of the entrepreneur is not assured. This is the

---

[7] J. J. Rousseau, *The Discourses' and Other Early Political Writings*, Cambridge: Cambridge University Press, 1997, p. 170.

argument used by liberal thinkers to denounce not only monopolies, collusive behaviour among entrepreneurs, and political interventions to limit competition, but also clan-based and oligarchic systems of power such as those represented by the different international mafias. It is not so much the economic (and debatable) inefficiency of these structures that concerns us here, but the fact that they ruin the political system of governance upon which the legitimacy of the modern entrepreneur is built.

The confrontation of liberties: a political dilemma

On the one hand, entrepreneurial direction is considered legitimate and indeed indispensable to the development of modern society; on the other hand, entrepreneurial direction poses a threat to individual freedom and needs to be continuously counterbalanced by the fragmentation of society. How can the two be reconciled, the direction of the entrepreneur and the fragmentation of society? Freedom makes entrepreneurial governance possible, but freedom can also lead to the suppression of the individual liberties of the weak by the strong.

If individuals are free, and if entrepreneurs are the most able individuals, it is natural that entrepreneurs further their self-interest by attempting to prevent competition. The freedom to become an entrepreneur is the enemy of the existing entrepreneur, because it threatens property and power. This is why it is natural to think that established entrepreneurs will do everything in their power to limit entrepreneurial freedom. Again, in the logic of liberalism, the freedom to enter into business limits the excesses of entrepreneurs. One can equally well argue (and recognize in practice) that the excesses of entrepreneurs limit entrepreneurial freedom. In fact, the rational entrepreneur seeks to make his/her enterprise larger, to accumulate resources and, finally, to attain a position of competitive dominance. It is not surprising to observe that the development of capitalism has gone together with an increasing level of concentration of the means of production in corporations which have become ever larger.

Thus, if the free markets are supposed to recreate the state of nature in society in which property is always new – a kind of inexhaustible Far West – then all the negative aspects of the state of nature (and of the Far West) are also to be found there. In particular, we are likely to find those negative aspects or drawbacks which have been at the centre of modern political reasoning since Hobbes, and which we outlined in the previous chapter: without a superior authority, the state of nature (i.e. the markets) leads to competition, to the domination of the strongest over the weakest, and finally to a 'war of every man against every man' in which the first battle consists of depriving others of the right to enter freely into business. In the end, the same liberty that is at the basis of entrepreneurial direction can also lead to an abolition of the liberties of those people who are too weak to become entrepreneurs themselves.

The markets cannot be left entirely to their own devices. Rather, society must prevent individual entrepreneurs from controlling markets and thereby establishing excessive power. There is a need for a superior political organization that watches over the rules of individual liberty, of which the first rule is the freedom to enter into business. Such a political institution must include both entrepreneurs and non-entrepreneurs, in order to be able to limit the possible excesses of those already in positions of entrepreneurial power and maintain the fragmentation of society. The name given to this political institution is modern democracy.

2 The institution of democracy or how to regulate a fragmented society

Historically, the emergence of capitalism and the ascendance of modern democracy in the Western world coincide. In terms of corporate governance, this means that the system of legitimate governance built around the entrepreneur and the democratic principles of power sharing come to fruition at the same time. At first glance, governance by democracy would appear to be in opposition with governance by the entrepreneur. The entrepreneur governs by virtue of superior qualities, while democracy governs on the basis of sovereign power equally distributed to a fragmented society of individuals. Whereas the entrepreneur orients collective action by drawing on his/her authority, democracy implies debate, refutation, and criticism. This opposition of forces looks like a contradiction. And yet, as paradoxical as it might seem at first sight, in terms of political reasoning, democracy is indispensable to establishing the legitimacy of entrepreneurial direction. Democracy is necessary to make entrepreneurial direction compatible with the norms of modern society and hence acceptable to those who are governed by it.

Democracy as a technique of government

In the modern mentality, the word democracy is laden with a variety of values, political, economic, and emotional. Therefore, it is necessary to be very precise in using the term. Stripped of the values people associate with it, democracy is nothing more than a technique of government – one among several – a manner of legitimating the governing powers and the decisions they reach. In this definition, we follow Schumpeter: 'The eighteenth-century philosophy of democracy may be couched in the following definition: the democratic method is that institutional arrangement for arriving at political decisions which realizes the common good by making the people itself decide issues through the election of individuals who are to assemble in order to carry out its will.'[8] In a very similar vein, Michel Foucault says that democracy represents 'techniques and procedures' of government,[9] a set of institutional tools for making authority acceptable to the governed.

What distinguishes democracy from other techniques of government is the emphasis on fragmenting every exercise of power in order to prevent one individual or one group of individuals from imposing authority and depriving others of their liberty. In contrast to governance by monarchy based on the unity of the social body and in contrast to governance by oligarchy based, in turn, on set differences between classes or castes, democracy is a technique of government that bases control on the division of society and that draws strength and coherence from social fragmentation. Democracy is reinforced by the individual liberties which it ensures, and this is why it develops fully with the modernization of societies. The more modern a society becomes, the more individuals in that society will be likely to base their identity on individual liberty, that is to say on the free choice of those who will command them. In order to guarantee that this choice is always available, it is necessary that all individuals can be sure that the same rules are in place to maintain their individual liberty and that nobody can take this liberty away from them for personal benefit. Conversely, greater availability of free choice consolidates the position of democracy as a technique of government. This is how the coherence of the political system is established. Individual liberty, free choice,

---

[8] Schumpeter, *CSD*, IV, XXI, 250.
[9] M. Foucault, *Du gouvernement des vivants*, Paris: Annuaire du Collège de France, 1979–80, pp. 449–52, our translation from the French text.

fragmentation of power, and safeguards to protect individual liberty –
such are the key elements of a general demand for democracy as it
emerges over the course of the Enlightenment.

Underlying this general conception are three concrete procedures for
implementing the maintenance of individual liberty: equality of rights,
separation of powers, and representation with public debate.[10] In
further articulating the three procedures of democracy, we will cite
extensively from Tocqueville's famous book *Democracy in America*.
The United States was the first country to be created on the basis of
modern liberal thought. In the United States of the time, modern
democracy was visible in its original, pure state. As Tocqueville
wrote so lucidly at the time, conscious of the historical importance of
his observations, 'I confess that in America I saw more than America;
I sought there an image of democracy itself, of its penchants, its character, its prejudices, its passions; I wanted to become acquainted with it
if only to know at least what we ought to hope or fear from it.'[11]

Equality of individuals: establishing social fragmentation

The first procedure of democracy is equality of rights among individuals. In the classic position of the philosophers of the Enlightenment
who sought to establish the necessary conditions for personal liberty
(Locke; Hume), the law must be based upon perfect equality. In very
concrete terms, the law establishes not only civic equality, but also
economic equality on the basis of property ownership. As we have seen,
the possibility to acquire property freely is indispensable to personal
liberty and the freedom to become an entrepreneur; the modern liberal
society is built around law – a law before which all are equal and which
all have an equal interest to defend. This is the foundation of the liberal
social contract, as described by Tocqueville:

the idea of rights is nothing other than the idea of virtue introduced into the
political world. It is with the idea of rights that men have defined what license
and tyranny are; enlightened by it, each could show himself independent

---

[10] For a recent synthesis, see D. Rueschemeyer, E. Stephens, and S. Stephens,
   Capitalist Development and Democracy, Chicago: University of Chicago Press,
   1993, pp. 43–6.
[11] A. Tocqueville, *DA*, Introduction, p. 13.

without arrogance and submissive without baseness ... Each one, having a particular good to defend, recognizes the right of property in principle.[12]

Then with none differing from those like him, no one will be able to exercise a tyrannical power; men will be perfectly free because they will all be entirely equal and they will be perfectly equal because they will be free. This is the ideal toward which democratic people tend.[13]

Equality fragments the society, because with equality every individual has the same right to act as everyone else. Modern society can be thought of not as a single social unit, but rather as an aggregation of autonomous individuals. In much the same way as Newtonian physics reintroduces the ancient Greek notion of the atom (in ancient Greek, a-tomos means that which cannot be divided), liberal society introduces equality among individuals (in-divis, in Latin, means that which cannot be divided). To affirm the equality of every individual before the common law is to build a society on the principle of fragmentation. Equality before the law alone, however, cannot prevent certain individuals from orienting the law to their personal advantage. This is why the separation of powers takes on such importance under democracy.

Separation of powers: protecting social fragmentation

Equality of rights can only be maintained if no single power can impose itself upon society. As Montesquieu so forcefully put it in arguing against despotism: 'power should be a check to power'.[14] To prevent the abuses of autocracy and to ensure the protection of individual freedom, political government legally institutionalizes the separation of the powers of direction (the executive) and oversight (the legislature and the judiciary). Again, in Tocqueville's words, 'the right to direct the official presumes the right to discharge him if he does not follow the orders that one transmits to him, or to raise him in grade if he zealously fulfills all his duties ... One should indeed be careful, for an elective power that is not to be subject to a judicial power sooner or later escapes from all control or is destroyed.'[15] Thanks to the separation of powers, social fragmentation is protected: the powers to be exercised

---

[12] *DA* I, 2, 6, pp. 227–8.   [13] *DA* II, 2, 1, p. 479.
[14] C.-L. de Montesquieu, *On the Spirit of Laws*, 1748, Book 11, Section 4, in the translation of Thomas Nugent, 1752.
[15] *DA* I, 1, 5, pp. 69–70.

over individuals are necessarily also divided. Just as importantly, the concentration of powers is considered oppressive and incompatible with the principles of modern governance. However, equality and separation of powers are not sufficient, if individuals are publicly to be able to manifest and defend their personal liberty; modern liberal society also requires a forum for the representation of different interests.

Fragmentation takes centre stage: representation and public debate

In effect, in order to support and protect equality of rights and separation of powers, the process of governing must be rendered visible to the citizens. This is why it is essential that public expressions of the individual voice are organized, either directly (direct democracy) or by the intermediary of representatives (participative democracy). In contrast to authoritarian regimes built on uniformity of opinion and the maintenance of secrecy, democracy welcomes differences of opinion, and the expression of differences through debates among representatives reinforces consent to decisions made by demonstrating the persistence of individual freedoms. These debates provide public proof that no single individual or elite is monopolizing power or preventing others from contesting the existing power structure. In other words, the *content* of such debates is often less important than their *representation*, or the process of putting the discussion on the public stage with the people's *representatives*. The existence of politics as a public theatre makes the rule of individual liberty visible to all. The importance of the dramatization of differences, of representation, and of public debate is also recognized by Tocqueville:

In America, the people name those who made the law and those who execute it; they themselves form a jury that punishes infractions of the law. Not only are institutions democratic in their principle, but also in all their developments; thus the people name their representatives directly and generally choose them every year in order to keep them more completely under their dependence. It is therefore really the people who direct, and although the form of government is representative, it is evident that the opinions ... can find no lasting obstacles that prevent them from taking effect in the daily direction of society.[16]

[16] *DA* I, 1, 3, p. 165.

And, a little further on, 'when one accords to each a right to govern society, one must surely recognize his capacity to choose among different opinions that agitate his contemporaries and to appreciate different facts, the knowledge of which can guide him'.[17] He concludes that 'the moral empire of the majority is founded in part on the idea that there is more enlightenment and wisdom in many men united than in one alone, in the number of legislators than in their choice. It is the theory of equality applied to intellects.'[18]

By demonstrating that numerous different interests exist, are represented and can confront each other, democracy puts itself on stage, as a show of social fragmentation and personal liberty. In democratic society, a decision that is not debated and therefore not criticized and amended is not considered legitimate – such a decision has the tint of tyranny. Even the most straightforward questions are put on stage and subject to the test of differing opinions. This is not a weakness of democracy, but a condition for its acceptance as a just system of governance. Democracy implies criticism of decision makers and thereby reinforces their power. Finally, in the dialectical tug of war between private interests and the general interest that characterizes liberal society, democracy is the government technique that prevents the general interest from imposing itself upon private interests.

Equality of rights, separation of powers, and representation with public debate – these three procedures form a trinity that allows the imposition of laws and regulations that are binding for all and makes it difficult for a single individual (or group) to use power to personal advantage. According to Schumpeter, democracy works like a religion.[19] In effect, it creates the conditions for general obedience and a standardization of practices based on rules that no one feels are imposed. In this way, it contributes to ensuring modern individual liberty, including the liberty to become an entrepreneur. The emergence of the entrepreneur as the heroic figure of capitalism is paralleled by the emergence of democracy as the institutionalization of social fragmentation.

In this chapter, we have seen that the distinguishing characteristic of modern liberal society is the institutionalization of social fragmentation to prevent the exercise of concentrated power in a manner incompatible with individual liberty. It is by this mechanism that governance by entrepreneurs is rendered acceptable to modern society.

[17] *DA* I, 2, 3, p. 174.   [18] *DA* I, 2, 7, p. 237.   [19] Schumpeter, *CSD*, pp. 265–6.

Fragmentation of society is assured by competition; competition which brings forth new rivals allows for the continuous redistribution of entrepreneurial power. However, for the discipline of competition to work in this manner, the conditions of competition need to be ideologically and politically stabilized. By institutionalizing a permanent division of powers through the procedures of equality, separation of oversight and control, and the representation of differences in public debate, the technique of democracy maintains fragmentation and thereby regulates society. In contrast to traditional societies, liberal society does not seek unity, but rather finds cohesion in the refusal of unity. This implies that the power of the entrepreneur, who seeks to unify productive forces, is only acceptable to the extent that it is systematically called into question. It is in terms of this general political context characteristic of modern Western societies that models of corporate governance are either considered legitimate or criticized as illegitimate and eventually reformed.

Conclusion to Part I

Political philosophy teaches us that the legitimacy of just governance in modern society has two possible sources. In the first instance, we refer to entrepreneurial direction and the founder of the business, who seeks to grow the corporation by virtue of hard work and unique talent, and, by pursuing his personal interest, contributes also to the general interest (Chapter 1). In the second instance, we refer to democracy as an effective technique of governance – a technique which safeguards individual liberty and finally institutionalizes social fragmentation by means of equality of rights, separation of powers, and representation and debate of different interests. Conversely, democracy ensures that the general interest does not supersede particular interests. These two sources of *legitimacy* are contradictory in that they oppose the concentration and the fragmentation of power. This dialectical contradiction constitutes the template of acceptable governance in modern liberal society in general, and in corporate governance in particular.

Modern man accepts to be governed in the corporation under the same conditions as he accepts to be governed by the other institutions of modernity. Whether a form of governance is just or unjust is a question that can only be answered in the context of modern opinion – what constitutes fairness in corporate governance has to derive from a definition grounded in the norms and values of society. We have shown that the source of legitimacy in governance is twofold: the entrepreneur and democracy. The evaluation of whether corporate governance is 'efficient', or 'just', or even 'good', will be made in reference to these two sources of legitimacy. Both the entrepreneur and democracy represent bases of power. One acts upon the other, like two antagonistic forces, and the resulting equilibrium defines acceptable governance (see Figure 1).

Both governance by the entrepreneur and governance by democracy stem from the defence of modern, individual liberty, that is to say the

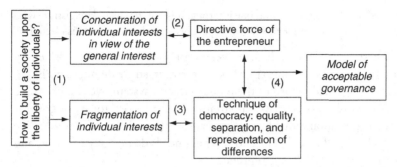

Figure 1 Dialectic of modern governance

individual's right not to have to submit to the control of anyone. However, the same quest to build society on the defence of individual liberty has given rise to two forms of governance that are at *opposite ends* of the philosophical spectrum: governance by entrepreneurial direction, a technique that builds on the assumption that there is a natural inequality among individuals to establish the legitimacy of power of a single person, stronger and more able than the rest; and governance by democracy, a technique that safeguards social fragmentation, takes on life through debates and ensures the absolute equality of all. These two sources of legitimate authority oppose each other in terms of the definition of power they represent – concentrated for the entrepreneur, fragmented for democracy – but are also complementary and, by synthesis, constitute the acceptable form(s) of governance.

Despite the apparent contradiction between the way governance by entrepreneurial direction concentrates power and the way governance by democracy emphasizes the social fragmentation of interests, this double form of legitimacy appears to work very well. Tocqueville explains away the contradiction by highlighting the role played by democracy in facilitating entrepreneurship and ensuring prosperity:

one would say that in the United States there is no imagination that does not exhaust itself in inventing the means of increasing wealth and satisfying the needs of the public. The most enlightened inhabitants of each district constantly made use of their enlightenment to discover new secrets appropriate to increasing the common prosperity; and when they have found any, they hasten to pass along to the crowd. When examining up close the vices and weakness often displayed in America by those who govern, one is astonished at the growing prosperity of the people – and one is wrong. It is not the elected magistrate who makes democracy prosper; but it prospers because the magistrate is elected.[1]

There seems to be a link between economic development driven by enterprise and the context of liberty guaranteed by democracy. Based on the historical record of the modern liberal system, we can conclude that the link between two apparently contradictory forms of governance is not anomalous but rather represents evidence of a productive equilibrium of forces. The entrepreneur needs democracy to work, and democracy needs the entrepreneur.

We have already shown why the entrepreneur needs democracy: democracy ensures the fragmentation of powers and limits the excesses of entrepreneurs. Thanks to public debates, democracy prevents entrepreneurs from monopolizing power and depriving others of the right to become entrepreneurs. In other words, democracy helps ensure the legitimacy of the entrepreneur in modern society. Tocqueville made this point quite clearly, when he noted that 'in democratic countries, as elsewhere, most industries are conducted at little cost by men whom wealth and enlightenment do not place above the common level of those they employ; these entrepreneurs of industry are very numerous; their interests differ; they therefore cannot readily agree among themselves and combine their efforts'.[2]

By maintaining equality between entrepreneurs and non-entrepreneurs, democracy prevents the more able from oppressing the less able and finally taking away their liberty. Democracy is what makes it possible for people from the lower rungs of society to rise, the process that so fascinated Tocqueville, a French aristocrat. In the famous fifth chapter of the third part of *Democracy in America* (Book II), he describes in great detail how the democratic spirit stimulates the relationship between master and servant and encourages the former to compete against the latter. By providing a forum for the opposition of different interests, democracy maintains legal, regulatory, and social constraints on entrepreneurs and, in this way, makes it possible for new, better entrepreneurs to continue to come forth.

Conversely, democracy also needs the entrepreneur. In a democracy, free individuals have multiple, different interests. Given institutional character by the separation of powers and amplified by public debate,

---

[1] *DA* II, 2, 4, p. 488.   [2] *DA* II, 3, 7, p. 556.

this multiplicity of different interests can lead to irreconcilable differences and cause working majorities to split into a large number of minority interest groups. Under these circumstances, democracy can become inefficient, and society has difficulty reaching decisions pertaining to the common interest. Out of the potential anarchy of individual interests, the entrepreneur represents the force that succeeds in providing direction to social communities. By charisma and talent, the entrepreneur rallies individuals to a cause and organizes a cohesive group, identifying economic opportunities and sometimes even imposing decisions that individual interests, in their diversity, fail to see or cannot agree upon. From Schumpeter to Penrose and Kirzner, all the principal scholars of entrepreneurship have shown that the entrepreneur is *the* individual, alone among others, able to discover and implement the choice that best serves the general interest of progress.[3] Democracy needs the entrepreneur to identify and guide communities down the paths of progress and to avoid the quicksand of inefficient government by innumerable, opposing minority interests. The temporal coincidence of the rise of democracy and the crowning of the entrepreneur in the eighteenth and nineteenth centuries is not an accident of history. Democracy makes possible the existence of the entrepreneur, but, conversely, the entrepreneur provides the direction necessary for free individuals to work in the common interest, thereby making sure that social fragmentation does not result in paralysis.

Modern society is organized as a dialectic opposition of forces between entrepreneurial direction and social fragmentation bridged by democracy. The entrepreneur organizes and gives direction to economic activity; social fragmentation imposes the competition of markets on the entrepreneur. This opposition of forces is continuously renewed and plays out again and again. The entrepreneur concentrates power; social fragmentation dilutes power. This opposition of forces gives rise to a creative tension in the governance of modern society. It also plays a decisive role in determining the governance of the business corporation, a particular form of organization in modern society.

From the political viewpoint mapped out in this first part of the book, the entrepreneur and democracy need to be able to co-exist and to contribute equally to determining the corporate governance forms

---

[3] See G. Gilder, *Recapturing the Spirit of Enterprise*, San Francisco: ICS Press, 1992.

observed in practice. Nonetheless, as we have pointed out, the opposition between these two sources of legitimate power can be problematic: the modern corporation runs the risk of serious, perhaps eventually fatal, dysfunctions stemming from the tension between entrepreneurs and democracy. This risk is particularly pronounced in today's large corporation. How to maintain the legitimacy of entrepreneurial direction in a world of dispersed shareholdings where ownership and work are no longer connected? Does the force of social fragmentation win out over entrepreneurial direction's tendency to concentrate power, fatally weakening the ability to organize the corporation? In order to be able to address questions such as these, we have to obtain historical perspective. Focusing the next part of the book on the history of corporate governance under the dual pressure of the entrepreneur and social fragmentation, we will be able to see how these two forces tend to oppose and constrain each other, in a dialectic that constitutes the engine of evolution for corporate governance.

Understanding how corporate governance evolves: the contribution of history

Introduction to Part II

We have argued that corporate governance is built upon a dialectic opposition between entrepreneurial direction and social fragmentation that is bridged by democracy. In Part I, we described this opposition of forces in terms of the arguments developed by the philosophers who constructed the ideological foundations of modern liberal society. If our hypothesis is valid, we should be able to read the history of corporate governance as a dynamic resultant of the dialectic opposition we have described. As we will show in this chapter, the meaning of what constitutes legitimate corporate governance has evolved over time, with the emergence and transformation of the entrepreneur and the intensification of social fragmentation. The principles of corporate governance were established with the beginnings of capitalism, but the application of these principles has responded to developments in the economic context and modifications in the socio-political landscape. We do not propose, in this second part of the book, to do original historical research. We prefer to refer to the work of historians in the field, acknowledging our debt. By highlighting the major trends in the economic history of the corporation, as presented by historians, we can shed light on the process whereby models of corporate governance evolve and take hold. The objective is to provide an analytic synthesis based on the historical research that others have carried out.

In explaining the evolution of corporate governance in terms of the dialectic opposition of forces between entrepreneurial direction and social fragmentation, a dialectic that results in the adoption of democratic procedures over time, we are working with concepts that are themselves undergoing development, albeit in different dimensions. In particular, it is important to note that although the function of the entrepreneur was already relatively well established in the Western world by the beginning of the nineteenth century, the spread of the democratic technique of governance and its extension to multiple spheres of social life lagged behind.[1] Therefore, the historical evolution of corporate governance needs to be understood not only in terms of the dynamic between entrepreneur and social fragmentation, but also in terms of the different degrees of maturity of these opposing forces. In order to see how corporate governance evolves, it is necessary to describe the models of reference for what constitutes proper corporate governance in the principal economic eras of the last two centuries and to explain why these models emerged. By 'model of reference' we mean the form of corporate governance that is adopted by leading companies and comes to be seen as 'normal' (i.e. normative) in the period and countries under consideration, whatever the type of ownership. The legitimacy of a technique of governance is closely related to what is considered 'normal' at any particular time in history. In each period, concrete corporate governance forms are observed and evaluated as good or bad in comparison with the model of reference.

In our historical review, we identify three models of reference for corporate governance: the familial, the managerial, and the public. These three models correspond to three distinct stages of evolution, each of which marks the further extension of democratic procedures into the domain of corporate governance. The first stage traces its beginnings to the *enfranchisement of the entrepreneur* and the granting to all individuals of equal rights of starting and directing a business; this stage extends from the late eighteenth century to the early twentieth century and is dominated by what we will call the 'familial model' of corporate governance. The second stage has its roots in the late nineteenth century with the emerging *separation of powers* of ownership and control (direction) by professional managers in what is to become the modern corporation by the time of Berle and Means; this stage is described in the literature as the 'managerial model' of corporate governance, and we will use the same term to speak of a period that is typically situated between the 1920s and the 1970s. Finally, we discern a third stage, emerging with the economic crises of the 1970s, characterized by the enormous growth of global capital markets and typified by increasing *representation and public debate*; we will call this the 'public model' of corporate governance and follow its evolution to

---

[1] We refer here to the classical work of Thomas Marshall, 'Citizenship and social class', in T. Marshall, *Citizenship and Social Class and Other Essays*, Cambridge: Cambridge University Press, 1950, pp. 1–85.

the present. Although the basic function of the entrepreneur has remained the same, namely to direct business activity, the actor(s) who fulfils the function of the entrepreneur has changed over time, from the business founders of the nineteenth century to the professional management of the twentieth century and, latterly, shareholders in financial markets, who impose strategic choices upon the corporation. Our three-stage description of the evolution of corporate governance traces the dialectic opposition between entrepreneurial force and social fragmentation over two centuries and articulates how the three principal procedures of democracy gradually come to be applied in corporate governance.

3 | *Familial governance (c.1800–1920): economic enfranchisement and the founder as entrepreneur*

The first stage of the evolution of corporate governance we shall describe coincides with the birth of modern society and the beginnings of capitalism. As we have already pointed out in Part I, this period saw a redefinition of the meaning and significance of property, with important consequences for all of society. Entrepreneurship was liberalized, a right to be granted equally to all citizens. The emancipation of the entrepreneur was a first step, both in the deployment of the liberal political project and in the establishment of the technique of democracy in the governance of the activities of production (1). The privatization of the means of production led to a definition of the rules of governance in the private corporation centred on the founder entrepreneur. He (we will use the masculine pronoun throughout this chapter in line with the historical context) was the one who exercised the entrepreneurial force in the development of the corporation, either by being personally involved in the founding, or by virtue of inheritance. The extended discretionary power accorded to the owner was based on his *genetic* ties to the corporation. This power was constrained by a counterweight that was also private and genetic, namely the institution of the family. Modern liberal society of the nineteenth century made the family the institution of reference in the maintenance of social equilibrium. The result was a familial model of governance in which the entrepreneur and father represented the exemplary figure (2). By balancing private power with a private counterweight to power, this model responded to the expectations of the liberal political project. Nonetheless, from the outset, the familial model of governance contained contradictions, suffered from criticism, and was subject to the eroding effect of the second constitutive force of modern society, social fragmentation (3).[1]

---

[1] For this chapter, we will refer extensively to P. Mathias and M. Postan (eds.), *The Cambridge Economic History of Europe*, Vol. VII, Part 1, Cambridge:

1 The entrepreneur – a child of modernity

Traditional conceptions of property: the partition of rights

For centuries, in the pre-modern West, ownership of the means of production was closely tied to social hierarchy. Only the aristocrat had the right to own land. Thus, until the beginning of the modern age in most Western countries, commoners needed to obtain royal permission and often also a title of nobility in order to purchase land. By contrast, commoners who worked the land did own the *tools* of production necessary for value creation; during the latter part of the Middle Ages, even the serf attached to a master owned his own tools and could pass them on to his descendants. Artisans, too, owned their own tools. Each social group exercised hereditary property rights over the possessions that characterized them as a distinct class: land, tools, the right to hunt, the right to bear arms, the right to raise taxes, etc. In pre-modern society, ownership was a technical attribute and a consequence of social status. In the traditional concept of property, it was social status that determined property, not property that determined feudal social status.[2] A man was born noble, because he was a land owner, or a person was born an artisan because he inherited his father's tools.

Traditional property rights law made a distinction between property and tenancy. Property attached a social status to an object, whereas tenancy referred to the work performed on an object. Generally, the nobility or aristocrat was the owner of lands exploited by tenant farmers. By the definition of social status, the aristocrat *could not work* the land. Typically without a formal contract, the tenant farmer worked the land, often over several generations, but he *could not sell* the land. On the other hand, the tenant farmer could cede the right to exploit the land to another tenant farmer.

From Roman times, property rights theory has distinguished between three types of rights – the right to make use of a property (*usus*), the right

---

Cambridge University Press, 1974, pp. 180–230, and K. Polanyi, *The Great Transformation*, New York: Rinehart and Co., 1944.

[2] F. L. Ganshof, *Feudalism*, New York: Harper and Row, 1961; G. Duby, *Guerriers et paysans, vii–xiiᵉ siècle: premier essor de l'économie européenne*, Paris: Gallimard, 1973.

to benefit from the fruits it yields (*fructus*), and the right to destroy it or sell it (*abusus*).[3] We can say that, in pre-modern times, the aristocrat owned the rights of *fructus* (in part) and *abusus*, but not the rights of *usus* (the aristocrat was forbidden to work); the tenant, on the other hand, owned the rights of *usus* and *fructus* (in part), but not the right of *abusus* – he was not an owner, but merely a tenant of property. In the feudal order, never could a single individual, even the king, own all three of the rights associated with property. The function of this partition of property rights was to limit the excesses of power. This strict partition of property rights ownership constituted an essential building block of an ordered society, a society in which the *complementary* nature of (property rights) positions provided for harmonious relations. Taken as a whole, traditional property rights law formed the basis of a society organized around a clear and impermeable hierarchy of social status. Solidarity between the different classes of traditional society was maintained by reciprocal dependence and the need to cooperate in exercising the different property rights that no one individual or class could hold alone. However, this reciprocal dependence also gave rise to regular conflicts over the division of the *fructus* (over which part was to go to duty, to tax, or to tithing, etc.), conflicts which are characteristic of a society built on the interdependence of stakeholders. In order to rein in the potential for conflict, the governance of property required numerous contracts, written, or more commonly based on a man's honour, and these contracts maintained a dense network of relationships between the holders of the different rights to property, often from generation to generation.[4] In order to understand in what sense modern society constituted a radical revolution it is necessary to bear in mind the medieval conception of partitioned property rights that we have sketched here.

---

[3] Part III discusses the implications of this distinction more fully.
[4] One often forgets that feudal society was permeated with legal and contractual concerns, with a multiplicity of legal sources and jurisdictions. As a consequence of the partition of property rights, differences of opinion over the exercise of property rights and over their limits make up the bulk of a considerable body of medieval legal production. This understanding helps us gain a better appreciation of the contemporary period, for, as we will show in the ensuing chapters, the contemporary period is also beset with challenges arising out of the partition of property rights.

The great legal revolution

The decline of the traditional form of social organization began in thirteenth-century Europe, with the ascendance of the towns. As the centre of economic gravity shifted towards the merchant cities, the hierarchical society based on land as the only significant means of production started to show cracks. With the development of international trade and commerce and the first wave of industrialization in the fifteenth century, the traditional notion of property in which work and ownership were separated could not be uniformly maintained: increasingly, there started to be a confounding of work (principally manufacturing and banking) and the ownership of capital. The merchant economy opened the door to the beginnings of a pre-capitalist economy.[5] The Florentine banker or the English merchant worked (*usus*), managed his fortune (*abusus*), and benefited from its fruits (*fructus*). In other words, he exercised all three rights to property. The traditional, hierarchical organization that forbade work in order to limit the power of those who owned property was resented by the emerging class of bourgeois (literally, people of the town) as a hindrance to economic development and political renewal. As Berman has shown, the liberal ideas of Hobbes and Locke and the philosophers of the Enlightenment came to the fore in a context of political continuity and legal rupture.[6] These political philosophers sought to found a new social order based on the individual defined as an owner of property – liberalism.

Inevitably, since traditional society based the legitimacy of power on the partition of property rights, liberalism had to formulate its own theory of property in response. As already discussed, the work of Locke defines the modern individual around the notion of private property. This was historically necessary – to create a new political society, the hierarchical basis of the old society had to be fundamentally questioned. The traditional society was based on a *collective* notion of property: each member of society held a part of the common property and was therefore dependent upon the others. Solidarity among individuals was a consequence of the partition of property rights and the

---

[5] See F. Braudel, *Civilization and Capitalism, 15th–18th Century*, Vol. II: *The Wheels of Commerce*, New York: HarperCollins, 1982.

[6] J. H. Berman, *Law and Revolution: The Formation of the Western Legal Tradition*, Cambridge, MA: Harvard University Press, 1983.

ban on concentrating ownership of all the rights to property in a single person.

The great legal revolution that prefigured and then accompanied the industrial revolution of the eighteenth century, typically (but not in all cases, i.e. Germany) eventually also drew strength from political revolutions: first the English revolution of the seventeenth century (1649–88), then the American Revolution (1776), and finally the French Revolution of 1789. In each of these countries, the revolution redefined private property in the modern sense. Thus, the French Declaration des Droits de l'Homme (1789) states, 'since property is an inviolable and sacred right, no one shall be deprived thereof except where public necessity, legally determined, shall clearly demand it, and then only on condition that the owner shall have been previously and equitably indemnified' (article 17). In almost identical fashion, the United States Bill of Rights (1791) states that '[No person shall] be deprived of life, liberty, or property, without due process of law; nor private property be taken for public use, without just compensation' (article 7). *Private* property became established as an essential characteristic of modern society – essential because private property permitted the full exercise of individual liberty, emancipating the individual from dependence towards the holders of other rights to the same property and thereby making him *autonomous*.

In the name of liberty and modern equality, the legal revolution makes it possible for an individual to work with property, benefit from its fruits, and sell it as he pleases. In order to legitimize this revolution, liberalism emphasizes the primordial function of the right of *usus*: he/she who *works* has the right to harvest and to sell *because* he/she works,[7] for individual property cannot be acquired without individual work. The new importance ascribed to work turns the old hierarchy based on the pre-eminence of the 'non-working' class on its head and forms the basis for the political acceptance of the entrepreneur in modern society. Impressed by a variety of experiences that demonstrate the powerful importance of work in America, the modern liberal society par excellence, Tocqueville describes this reversal of perspective in a particularly memorable way. Observing the different

---

[7] See Part I for a discussion of the key significance accorded to the right of *usus* in the writings of liberalism since Locke.

conditions on the two banks of the Ohio River (the boundary separating states with slavery from states free of slavery), the French visitor perceives how slavery, that is to say the debasement of work, goes a long way towards explaining how the two societies differ in terms of resource usage and wealth.

On the left bank of the Ohio work is blended with the idea of slavery; on the right bank, with that of well-being and progress; there it is degraded, here they honor it; on the left bank of the river, one cannot find workers belonging to the white race, for they would fear resembling slaves; one must rely on the care of the Negroes; on the right bank one would seek in vain for an idle man: the white extends his activity and his intelligence to all his works.[8]

These remarks poignantly anticipate the ideas of liberal economists from Say to Demsetz: the link between private property, its exploitation through work, and the creation of wealth.

The aristocrats who benefited from the right of *fructus* and exercised the right of *abusus*, but not the right of *usus*, were stigmatized as unproductive and illegitimate by the new powers. The old leisured class was politically marginalized with the advance of liberalism, through a gradual process of integration into the new bourgeoisie in England and Germany, through violent upheaval and revolution in France, and through proscription in the United States. In parallel and with the same methods, the rise of liberalism led to the disappearance of the commons and to the closure of the guilds and craft unions that had controlled the activity of artisans and prevented free access to the professions; another traditional way of limiting the freedom to work and the right of *usus* was abolished. At the same time, those who refused to work were stigmatized. As Michel Foucault has shown, the ideology of work was accompanied by exclusion and, not infrequently, incarceration or putting away, for those who refused to enter into the new order and work for a living:[9] the United Kingdom saw the creation of workhouses for the unemployed (1834); the United States also had its poorhouses or almshouses.

Between the 1650s and the 1850s, most Western countries underwent their own legal revolutions and formulated new statutes for

---

[8] *DA* I, 2, 10, p. 332.
[9] See, for example, M. Foucault, *Discipline and Punish: The Birth of the Prison*, New York: Random House, 1975.

property rights.[10] In the new laws, the social partition of property rights was eliminated and the individual was authorized to hold all of the property rights. Based on this legal and political rupture, the traditional relationship between social status and property was completely reversed: no longer did social status determine property, but, on the contrary, it was property that now determined social status. This reversal established the conditions of free enterprise and paved the way for the modern entrepreneur.

A *new hierarchy based on property*

By the definition of modern liberty, every citizen could freely assure his/her own subsistence by work, and work was enthroned as the essential means for acquiring (new) social status. The liberal movement led to economic enfranchisement, giving every citizen equal access to property ownership.

The *founder entrepreneur* was the principal beneficiary of this general movement for political and economic emancipation. The founder entrepreneur entered into the culture of liberal society as the heroic prototype of the new regime – a regime that made the individual capacity for action of the *self-made man* the basis of modern authority. The founder entrepreneur did not inherit from the past, but rather, thanks to the redistribution of property, transcended the ancient social order. Sanctioned by new rules permitting the acquisition and holding of property, daring individuals proceeded to carve out vast private fortunes and create a new class of *bourgeois*. The modern entrepreneurs of the eighteenth and nineteenth centuries can be compared to the conquistadores of the sixteenth century in the Americas who created great domains in the new economic and social space that hunger and turmoil motivated them to seek and arms permitted them to conquer. Once again in history, important changes in the rules governing property made it possible for a redistribution of the means of production to

[10] D. North and L. Davis, *Institutional Change and American Economic Growth*, Cambridge: Cambridge University Press, 1971; D. North and R. Thomas, *The Rise of the Western World: A New Economic History*, Cambridge: Cambridge University Press, 1973. Concerning the early history of property rights in the United States see D. Schultz, *Property, Power, and American Democracy*, New Brunswick, NJ: Transaction, 1992, especially Chs. 1, 2, and 3.

occur.[11] Driven by personal energy and supported in their efforts by industrial advances, the entrepreneurs established great businesses in the virgin spaces opened up by the recomposition of ownership. Instead of conquering land by means of war, these modern adventurers appropriated markets by means of innovation. In the new political landscape in which the very notion of property was being redefined, modern entrepreneurs created the rules of the game for private property. They were able to exercise the new economic and political force represented by entrepreneurship in a sovereign manner. In this golden early age of capitalism, the spirit of entrepreneurship of the founder entrepreneur became established as the engine of social progress, equalled in prestige by no one except perhaps the *savant*.

We hasten to stress that the enfranchisement of the entrepreneur is a *consequence of the liberal political project*, made possible by the application of the first of the great principles of democratic government, the equality of rights. Upsetting the traditionally ordered society, equality of rights translates into equality of the right to enterprise for all. As historical studies have shown, even in Europe entrepreneurs generally 'came from every social class and from all parts of the country . . . it is still permissible only to affirm that the body of known industrialists contained representatives of every stratum of society, every county, and virtually every category of economic activity'.[12] This was especially true of the United States, the country in which even the proverbial shoe shine boy could hope to become a millionaire by his own industry. One can therefore say that the founder entrepreneur is a child of modern liberal society and the emerging political democracy: without *civic equality*, there would have been no freedom of enterprise, and therefore no entrepreneurs.

Incorporation – the birth of the corporation as an artificial individual

The enterprise as a collective unit of production that assembles workers under the authority of leaders is not a modern invention. The history of great organizations of production is very long. The enterprise as an

[11] See Marx, *Capital*, section VIII for many further examples.
[12] P. Payne, 'Industrial entrepreneurship and management in Great Britain', in P. Mathias and M. Postan (eds.), *The Cambridge Economic History of Europe*, Vol. VII, Part 1, Cambridge: Cambridge University Press, 1974, p. 181.

organization (including the very large organization) has existed ever since it was necessary for economic reasons to join together workers for collective tasks: bridges, canals, mines, forest work, etc. From the age of antiquity, one finds tasks of various kinds organized in this manner: the great public buildings in Egypt, the Greek arsenals, the medieval cathedrals, and the royal manufactures. However, with the exception of slavery (the slave himself being considered a simple tool of production), these efforts always grouped together actors who held property rights to a part of the means of production that they would temporarily put into the service of a collective project such as the construction of a castle or a cathedral.

The real breakthrough of the early nineteenth century was the invention of the corporation as an institution in support of *private property*. For centuries, indispensable means of production such as pasture land, mines, or mills had been considered to be collective – *social* communities belonging to all (the *commons*) or to a lord who oversaw it in the name of all (the common property of mills and ovens), with workers owning their own tools and participating of their own volition. This state of affairs reflected the principle of property rights partition that was fundamental to the feudal order and forbade privatizing the entirety of the means of production. The guilds of the Middle Ages played an intermediary role between those who gave orders and those who took orders, but the guilds did not contract directly and therefore did not restrict the liberty of their members to participate or abstain from any particular job. The institution of the corporation (from Latin *corpus*, a body) for the first time allowed the collective unit of production to be considered as a separate entity of private property, governed by a single owner who could exploit it with others, but retained exclusive property rights. Although the corporation could (typically) constitute a collective of work, as an institution it was separate from the workers, owned and hence governed by a single individual – a *private* community in which workers no longer owned their own tools. Today, we are very used to thinking of the enterprise as a separate entity of private property, and we often forget what a radical social innovation this represented at the time and underestimate the deep changes in social attitudes and legal structures concerning the relationship between work and property that went with it.[13]

---

[13] The debate over the legal status of the corporation and, especially, over its position relative to that of other stakeholders, namely social partners, employees, and owners, continues to this day with work in the fields of corporate

Private property is the basis of political liberalism, but the corporation gathers under its roof workers without ownership of the means of production; this is not compatible with the spirit of individual freedom that underlies liberalism. The build-up and vast expansion of productive organizations considered as private properties required the creation of important supporting institutions in the law. In much the same way as medieval law provided for physical territories hereditarily directed by nobles, with the codes of incorporation modern law created legal territories governed by entrepreneurs and considered as their private economic spheres. The institution of the right to *incorporation* represented a critical advance in the history of modern Western society. With this right an individual could create a private society (corporation) of which he was the sole director, to the exclusion of all other stakeholders. At the time, granting the right to incorporation to private individuals seemed just about as incongruous as granting the right to coin currency and was strongly attacked – both by political conservatives and by socialists.

In order to make the corporation politically acceptable, it was necessary to construct a legal definition that gave it the same status as an individual, albeit an artificial individual, with the same rights and freedoms. Of course, such an ideologically weighty reframing did not pass without resistance: it took several decades to become established. The legal emancipation of the corporation as an individual took shape over battles in the courts to determine the degree to which the notion of individual could be extended to a community. In the United States, this conflict played out over a sixty-year period, between 1819 and 1886. In 1819 the US Supreme Court overturned a New Hampshire court decision to revoke the charter granted to Dartmouth College by King George III. The Court claimed that since the charter contained no revocation clause, it could not be questioned, even by courts of law. In other words, the statutes of a private organization could supersede public law. This decision was the starting point for a power struggle between public and private concerns. Initially, the individual States

---

law and stakeholder theory. For a deeper historical treatment, see R. Seavoy, *Origins of the American Business Corporation, 1784–1855: Broadening the Concept of Public Service during Industrialization*, Westport, CT: Greenwood Press, 1982, as well as B. Gardner, *The East India Company: A History*, London: Hart-Davis, 1971, Ch. 7, which addresses these questions from the point of view of economics.

responded by constitutional amendments that introduced the possibility of getting involved in the statutes of corporations. In 1855, the Supreme Court decision handed down in the case of *Dodge v. Woolsey* gave the legal advantage over corporations back to the States, stressing the law's powers over 'artificial bodies'.

However, the battle was not over yet. The 'individual' character of the corporation remained in doubt, until 1886, when the United States Supreme Court decided upon the case of *Santa Clara County v. Southern Pacific Railroad* by citing the 14th Amendment that guaranteed the rights of freed slaves to affirm the rights of 'the person' of the corporation. This ruling established the basis for defining the 'moral person' of the corporation, as a counterpoint to the physical person of the entrepreneur. Thus, the emancipation of the founder entrepreneur, that is to say the enabling of free enterprise, came to be complemented by the emancipation of the corporation itself considered as an artificial individual. This conflation between the physical person and the legal support to entrepreneurship allowed the entrepreneur to take full control of his private space, while still respecting the ideological boundaries of liberalism.

Over the course of the nineteenth century, the right to incorporation was institutionalized in the legislation of all of the European countries under consideration here: in France, by the Code du commerce (1807), the Loi sur les sociétés en commandites par action (1856), and the Lois sur les sociétés (1867); in the United Kingdom, by the Act for the Registration, Incorporation, and Regulation of Joint Stock Companies (1844), the Limited Liability Act (1855), and the Companies Act (1867); in Germany, finally, by the legislation covering the Kommandit-Gesellschaft auf Aktien and the Aktiengesellschaft (1870). By the end of this first phase of capitalism (c.1920), a significant part of the world was living under a regime of governance that differed dramatically from anything ever seen before: free individuals could create their own collective units of production and employ other free individuals to work in them, with the common (civil) law as the only restriction on the entrepreneur's freedom of direction. What is more, the form of organization thus created was legally considered like a social individual, autonomous and subject to the same regime of free choice as every individual in the liberal society. In other words, a double emancipation took place – that of the founder entrepreneur as an individual and that of the corporation he owned as an artificial individual.

The idea that a specific part of the society (i.e communities of production) obeyed private rules of governance that could differ from those pertaining to the rest of society became established in the modern mindset at the same time as the affirmation that the corporation, *as an organization*, had the same rights as any individual. The economy was conceived of as the *privatized* part of the public space, directed by individuals according to their own interests with a conflation of the entrepreneur as individual and the corporation as individual. The fundamental legal separation of public and private spheres is a reflection of the political separation between the social and the economic that characterizes modern society.[14] Consequently, it implies the formulation of its own rules of private corporate governance.

2 Discretionary power and its counterweight: the familial model of governance

Under the influence of liberal ideology, from the middle of the eighteenth century onwards, Western societies began to put in place democratic systems of political government. As we showed in Part I, democratic government is best suited to satisfy the constraints of liberalism. Thus, in the United States, universal suffrage was introduced from the end of the eighteenth century, albeit with restrictions by State, in order to prevent new immigrants from voting. These restrictions were slowly eliminated over time, but true universal suffrage took until 1865 and the Civil War before it extended to all States. In the United Kingdom, political citizenship extended progressively over the course of the nineteenth century: the Reform Act (1832) gave the right to vote to almost all men who possessed property. Suffrage was extended in 1867 to workers who were heads of household, and in 1884 to the majority of the male population. In France, the law of 1815 gave the right to vote to rich men over forty – a restriction that was later eased, until, in 1848, universal suffrage was declared (for all males over twenty-one years of age). In Germany, finally, universal suffrage was acquired in 1871, under the authority of the Empire.

---

[14] The notion of a separation between public and private as characteristic of modernity can be found in the writings of many of the most influential observers of modern society: Polanyi, Hirschman, Foucault, Arendt, etc. In this context, it is worth recalling that the Greek etymology of the term *oeconomia* relates to the governance (*nomos*) of the private domestic sphere (*oikos*).

The corporation, by contrast, although it emerged from the same liberal current, escaped implementation of the democratic practices that were becoming the norm in the political sphere: separation of powers and public representation of divergent interests. Ignoring this trend, the corporation was built upon the all-powerful founder entrepreneur. In order to understand this apparent paradox, we need to delve deeper into the split between public and private, specifying the distinctive rules of governance in each of these spheres. The corporation was supposed to govern itself according to the new rules of the private sphere: extended power of the 'master of the house', limited by a counterweight which was also private, namely the institution of the family. The result was a paternalistic model of governance in which the figure of the founder entrepreneur was explicitly associated with that of the good father of the family, who founded, governed, and protected his corporation as family. This model constituted an ideal equilibrium from the point of view of the liberal political project, because both power and its counterweight were part of the private sphere, but it contained internal contradictions that would eventually lead to its decline.

The all-powerful founder as entrepreneur

The businesses of the nineteenth century were essentially personal. The most widely used form of incorporation was the partnership (*societé en commandite* in France, *Kommanditgesellschaft* in Germany, *corporation in commendam* in England). In most cases, the founder entrepreneur had unlimited liability and backed the commitments of the corporation with his personal assets. The entrepreneur's risk was real and could lead to bankruptcy and personal ruin. In the spirit of liberalism, it appeared only natural that the assets of the entrepreneur and the assets of the business should not be distinct. The business was understood as a private, personal matter, inextricably and genetically tied to the founder and his family. The personal legitimacy of the founder entrepreneur was based upon the initial act of creating the corporation and his heirs benefited from being genetically associated with that act. The majority of the industrial dynasties founded in the nineteenth century can be associated with significant technological breakthroughs. Thus, there typically existed a direct, politically acceptable link between the authority of the entrepreneur, the work he had accomplished, and the economic and legal responsibility he took.

Not shareholders, but providers of funds

The joint stock company remained rare until late in this period, making up less than 5% of European corporations at the end of the nineteenth century. The personal implication of the entrepreneur notwithstanding, the law authorized the corporation to seek outside financing by issuing shares that participated in the profits and could be freely sold. In order to respond to increasing capital requirements from the 1820s onwards, the corporation commonly took on the form of a partnership with outside shareholders; this form distinguished between the entrepreneurs as owners and the shareholders who had the right to a dividend but not to directing the corporation. This separation allowed for financing without further involving financiers in the running of the corporation. The entrepreneur as owner (Fr. dirigeant commandité) maintained unlimited personal liability. The theoretical 'power' of shareholding appeared relatively early on in the history of capitalism, but stayed marginal and developed significantly only later, in the legal context of the limited partnership. In France, for example, the société anonyme (Code of 1807), remained strictly controlled and a founding required government authorization. Between 1850 and 1870 fewer than twenty such authorizations were granted, whereas partnerships numbered over 3000.[15] In the United States, when Charles Dow established his first Dow Jones Index on 3 July 1884, he listed just eleven corporations, nine of which were railways.[16] Until the end of the nineteenth century, the 'outside' shareholder remained suspect: he did not fit the original spirit of capitalism, a spirit which insisted upon conflating the entrepreneur as individual and the corporation as individual.

The unlisted stock company (private company) would only be fully adopted in Great Britain in 1907, and not until 1927 in France, more than 150 years after the birth of industrial capitalism. In the spirit of early capitalism, shareholders were seen purely as providers of funds, and, even if ownership was (relatively) diluted, the entrepreneur remained solely responsible and master of the enterprise, the only person with the right to direct. Common shareholders did not get

---

[15] For more background material on France during this period, see C. Freedeman, *Joint-Stock Entreprises in France (1807–1867)*, Chapel Hill: University of North Carolina Press, 1979.

[16] P. Frentrop, *A History of Corporate Governance*, Amsterdam: Deminor, 2003, p. 188.

involved in the affairs of the corporation they invested in, except in extreme situations, when they judged that their investment was at the peril of total loss. The present-day idea that the corporation is accountable to outside shareholders cannot be found in the literature of the nineteenth century.[17] A telling example is that of the near bankruptcy, in 1873, of Krupp, then Europe's largest industrial company. Rather than transform his firm into a limited company during a liquidity crisis, Alfred Krupp took to his bed, feigning illness, in an attempt to escape his bankers. In his words, 'we do not have shareholders who are out for dividends and we never will'.[18]

Shareholders played the passive role of fund provision and often were not vigilant enough to avoid losing a large part of their investments. With very poorly developed capital markets, shareholders were only few in number and typically came from the same circle as the owner entrepreneurs themselves, but there was no effective shareholder oversight:

The principal entrepreneurs were associated with others in the same or related business; and the entire system was apparently very adaptable and extremely flexible; Arkwright, as is well known, numbered among his partners John Smalley, Samuel Oldknow, David Dale, Samuel Need, the Strutts, Richard Arkwright jr., Thomas Walshman, John Cross, and others [that is to say the principal entrepreneurs of the day in Great Britain].[19]

Similarly, in Germany:

it is necessary to distinguish between two 'inner circles' among shareholders. The 'founders' of companies – who normally took over large portfolios of equity capital, sat on the board, and were involved in basic entrepreneurial decisions . . . and many outsiders and pure capitalists. Within this group there was a smaller 'inner group' of local people, [who] accumulated seats on board and concentrated fully on the direction of various mining enterprises

---

[17] In the literature of that era, shareholders were considered with some disdain, as lowly agents or brokers. For the most part, economists of the time ignore the shareholder and speak simply of the owner entrepreneur. This does not mean that there were no outside shareholders, or that the law did not allow for the distinction between entrepreneur and shareholder. Rather, in the spirit of liberalism, the owner entrepreneur was the only true economic actor (see Chapter 1).

[18] Frentrop, *History*, pp. 166–7.

[19] Payne, 'Industrial entrepreneurship', p. 192.

in which they had influence. ... They were mostly members of old commercial and entrepreneurial families (Stinnes, Grillo, Servaes, Haniel, *et al.*).[20]

The appearance of legal control by the shareholding body was merely a by-product of the sociological proximity of the owner director and his shareholders. This was really a kind of optical illusion: the legitimacy of the founder entrepreneur (and of his descendants) was based on work, talent, and personal authority, and more broadly on the idea of contributing to the progress of society. Shareholders were merely suppliers of capital, with little or no influence on the discretionary powers of the owner director, except inasmuch as they belonged to the same social and familial networks.

Since, in the preponderance of cases, the founder entrepreneur held the major part of the rights of *usus*, *fructus*, and *abusus* and also was held personally responsible in case of bankruptcy, he had extended discretionary power. Within the general framework of rules for the transmission of private property, the law required the founder entrepreneur to pass on the responsibility for bankruptcy and the power associated with it to his heirs, who thus inherited both the risks and the rights associated with property. There was a doubly tied genetic link between, on the one hand, the legitimacy of the owner director and the exercise of the entrepreneurial function, and, on the other hand, the legitimacy of the owner director and the pursuit of the founder entrepreneur's lineage.

How to govern a private community?
Although the law had established the entrepreneur's legitimate right to exert the force of entrepreneurial direction it did not tell the entrepreneur how to govern the corporation. Establishing authority by the conflation of the notions of entrepreneur and of corporation is one thing, maintaining authority inside the firm over 'free' employees quite another. In the new liberal society, the entrepreneur could not *force* employees to obey. The entrepreneur did have the coercive power of granting or not granting employment, according to his economic choices, and in this way deciding over the personal fate of employees. Indeed, there are a number of historical cases to provide evidence of

[20] J. Kocka, 'Entrepreneurs and managers in German industrialization', in *The Cambridge Economic History of Europe*, Vol. VII, Part 1, p. 542.

this kind of behaviour, and the European novel of the nineteenth century regularly invoked the extreme figure of the heartlessly utilitarian director of business, such as Balzac's Nucingen (*Le Père Goriot*, 1835), Dickens' Bounderby (*Hard Times*, 1855–7) or Zola's Grégoire (*Germinal*, 1885). More or less dramatically expressed in different countries, a cultural tradition emerged built around the figure of the heartless entrepreneur, a tradition that also reflected the socialist critique of capitalism. However, the form of governance by 'economic terror' described in this tradition could only be of limited effectiveness over the long term: on the one hand, it did not encourage productivity or quality; on the other hand, it required constant and costly control of those who worked only under threat and stood in philosophical opposition to one of the basic values of liberal society, individual freedom.

Interestingly, throughout the nineteenth century, one of the major problems of the corporation was the lack of qualified labour. The market for work uprooted the new workers and made them dependent upon the offer of the industrial corporation; at the same time, it gave rise to a new balance of forces, pitting the liberty to be an entrepreneur against the liberty of work, and forced a redefinition of authority in the liberal society. As Tocqueville fittingly observed, the individual character of property and the civic emancipation upset existing hierarchical relationships. Bases of individual liberty, both property and work give each person a certain measure of power in the public space to which he or she belongs. 'As the rules of social hierarchy are less observed, while the great are pulled down, while the small rise and poverty as well as wealth ceases to be hereditary, one sees the distance in fact and in opinion that separates the worker from master decrease each day.'[21] Quite clearly, the division of labour was at the origin of the efficiency of the modern enterprise (as Smith had already established in 1776); at the same time, the division of property between capital and labour became a constraint on corporate governance: the decisions made by the director (entrepreneur) had to be sufficiently well accepted by the employees if they were to be effectively put into practice. This was the price of success in the modern enterprise.

---

[21] *DA*, II, 3, 7, pp. 555–6. For a treatment of the new dialectic between master and servant established by liberal society, we refer to Chapter 5 in the third part of *Democracy in America* (Book II).

It is too easy to be biased by the devilish caricature drawn of the nineteenth-century entrepreneur, the image of a mean exploiter of people without human pity made popular by the anti-capitalist criticism of the day. Undeniably, a sizable number were cruel and pitiless. Industrialization was (and is) a very harsh process, especially as it affected the weak. Nonetheless, it must also be said that the human, philosophical, social, and economic questions generated by this process also disturbed the founding entrepreneurs from very early on and constituted an important part of their struggle for personal legitimacy and social standing. The nineteenth century was marked by a very intense questioning of the legitimacy of authority in the corporation, and this search for answers was often led by the entrepreneurs themselves. Thus, from the early 1800s onwards in the United Kingdom, an entrepreneur as well known as Robert Owen began to reflect upon the responsibility of the entrepreneur towards employees and upon the need to take care of their education and their health – this reflection led him to a kind of 'patriarchal socialism'; in France, an important movement of 'philanthropic' entrepreneurs developed, including such figures as Benjamin Delessert (who founded the first savings bank in 1818) or Joseph-Marie de Gerando, who focused his attention on the question of how employees could accumulate wealth. More generally, the employee question became a central issue in the political development of capitalism and in the legitimacy of the corporation.

By what values, moral foundations, economic principles, and social considerations should a corporation be run? In an economic world that was new, what principles could be drawn upon? Reading the memoirs and private correspondence of the great entrepreneurs of the age provides fascinating insight on these questions. One remarks an almost obsessive concern with finding an anchor for the entrepreneur's duties and responsibilities, and the search extends over a broad area – political thought, scientific proposals, and often religion. What renders power *respectable*? More than one might think, the mighty captains of industry of the day seemed haunted by moral questions: this questioning led many of them to believe that the mission of the entrepreneur must be to provide for the *good* of those who are working under his direction. However, beyond moral principles, the exercise of power by the entrepreneur raised political challenges in the emerging liberal and democratic context, for it had become necessary to develop a coherent way of thinking about the corporation as a *private* community. To what point did private authority over others extend? What was to prevent the entrepreneur from becoming an absolute, authoritarian master in his own corporation, who disregarded the liberal principle of individual autonomy upon which his own legitimacy was based? Power can only be respectable within limits set by an established counterweight to power. We will show that the role of legitimate counterweight to power was to be assumed by an institution that was both traditional and new – the family.

The political invention of the modern family as a private community[22]

As a productive organization, the family represented a very traditional form; with the liberal transformation, it metamorphosed into a modern institution. The industrial revolution(s), along with the resulting immigration and rural exodus, destroyed the traditional notion of family as clan, built on the common need to exploit the land, passed on from generation to generation. Obliged to leave their original homes and workplaces for cities and other countries, the traditional family as clan was dislocated and split apart. However, the family was also reconstructed, for this traditional institution was to serve as a key enabling factor in the implementation of the liberal political project. The philosophical and political literatures of the eighteenth century are replete with hymns to the family, and, notably, to the *private* form of happiness to be found in the family. Liberal thinkers did not see in the family an obsolete form of clannish social organization, but on the contrary, the unit of social structure that was most compatible with the virtues of the liberal individual and the pursuit of private interest. The family is, of course, a natural consequence of individual freedom, since it allows for the association of individuals by reasons of *natural* choice rather

---

[22] For this section, we draw heavily on the work of historians of private life, especially R. Sennett, *Families Against the City*, Cambridge, MA: Harvard University Press, 1970; E. Shorter, *The Making of the Modern Family*, New York: Basic Books, 1975; E. Hobsbawm and T. Ranger (eds.), *The Invention of Tradition*, Cambridge: Cambridge University Press, 1983; M. Foucault, *The History of Sexuality*, Vol. I: *An Introduction*, New York: Vintage Books [1978] 1990; P. Bardaglio, *Reconstructing the Household: Families, Sex, and the Law in the Nineteenth-Century South*, Chapel Hill: University of North Carolina Press, 1995; G. Duby, G. Fraisse, and M. Perrot, *Histoire des femmes en Occident*, Tome IV: *Le 19ème siècle*, Paris: Perrin, 2002.

than by reasons of constraint. Thus, the family is entirely compatible with liberal autonomy; better yet, it represents a guarantee of this autonomy against eventual oppression, for example from the state.

The vision of Hegel, put forth at the beginning of the nineteenth century, represents the most complete modern political theory of the family.[23] The family is one of the 'circles' of society that allow the individual to resist the pressures of civil society and the state; in the words of the historian Perrot, 'the family becomes a rational and voluntary construction, tied to strong spiritual ... and material relationships; the inherited wealth of the family is both an economic necessity and a symbolic affirmation'.[24] The family is viewed as an intermediary between the totally autonomous individual and the state; it puts women, considered at the time to be only insufficiently rational, and children, not yet considered to be autonomous, in a special position, affording them some degree of protection. The legal and political reflections of Hegel provide an illuminating translation of the general meaning and the importance accorded to the family by the new ideology: the family served to maintain the autonomy of the individual, especially that of the father of the family, to protect the less autonomous individuals, and to ensure 'private happiness'. It is the smallest 'social contract' necessary for society to function, and in most cases it effectively appeared as a contract in which notions of affection and love did not have any place. Thus, at the time when the entrepreneur was emancipated, the family took on a new economic function, because, by the mechanism of family alliances (marriages), it permitted the primitive *private* accumulation of assets and capital among individuals.

In a period of profound social upheaval marked by the modern fragmentation of powers, the family also appeared as an ideally stable entity, based on a *natural* hierarchy of blood ties and generational passing. Even socialist thinkers adopted this view. 'The Saint Simon movement ..., the majority of communists, socialists inspired by Christianity ..., they all propound a modernization of the institution of the family, equality of the sexes, including education, and the right of divorce; however, monogamous marriage remains the basis of the

---

[23] Hegel, *Principles of Legal Philosophy*.

[24] M. Perrot, 'La famille triomphante', in P. Ariès and G. Duby (eds.), *Histoire de la vie privée*, Tome IV: *de la Révolution à la Grande Guerre*, Paris: Seuil, 1987, p. 94, our translation.

affective nuclear family in their eyes.'[25] Not until the arrival of Marx in the second half of the nineteenth century did the socialist ideology begin to think of the family as a bourgeois and reactionary institution.

The philosophical support for the family was echoed by political programmes aimed at institutionalizing the modern nuclear family: the father was considered as all powerful and responsible for the group; the mother, at least in the higher classes and in the second half of the nineteenth century, was not expected to work anymore; and the children were treated as incapable minors, to be excluded from the workplace, in other words to be kept out of the public sphere. Here again, the liberal legal revolution provided support by making family laws the centrepiece of civil codes in all of the Western countries: the French Civil Codes (1804), that establish in a systematic manner the principles of governance of the nuclear family dominated by the 'father of the family', are exemplary here. In the liberal logic, the family allows for a separation of the private sphere, entrusted to the woman, and the public sphere in which the man, as the primary breadwinner, is the principal actor. The private/public separation leads to a new division of the sexes, but also to a new division of roles and responsibilities. Women are excluded from work, and as Pateman notes, in comparing the English census of 1851 with that of 1911, whereas in 1851 women who stayed at home were classified in the same manner as those who had comparable work (housekeeper or maid, for example), by 1911 they had come to be classified as 'inactive'.[26] By contrast, the considerable power accorded to the father of the family in the law of the early nineteenth century has the corollary of responsibility for the survival of the family for which, increasingly, the father alone is supposed to provide. The new bourgeois family that emerged over the course of the nineteenth century represented a new ideal type for governing all matters 'private'.

We can only broadly sketch the evolution of the family as a political institution here – in the intention of emphasizing that the family holds a very important place in the implementation of the liberal political

---

[25] Perrot, 'La famille triomphante', p. 101, our translation.
[26] C. Pateman, *The Disorder of Women: Democracy, Feminism and Political Theory*, Cambridge, MA: Polity Press, 1989.

project.[27] This evolution is also central to understanding why· the founder entrepreneur finds in the family both the legitimation and the ideal institutional counterweight to his discretionary power. On the one hand, the family is a *private* institution; as such, it corresponds to the same movement of privatization that establishes the entrepreneur, and it is not in any contradiction with him. On the other hand, the family allows for the setting of limits: responsibility towards the family represents a constraint on the power of the entrepreneur. The same norm that legitimizes the entrepreneur as the 'head of the family' also obliges him to assume the duty of maintaining the family, a duty that limits his freedom of action. Thus, 'bankruptcy' was punishable by imprisonment in all of the countries under study and led to public scandal and dishonour – at least until the 1860s – not only because failure led to doubt about an individual's honesty, but also because it demonstrated the incapacity of a 'father' to provide for the needs of the family he had been entrusted with.

Finally, the family accentuates the *genetic* nature of the link between the founder entrepreneur and his business. It implies that governance is meant for the long term, for the survival of the inheritance, and in this way lets the descendants share in the same legitimacy as the founder. In sum, it is not surprising that, as a corollary to the emergence of the entrepreneur, the family establishes itself in corporate governance as the ideal counterweight to power.

External counterweight: the role of the family as social institution

It is important to stress that – legally and politically – the emancipation of the entrepreneur and the emancipation of the corporation as an artificial individual, on the one hand, and the institutionalization of the patriarch-led family as the stable core of liberal society, on the other, occurred in parallel. Following directly from the logic of the liberal political project, these contextual factors help explain why the corporation of the nineteenth century tended to represent itself as a

---

[27] Here we can only touch upon the link between family structure and the development of the liberal project, a much larger question. For an in-depth and very well nuanced analysis, see E. Todd, *The Explanation of Ideology: Family Structures and Social Systems*, Oxford: Blackwell, 1985; E. Todd, *The Causes of Progress: Culture, Authority and Change*, New York: Basil Blackwell, 1987.

family. The corporation emerging in those days was also a private space, just like the family: in the same private sphere, the institution of the entrepreneur and the institution of the family both supported and limited each other. The family gave the legally all-powerful entrepreneur a socially respectable framework of governance. Governance could follow domestic patterns and power be exercised in a paternal manner, in parallel and in harmony with the forms of interaction adopted in the strictly familial sphere.

The corporation as family

At the head of the corporation, the owner-father (in French *patron*, from the Latin *pater*, father) acted not in his personal interest, but in the interest of ensuring the continuity of the extended family (including work for the employees) which the corporation came to stand for and for which the owner was responsible. The owner worked in the corporation himself and devoted his life to it. In the genealogy of a corporation, a heroic ancestor vouched for the fact that the corporation was founded on work and represented a genetic enterprise that was being pursued by his successors. As a consequence, children of the founder, nephews and cousins held all the key posts, and corporations were named after the family: Krupp, Wendel, Rockefeller, or Cadbury. And as the 'modern' family became the norm, the woman was increasingly excluded from corporate tasks and charged with managing the house of the entrepreneur. Often, she also played an auxiliary role, tending to social and charitable works – that is to say the most 'private' portion of the corporation's activities.[28]

Employees were also typically considered to be members of the larger corporate family (as a latin *cliens*), living by the same values of loyalty and filial obedience. Characteristically, Jacques-Joseph Harmel, the creator of the modern steam engine, was known as *le bon père* (the good father). 'He had instituted a system of collective pay by family, directly carried out by himself, taking payday as an opportunity to maintain personal contact with his workers, finding out about the progress of the children or of ill relatives, and offering advice

---

[28] For more details, one finds an interesting description of the evolution of the Cadbury family from the eighteenth to the nineteenth century in C. Hall, 'Sweet Home', in Ariès and Duby (eds.), *Histoire de la vie privée*, Tome IV, pp. 62–70. See also L. Davidoff and C. Hall, *Men and Women of the English Middleclass*, London: Routledge, 2003, especially pp. 272–316.

or help.'[29] The work contract did not yet exist; it appeared only much later.[30] It is interesting to note that generations of employees often corresponded to generations of owners, with members of the same worker families fulfilling the same tasks over several generations in the same corporation. For example, in 1867, at de Dietrich, in France, 'the population is as attached to the business leaders who have provided it with work for so many years as it is to the earth. The stability in the factories is remarkable: [of 1074 permanent workers] 249 have thirty years of service and 228 are sons or sons-in-law of company workers.'[31] The family enterprise represented a very important source of local employment and was hence also deeply rooted in its local region. In most of the Western countries, the topology of the larger nineteenth-century factories directly mirrored the family model: the main building of the master in the centre, the workshops adjacent, and, surrounding these, the buildings for the workers and for collective services (schools, stores, etc.), together constituting veritable new industrial cities of their own – the company towns. Social policies were privatized following a paternalistic logic of benevolence towards the employees, and the corporation became an important social actor. Thus, for example, in 1908, 45% of the profits of the great steel works of Longwy in France's industrial Nord went to 'social works'.[32] Even some socialistically inspired utopias were founded on the ideal of the family, such as, for example, the *familistère*, the veritable family monastery of Godin, constructed around the middle of the nineteenth century in Guise, France, whose founder, François Godin, was a benevolent and autocratic 'father'.[33] With different nuances and

[29] L. Bergeron, *Les capitalistes en France, 1780–1914*, Paris: Gallimard, 1978, p. 147, our translation.

[30] In France, for example, the work contract for people employed on an indefinite basis only became obligatory in 1993, following a European directive set out in 1991. Until 1993, the obligation to write out a work contract only pertained to people employed on a limited, predetermined basis.

[31] Bergeron, *Capitalistes*, p. 153, our translation.

[32] G. Noiriel, 'Du "patronage" au "paternalisme": la restructuration des formes de domination de la main-d'œuvre ouvrière dans l'industrie métallurgique française', *Mouvement Social* 144 (1988), 17–36. See also G. Noiriel, *Les ouvriers dans la société française, XIXe–XXe siècle*, Paris: Seuil, 1986.

[33] Further examples along these lines can be found in Harold James, *Family Capitalism: Wendels, Haniels, Falcks and the Continental European Model*, Cambridge, MA: Harvard University Press, 2006. For Germany, see D. Crew, *Bochum: Sozialgeschichte einer Industriestadt 1860–1914*, Frankfurt: Ullstein, 1980.

specificities in each country, a kind of paternalistic welfare capitalism developed, of considerable political and social importance.[34] Of course, these systems of benevolence remained under the charismatic and indisputable authority of the founder father who disciplined his employees with the same rigour as he disciplined the family (albeit frequently with more force): disciplining and punishing according to the meanings given to these terms by Foucault were principles of governance that the father considered only natural.

Inside the corporation, hierarchical relations resembled those in a family, based on ties of deferential fear and obligation. In the name of the director owners, foremen provided instructions to the employees. Their function was one of maintaining the economic order, rather than one of entrepreneurship or management. Foremen drew legitimacy from being singled out by the capitalist entrepreneurs, either for their experience or for their loyalty, rather than from any science of manage-ment – such a science did not yet exist. These men of the middle acted like intermediate guardians of the family, often enforcing high levels of discipline, precisely because they did not have family ties to the employ-ees.[35] As Payne has noted for England,

the familial structure of business enterprise inhibited interest in any collective body of management thought and militated against its acceptance even on the rare occasions when the publication was undertaken. This is hardly surprising in an age when the majority of entrepreneurs were their own managers and when sons or near relatives who were to succeed to the control of the firm learned the mysteries of the trade by experience within the family enterprise.[36]

During the same period in Germany,

employers found loyalty and honesty even more important criteria in the selection of staff than training and ability ... often the senior salaried employee of a company was the brother or cousin of the founder, and the first general manager his closest friend from school or military service ... the

---

[34] A. Tone, *The Business of Benevolence: Industrial Paternalism in Progressive America*, Ithaca, NY: Cornell University Press, 1997.

[35] S. Jacoby, *Employing Bureaucracy: Managers, Unions, and the Transformation of Work in American Industry, 1900–1945*, New York: Columbia University Press, 1985, p. 20.

[36] Payne, 'Industrial entrepreneurship', p. 198.

family loyalty provided the control – albeit informal – necessary for successful decentralization of responsibility and authority.[37]

Familial governance

Familial governance of the corporation was as informal but also as
sophisticated as the governance of a family. In the context described,
directors were formally accountable only to the small circle of family
members concerned with the business. Even in the largest corporations,
major issues were decided upon around a table, over the course of
informal gatherings. The institutions of corporate governance such as
they existed at the time were established in a form which suggested a
family gathering. Thus, an annual general assembly and an informal
meeting of the board (table) of directors were the norm, a formal board
not being required in a country like France until much later (1940). As
late as 1906, more than a century after the emergence of the capitalist
corporation, the case of *Automatic Self-Cleansing Filter Syndicate Co.
v. Cunningham* required the English Court of Appeal to decide whether
it was the annual general meeting or the board of directors that was
authorized to direct the affairs of the corporation (the Court ruled in
favour of the board of directors). Where there was a board, the law
typically required that decisions be taken unanimously. The directors
were assumed to be few enough in number and personally well enough
acquainted to make any public discussion superfluous. This absence of
formalism is a necessary consequence of the private, therefore non-
transparent, secret, and self-regulating nature of the corporation. It is
also a corollary of its efficiency and of its close adherence to the
liberal logic.

However, one should not be misled into thinking that the informal
nature of familial governance implied unlimited or uncontrolled power
for the entrepreneur directing the corporation. Such an interpretation
would erroneously underestimate those activities and behaviours not
covered by explicit rules and visible forms of control: his membership
in the family significantly constrained the entrepreneur. The entrepreneur of the nineteenth century was not an isolated individual, but
rather an individual integrated in a family. He was the head of the
family and, as such, was predisposed to act in a manner that reflected
socialization in a family and its values. The autonomous authority of

---

[37] Kocka, 'Entrepreneurs and managers', p. 554. Examples are provided.

the entrepreneur was embedded in a locus of legitimacy that made it socially acceptable and thus efficient. Four fundamental principles established limits on the founder's exercise of the entrepreneurial force: first, the objective of assuring the *durability* of the economic project associated with the name of the family and its existence as an extended family group; the family was not content to own, rather it developed with the corporation, living with it and, indeed, becoming one with the corporation. The corporation was an integral part of the family identity, and the family therefore felt responsible for its well-being. The director (father) assumed this responsibility in the name of the family, to ensure the survival, not only of the assets, but also of the entire family group, employees included, and made economic choices that reflected this responsibility.

The second principle was the requirement to display and live by *moral values*; these moral values were indispensable for likening the authority of the father director to that of the head of a family and took the form of ethical commitments that went beyond the person of the director and publicly constrained him/her. Here we refer to the honour of businessmen, the sanctity of the founder's word, the importance of loyalty, etc. The founder or father director could be considered as a good father of the family, because he lived an exemplary life – or tried to. These values both confirmed and limited the entrepreneurial power of the father director. As a perfect illustration, in 1900 George Westinghouse introduces the slogan: 'The Name of Westinghouse is a guarantee.'[38]

As a third principle, we would identify the care given to *succession*. The rigorous preparation of family successors, the games of power played in the background, but also the durability of power suggest a comparison between the families of entrepreneurs and monarchies, and underline, more generally, the prevailing notion of the clan and the concern for permanence and respectability over the long term. The logic of genetic legitimacy implied that entrepreneurial power issued from the founder and did not leave the family; as a consequence, it was critical to find deserving successors. The requirement to transmit power to deserving successors exercised an important regulatory

---

[38] Quoted in R. Monks, *The New Global Investors: How Shareowners Can Unlock Sustainable Prosperity Worldwide*, Oxford: Capstone 2001, p. 11.

function during this first period of capitalism, ensuring that the director maintained a long-term perspective and organized carefully for a viable succession.

Finally, we would mention the importance of *independence*, the real key word of familial governance. The family intended to remain the master of its own house, and this implied managing growth without external shareholders, except perhaps by means of alliances (typically by marriage) between friendly families. As a result, the margins for strategic manoeuvre were reduced and the acceptable path of growth was considerably narrowed: it was necessary to find markets and make investments that did not overstretch the corporation's capacity to finance growth on its own, or at most with a minimum amount of debt. Thus, the scope for exercising the entrepreneurial force of direction was clearly framed by resource constraints imposed on the entrepreneur by the familial context.

In sum, the large amount of discretionary power accorded to the entrepreneur was socially and morally respectable because it reflected the spirit of responsibility and concern for the common well-being attached to the father of the family. The 'domestic dictatorship' (Tocqueville) of the entrepreneur is circumscribed by his complex responsibility as the father of a family. It is not so much the formal law that constrains the entrepreneur during this period, but the informal, moral duty and the embeddedness of the corporation in the family structure. Consistent with the governance of the corporation as family, many alliances between corporations were based on marriages or interfamily collaborations (between uncles and nephews, for example). The directors of the corporations in a region knew each other and formed a tight network of control over markets. Often, 'they belonged to extended kinship families that gave them access to credit, which permitted their firms, and their records, to survive while others, less well connected, went to the wall'.[39] Familial governance cannot be fully comprehended without an appreciation of the socio-political context it evolved in. In this context, the traditional institution of the family fulfilled the function of limiting the entrepreneur's exercise of power and providing a framework that rendered that power acceptable to employees and society.

---

[39] Payne, 'Industrial entrepreneurship', p. 183.

3 Familial governance: a politically fragile equilibrium

The intensification of research and dialogue concerning corporate governance observed in recent years has not added much to our understanding of the long period during which the familial model of governance held sway. On the contrary, contemporary writing typically considers this model to be archaic, incompatible with modern liberal society. This conception makes a caricature of the model and is conceptually wrong, as we have tried to show. The family corporation was entirely consistent with the liberal political project, contributing in an important way to getting capitalism off the ground and representing an ideal equilibrium in which both entrepreneurial power and its counterweight belonged to the private sphere. Nonetheless, it is also clear that, from its origins, this model contained contradictions with the liberal project – internal contradictions that would inevitably undermine it.

An entirely private model of governance

At the time when the corporation became established, familial governance emerged to form a particularly harmonious equilibrium between power and counterweight. On the side of power, the enfranchisement of the entrepreneur allowed for free enterprise on the basis of private property. The birth of the corporation and the enfranchisement of the entrepreneur gave the entrepreneur very broad discretionary powers: he could freely make all the necessary economic decisions, and his scope for entrepreneurial action was very open-ended: after all, he held all three of the rights to property – *usus*, *fructus*, and *abusus*. It is important to stress again that the power of the entrepreneur is inextricably tied to his work and his personal commitment to the corporation that will be genetically transmitted to his successors. Early capitalism cannot abide the rentier: in the pure spirit of political liberalism, the accumulation of property is only acceptable to the extent that it represents the fruit of efficient work. This notion is famously evident in the philosophy of Adam Smith, particularly in his condemnation of a separation of ownership and control:

The directors of such [stock] companies, however, being the managers rather of other people's money than of their own, it cannot well be expected, that they should watch over it with the *same anxious vigilance* with which the partners in a private copartnery frequently watch over their own . . . It is upon this account that joint stock companies for foreign trade have seldom been able to maintain the competition against private adventurers.[40]

Only ownership justifies vigilant direction. On the side of the counterweight to power, the family lent corporate governance respectability and a strict framework of evaluation. The family (in the modern sense of the term) exercised an effective influence on corporate governance, because it represented a private dimension at the time when liberal ideology imposed privatization and separated the economic sphere from the social sphere. Economic interests and private interests were identical. The family moderated the power of the entrepreneur, *morally*, by imposing the obligation of being a good father and remaining loyal to the values of the corporation, and *economically*, by setting constraints that ensured the independence of capital and the long-term survival of the common enterprise.

This exceptional political equilibrium was not based on the division of power, but, rather, on its unification. The function of the entrepreneur, the corporation considered as an artificial individual, and the family of the entrepreneur came together to ensure coherent economic actions and socially acceptable limitations to power. Economic power *and* moral obligation were combined in the entrepreneur and his successors, genetically tied to the founder. The familial model of corporate governance established itself based on the new equality of rights and the resulting emancipation of the entrepreneur, but did not go any further in the consideration of democratic procedures. Under familial governance, the corporation was thought of as a purely private affair, privately controlled, and hence it largely escaped the democratic political pressures which characterized the nineteenth century. No doubt this is why this period of capitalism under familial governance is sometimes thought of as a golden age during which an 'authentic' form of capitalism could flourish – the liberal ideal of a *private* community built by a founder entrepreneur, the continuity of which was genetically assured.

It is important to specify that family ownership or family *capital* does not equate with familial *governance*. The definition of corporate governance is partially tied to the power conferred by the ownership of

---

[40] A. Smith, *An Inquiry into the Nature and Causes of the Wealth of Nations*, 1776, Book V, Ch. I, Part 3, Article 1, our italics.

capital, but corporate governance is essentially a question of the relations of authority (in this case, that of the father of the family as the
director) that are considered socially acceptable by the governed. Thus,
it is because the family (in general) was accepted as a legitimate structure of governance that familial governance itself was considered legitimate during this period of history. The ownership of capital
establishes a hierarchy within the (extended) family that is the corporation, but it is not *sufficient in and of itself* to render governance by the
father of the family acceptable.

Latent forces of contradiction

In equilibrium between private power and the institution of the family
as counterweight, familial governance conformed perfectly well to the
liberal logic of the beginnings of industrial capitalism. However, the
two pillars of power and counterweight, the founder entrepreneur on
the one hand and the institution of the family on the other, were both
subject to criticism and social fragmentation, in a manner that is typical
of liberal society. We pointed out that the nuclear bourgeois family was
supported as a modern institution by liberalism, because it permitted
the individual to exercise some degree of autonomy, in particular
towards the collective and the state. However, this institution also
supposed that its members were unequal, allowing the head of the
family to exercise a pre-eminent function. This principle, in turn, was
incompatible with the foundations of liberalism that established the
absolute equality of individuals and, consequently, equality between
men and women. The gradual emancipation of different members of
the family carried the seeds of crisis in the institution of the family, at
least as it was initially conceived.

Furthermore, the nuclear family, by the mechanisms of inheritance
and generational continuity, also contradicted the values of modern
liberty – the right of blood (*abusus* by inheritance) was given precedence over the right of work (*usus* by the direction of the corporation).
Recall that the legitimacy of private property as affirmed by liberal
thought was deeply tied to the right of work. As long as the descendants
of the family worked in the corporation and were considered compe-
tent, the situation may have been ambiguous, but was still acceptable.
The context changed decisively when the family grew larger and the
number of heirs who were not directors of the corporation or even

participating in its activities increased. This recalled the pre-liberal scenario in which the rights to property were partitioned between those who owned the right of *abusus* (heirs grown lazy) and those who exercised the right of *usus* (directors who were now owners). The inherited ownership of capital and the foundational principles of liberalism were not easily reconciled, and, over time, the familial model lost much of its initial coherence.

However, and even more radically, in the name of the same individual liberty defended by liberalism, anti-capitalist criticism denied the entrepreneur the right to exercise authority over the means of production. This criticism is a child of liberal society: the individual freedom which is the hallmark of modernity includes the freedom to question, to oppose, and to offer new ideas, in the pursuit of social fragmentation which is necessary for the defence of individual liberty and the emergence of a democratic technique of government. Thus, the fact that the entrepreneur's birth can be traced to liberalism also implies that this new creation of liberalism was immediately questioned – such questioning was an integral part of individuals' new freedom to express and act upon their thoughts. In light of the enormous human misery engendered by the industrial revolutions and the mass migrations that accompanied them, anti-capitalist criticism focused on the plight of the workers who had no property of their own and were forced to sell their work to entrepreneurs for very meagre wages. The evidence that so many people were suffering from the economic transformations of the time and had little hope of acquiring any property appeared to make a mockery of the liberal promise of a new era of liberty and prosperity.

An inevitable transformation

Very early on in the development of capitalism, the asymmetry of forces between entrepreneur on the one hand and workers on the other became evident, in apparent contradiction to the principles of political liberalism upon which the legitimacy of the new entrepreneurs had been established. Two very different currents of criticism arose, each one in its own way promising to re-establish individual liberty.

The first current of criticism was a conservative reaction and proposed a return to the political equilibrium that had held sway before the legal revolution and political modernity. The reactionary argument held that the old regime had provided for a greater degree of personal liberty by preventing those at the top of the social ladder from exercising their authority without considering their own economic dependence on those people within their domain. The old system, although apparently unjust from a modern point of view, seemed preferable to the reactionaries, because it prevented the new entrepreneurs from concentrating in their hands all the rights to property: *usus, fructus,* and *abusus.* Since it proposed to go backwards and erase economic, social, and political evolution (often implying a refusal of industrial progress and a return to an agricultural economy), the reactionary criticism appears utopian and is often neglected in modern accounts. Its lack of realism and class-based appeal meant that its influence remained limited, leaving ideological traces and, more deeply, a profoundly anti-capitalist culture in some European classes.[41] From the point of view of our discussion of corporate governance, it is important to note that the reactionary criticism opposed the all-powerful entrepreneur and called for a return to a partition of property rights that would prevent any one individual from having too much power. This discourse against a concentration of power is echoed in many subsequent debates on corporate governance.

The second current of criticism drew its inspiration from socialist thought. We do not want to get into a comprehensive discussion of so large and so rich an area as socialism at this point – that would take us too far afield. Let us instead stick to the influence that the emergence of socialist thought had on the history of corporate governance. In a general sense, albeit with different nuances in the different schools, the socialist criticism concerns the notion of private property. Socialism does not fundamentally question the liberal evolution and agrees that individual liberty is the greatest good. However, in view of its consequences for individual liberty, the freedom of economic enterprise appears to socialism as harmful. Private property is necessary to ensure individual liberty, but private ownership of the *means of production* is not held to be essential to individual liberty. The socialist criticism argues that the freedom of economic enterprise on the contrary

---

[41] This anti-capitalist culture continued to exist for many years, resurfacing in the strife that led to the collapse of Weimar Germany in the 1930s and finding echoes in Vichy France in the 1940s; today, it still animates certain utopian ecologist groupings.

produces irreversible social disparities that in the final analysis deprive the greater part of the population of individual liberty. For the socialists, who do not want to go back to the pre-modern society, the only way forward is to forbid private enterprise, that is to say to forbid private ownership of the means of production for the economic activities upon which society depends. What would corporate governance under socialism look like? Socialist thought and practice have produced numerous alternative models, all the way from the creation of units of production that belong to all (Phalanstères, Saint-Simon), to provisional ownership by the government (Marx), with numerous intermediate forms inspired by the Christian principles of sharing (worker cooperatives, mutuals, etc.). We will not discuss the pertinence and the failures of these models here, but we do want to note that the socialist criticism has had a lasting effect on the history of corporate governance: socialist thought has been and continues to be a source of inspiration, ideas, and models for all those parties implicated in the corporation who are opposed to the power of the entrepreneur. This is an essential contribution, because criticism of this kind helped sap the legitimacy of the entrepreneur as sole master (father) of the corporation almost from the very beginning. Whereas the entrepreneur triumphed in the private space that he built and governed, in the space of public opinion, of contemporary thinking, and of politics, the power of the entrepreneur came to be questioned because of its private and therefore exclusive nature. As a *private* community, familial governance drew the attacking ire of those who wanted to defend their conception of *res publica* as community.

The same force of social fragmentation that, carried by the liberal political project, caused traditional society to explode and allowed both for the emancipation of the entrepreneur and the enterprise, and for the conception of the modern nuclear family – that same force of fragmentation continued to work *against* the founder entrepreneur and the familial model of corporate governance. From the 1850s onwards, familial governance's status as the model of reference began to be undermined. We do not mean to imply that the family corporation, that is to say the corporation that is majoritarily family-owned, disappears; of course, this is not the case. As we have said, it is important to distinguish between family *ownership* and familial *governance*. Family ownership is still very widespread today and includes some of the very largest, best-known corporations (representing 35% of the global Fortune 500 and accounting for 10% of medium-sized companies in the United States, 32% in France, 30% in the United Kingdom and in Germany[42]). The corporate governance of family corporations, on the other hand, today no longer, or only very rarely in the West, refers to the *bonus paterfamilias* and the ideology of the family in the way we have described him here.[43] The governance of family corporations today is not familial in the sense it would have been in the nineteenth century. The resilience of values of loyalty and common destiny may well be stronger in family corporations than in other forms of corporate ownership, but employees and other stakeholders are no longer considered members of an expanded family. Familial governance in the strict sense is considered archaically paternalistic and today only concerns a limited number of very small enterprises. The ideal equilibrium of private governance and the legitimacy of the founder entrepreneur were subjected to slow erosion by the social fragmentation which is characteristic of liberalism. The equilibrium was definitely upset, when family ownership was disconnected from the entrepreneurial function. This rupture coincided with the development of the large, modern enterprise at the end of the nineteenth and the beginning of the twentieth centuries.

---

[42] G. Bloom, *Inherited Family Firms and Management Practices: The Case for Modernising the UK's Inheritance Tax*, Centre for Economic Performance Policy Analysis, London: London School of Economics, 2006.
[43] In Chapter 8, we will show under what specific economic conditions the familial model can persist.

4 | Managerial governance (c.1920–1970): separation of powers and management as entrepreneur

Since Berle and Means, it has become a commonplace to state that the family corporation (owned by the family and governed according to the model described in the preceding chapter) declined with the emergence of the very large corporation. Since the middle of the twentieth century, this evolution from familial capitalism to managerial capitalism has been studied extensively, and we will of course refer to the authoritative findings of this research. However, in the context of this book, we also want to offer our own perspective on the following question: why was the large, modern enterprise incompatible with the familial model of governance? In other words, what were the factors that contributed to undermining the traditional legitimacy of the family and to strengthening the new managerial legitimacy based on expertise and knowledge, to the point that the latter model of governance came to be universally accepted as the standard for the large modern corporation? In order to understand the complex interplay of forces that results in the replacement of one model of governance by another, it is necessary to explore how the balance of forces breaks and reforms. At the conclusion of the preceding chapter, we observed that the familial model, although founded as an offspring of the modern liberal project also, contained seeds of contradiction with liberalism. In this chapter, we will describe how these contradictions played out and advance two sets of reasons for the decline and demise of familial governance. First, we will present a brief summary of the well-known economic and contextual explanation for the emergence of the large enterprise and managerial governance: the imperative for scale and size and the need for external growth capital. We will then offer an alternative explanation, showing how political developments and forces endogenous to the model undermine familial governance and hasten the advent of managerial governance (1). With the large modern corporation, a new model came into force, a model that confirmed a separation of the powers of ownership and control in coherence with the liberal vision and the democratic technique of governing. This new stage in the democratization of corporate governance corresponded to the increased fragmentation of ownership and to the fragmentation of the family under the pressure of modern, liberal society. It was also the result of a process whereby a class of employees – management – appropriated the force of entrepreneurial direction from the owners. From the 1940s to the 1970s, the economic power of management, now broadly extended, found a social counterweight in the power of unions, resulting in a new equilibrium, characteristic of managerial governance (2). As stable as this new equilibrium appeared, it, too, was exposed to the workings of the forces of social fragmentation, leading, over time, to new contradictions with the liberal project. By the 1970s, the managerial model would face its own crisis.

1 The demise of the familial model of governance

Exogenous factors: market size and its consequences for the corporation[1]

The demographic and economic environment in which late nineteenth-century business evolved required the pursuit of increased scale and size. On the one hand, there were a large number of major industrial projects to complete: most dramatically, the construction of transcontinental railways (in the United States, in Russia, and in the European colonies of Asia and Africa) leading to a tenfold increase in the number of railway lines in Europe and a twentyfold increase in the USA between 1850 and 1900, and the digging of transoceanic canals (Suez

---

[1] For the discussion of contextual factors behind the demise of the familial model, we refer to the following sources: S. Bowman, *The Modern Corporation and American Political Thought: Law, Power, and Ideology*, University Park: Pennsylvania University Press, 1996; A. Chandler, *Scale and Scope: The Dynamics of Industrial Capitalism*, Cambridge, MA: Harvard University Press, 1990; M. Wilkins, A. D. Chandler, and H. Daems (eds.), *Managerial Hierarchies: Comparative Perspectives on the Rise of the Modern Industrial Enterprise*, Cambridge MA: Harvard University Press, 1980; M. Sklar, *The Corporate Reconstruction of American Capitalism, 1890–1916: The Market, the Law, and Politics*, Cambridge: Cambridge University Press, 1988; P. Payne, 'Industrial entrepreneurship and management in Great Britain', in P. Mathias and M. Postan (eds.), *The Cambridge Economic History of Europe*, Volume VII, Part 1, Cambridge: Cambridge University Press, 1974, pp. 180–230; G. Ripert, *Aspects juridiques du capitalisme moderne*, Paris: Pichon and Durand-Auzias, 1951.

1869, Panama 1881–1914), but more generally the development of standardized national infrastructures (train stations, roads, schools, hospitals, and military equipments). Such large projects could only be carried out with the input of corporations that were able to produce standardized parts and solutions rapidly and cheaply. On the other hand, and in parallel with the industrial projects discussed, the growth of large cities and the concentration of the population imposed efficient, large-scale systems of transportation and distribution, also favouring large corporations with standardized, scale-efficient means of production and multiple, even international locations: in the United States, by 1890, 30% of the population was urban, versus a mere 4.5% in 1830; in France, the percentage by 1900 was 44.7%, versus 18% in 1800.[2] The story of how these developments cumulatively led to the emergence of the large, modern enterprise is well known.

The appearance of the large enterprise represented a major turning point in the history of capitalism and in the evolution of corporate governance. In the United States, the wave of industrial concentration peaked in the 1890s and led to the creation of the great trusts of communication, transportation, and energy (Western Union, Bell Telephone, Standard Oil Company, Vanderbilt, etc.);[3] in Europe, industrial concentration took place a few years later, accelerated by the need to standardize production for the military requirements of the First World War. The experience of the automobile industry was emblematic of this development: in 1900, there existed 600 different makers of automobiles in the United States, but ten years later over 80% of these had already closed or gone bankrupt; over the same period, Ford incorporated (1903) and grew to over 13,000 employees (1914). In France, Renault (incorporated in 1899) grew from 1660 employees in 1906 to 22,800 in 1918, with the number of cars produced rising from forty per year to 10,000. Similar figures can be found at several other nascent automobile giants. These figures do not surprise us anymore, but they are symptomatic for the extraordinary process of concentration that characterized the turn of the century.

---

[2] In 1890, the four largest cities in the world were London (1.5 million people), New York (3.4), Paris (3.9), and Berlin (2.4). Peking and Calcutta both had fewer than one million inhabitants at this time.

[3] N. Lamoreaux, The *Great Merger Movement in American Business, 1895–1904*, Cambridge: Cambridge University Press, 1985.

The emerging large enterprise presented a problem of coherence for familial governance. In nineteenth-century Europe, a business was considered large if it employed fifteen to twenty people. The enormous mining groups such as Wendel in France or Krupp in Germany that employed several hundred people clearly stood out as exceptionally large. Even if a business had exports or colonial outposts, the vast bulk of its production and hence also of its organization was concentrated in a clearly defined geographical region. In the majority of cases, businesses served local needs, with markets located within narrow geographic confines. 'It was in serving the domestic market – less volatile, less hazardous than overseas markets – that new entrants to the ranks of the entrepreneurs could acquire their business acumen and skill.'[4] Small and tightly contained, the corporation could be convincingly likened to an extended family – both the sociological and the geographical roots of the stakeholders could be reflected in the concept of family. With mass production requiring many thousands of employees and the growth of markets necessitating implantations very far from the home base in which the entrepreneur and his family were known, however, the reference to the corporation as an extended family became increasingly tenuous.

Of course, the massive growth of the corporation also required fresh capital, and the providers of such capital – the share-owning public in the United States, banks in Germany, and bondholders in all of the Western countries[5] – typically came from outside the circle of the family and had no historical, personal links with the corporation. The economic context put familial governance under pressure: first, the increase in the corporation's sphere of action stretched the family's naturally limited reach; and second, the increased reliance on external capital put distance between entrepreneurs and shareholders and weakened the power of a common, family destiny to act as a credible counterweight to the entrepreneurial autonomy of direction. The bigger the corporation became, the harder it was to maintain the basic tenets of familial governance.

---

[4] Payne, 'Industrial entrepreneurship', p. 187.
[5] For an analysis of the specifics of the American case, in particular the regulatory constraints aimed at limiting the power of banks, see M. J. Roe, *Strong Managers, Weak Owners: The Political Roots of American Corporate Finance*, Princeton, NJ: Princeton University Press, 1994.

These factors in the economic context have received a great deal of attention in the literature. However necessary they were for the evolution towards managerial governance, they do not strike us as sufficient for such an important shift. The contextual factors cannot explain why familial governance *did not successfully adapt*: in other words, why the family was no longer an adequate counterweight to the power of direction and therefore could not continue to ensure its legitimacy. This question is even more important in light of the fact that the emergence of large corporations has not signalled the end of small firms built on family capital. Quite the contrary: in the United States, family-owned corporations numbered 11 million in 1957 and over 17 million in 1980, far more significant in number than the few thousand corporations that were publicly listed.[6] Similar demographic statistics can be cited for the European corporate landscape. However, in spite of the persistence of the family-owned corporation the familial model of governance has receded into the background and is no longer considered a reference for 'good governance'. Economic reasons explain why familial governance could not adapt to increased size, but it is harder to understand why familial governance does not still hold for the small corporation. This is why it is necessary to go beyond economic explanation and examine political developments and forces endogenous to the familial model.

Endogenous factors: challenges to liberalism and the corporation as a private space

Liberalism challenged in the public sphere
The role model of the family helped make capitalism socially respectable, but it did not silence anti-capitalist criticism. Anti-capitalist criticism cannot be simply put off as a negligible force in the history of the corporation. Even though the criticism did not go as far in the West as it did in Russia and stop the development of capitalism, it did have a significant influence on the evolution of familial governance. Public debates concerned the extent of the power of the governing over the governed, with an emphasis on the limits and controls necessary to keep this power in check. Over the course of the nineteenth century in

[6] See M. Blackford, *A History of Small Business in America*, Durham: University of North Carolina Press, 2003, especially Chs. 1 and 2.

Europe and also in the United States, political upheavals further undermined traditional forms of power and authority (absolutism in Central
Europe, autocracy in Western Europe, and slavery in the United States)
and strengthened democratic aspirations compatible with liberal ideology, in the sense defined in the first part of this book.

The corporation often found itself at centre stage in these developments. For example, in the United States, the insurrectional strikes of
1877 spread from the railroad industry to all the larger cities of the East
Coast and forced the government to use federal troops against
American citizens for the first time in the history of the country. Over
the five-year period from 1881 to 1886 an estimated 3000 strikes took
place in the United States.[7] In Europe, the revolutions of the year 1848
represented a break in the evolution of liberal society, launching a
significant review of 'laissez-faire' as a political project based solely
on private initiative and giving rise to the idea that the public, political
sphere should supersede the private sphere in orienting collective action
towards the general interest.

From the time of the creation of the Working Men's Association in
London in 1836 onwards, professional and political demands were
inextricably bound together. Questions about public liberty and equality of rights, and concerns about conditions of work and life, were
presented as social problems of public interest in which a political
resolution rather than a private resolution ought to be imposed. This
way of framing the issues can be found in a broad variety of debates: on
slavery and on working conditions for immigrants in the United States,
for example, as much as on the state of the worker in Europe in the
second half of the century. In the United States, the liberal ideology
was challenged on racial and ethnic grounds, in Europe on professional and social grounds (these challenges were also present in the
United States).

Of course, the advance of socialism was an important factor in the
history of the liberal ideology – necessitating a response both to the
criticism of the injustice and misery generated by capitalism and to
the political movement of the anti-capitalist forces. The first workers'
international was held in 1864 in London, and its statutes were penned
by Karl Marx, who was to publish his major work, *Das Kapital*, just
three years later. The last third of the nineteenth century was

[7] M. Beaud, *Histoire du capitalisme*, Paris: Point, 1981.

characterized by an increasing amount of social violence, including anarchist terrorism; the social question and the very real risk of revolution it carried necessitated a fresh political response from liberalism.

Questioning the exclusively private nature of the corporation

The new uses of public power had important longer-term implications for the corporation: as long as it was considered an exclusively private space, the corporation could pretend to govern itself according to its own rules; autonomy of this kind was not realistic anymore once the corporation employed workers who, as citizens, made public demands for changes in the workplace, or when the corporation's activities became so large that they had an important effect on the public space. Even in the United States, the country with an unequalled tradition of private initiative and the most liberal reputation, the power of the corporation was the subject of a very lively discussion during this time, most famously, perhaps, in the debate between Henry Lloyd and Edward Atkinson. Whereas Lloyd condemned the large corporation in the name of protecting the general interest against the egoism of private property owners, Atkinson lauded the large corporation as a powerful source of innovation in the service of the general interest. In this symptomatic debate, the conditions under which society should accept the increasing power of economic organizations were at issue, with a focus on determining whether or not the corporation served the general interest. Once this line of questioning was adopted, one had also to consider the disparity between private methods of governance in the corporation that were often despotic and public methods of governance in society that were clearly in the process of democratization.

Of all the countries considered here, suspicion about the private methods of governance in the corporation was perhaps greatest in Germany: under the authoritarian administration of Chancellor Bismarck, laws were instituted (first in 1870, then further elaborated in 1884) that required large corporations to adopt a dual form of governance with a supervisory board (*Aufsichtsrat*) and an executive board (*Vorstand*).[8] Charged with controlling the directors, the

---

[8] On this topic, see K. Hopt, 'The German two-tier board (Aufsichtsrat): a German view on corporate governance', in K. Hopt and E. Wymeersch (eds.), *Comparative Corporate Governance: Essays and Materials*, New York: de Gruyter, 1997, pp. 3–20.

supervisory board was opened, for a mandatory third of its membership, to personalities outside of the shareholding body who were to
ensure public surveillance over large private corporations considered to
be sensitive (important to the public interest). The supervisory board
was initially intended as 'a substitute for the state charter and the
continuous state control which were abolished. This is the historical
reason why the *Aufsichtsrat* is an outside board, i.e. it links people
other than owners with enterprise.'[9] Even if this form of external
surveillance has not always worked as envisioned, it does reflect the
extent to which public interests began to penetrate the private sphere
during the second half of the nineteenth century.

Even where it did not directly concern the question of control, social
pressure on the private space of the corporation could be intense,
taking on a variety of different forms. Perhaps most clearly, the effects
of this pressure can be seen in the laws introduced to reduce the domain
over which private property had the *exclusive* say – making private
property obey an increasing number of constraints aimed at defending
individual liberty. In stages, but over roughly the same time period and
in all of the countries under study, legislation placed limits on the
legitimate authority of the father of the family. First, the choice of
who could be employed was reduced: decrees forbidding the employment of children and adolescents (1813, 1841, and 1874 in France;
1839, 1853, and 1869 in Prussia; Massachusetts Law 1842 and
Pennsylvania Law 1848 in the United States; and the Acts of 1802,
1833, 1874, and 1891 in the United Kingdom); and then limitations on
the work of women (United Kingdom 1842; Germany 1890; and
France 1900). Then, the organization of work in the corporation was
circumscribed: maximum number of working hours (Illinois, in 1864,
was the first State in America to legislate an eight-hour day; the United
Kingdom, in 1847, limited work in factories to ten hours per day;
France, in 1892, reduced the workday to twelve hours and subsequently, in 1900, to ten hours; Germany, in 1908, legislated for eight
working hours); weekly rest (1880 in the United Kingdom; 1891 in
Germany; 1907 in France); and the right of employees to organize

---

[9] Mary O'Sullivan, *The Political Economy of Corporate Governance in Germany*,
Insead Working Paper 226, p. 6. See also G. Jackson, 'The origins of nonliberal
corporate governance in Germany and Japan', in W. Streeck and K. Yamamura
(eds.), *The Origins of Nonliberal Capitalism: Germany and Japan Compared*,
Ithaca, NY: Cornell University Press, pp. 121–70.

themselves against their employer (the right to strike: France 1864; Germany 1871; United Kingdom 1875; and the right to unionize: United Kingdom 1824; France 1884; Germany 1890). This kind of societal pressure on the corporation does not contradict liberalism; on the contrary, it represents an intervention of public powers in the spirit of political liberalism to protect private interests (those of employees) within a private space (the corporation). This kind of intervention leads to a reduction in the domain of private property, and eventually to a partial *de-privatization* of the corporation.

From the latter years of the nineteenth century, the corporation became increasingly porous, and the concerns and demands of society entered into what was originally considered to be an exclusively private domain. Building on the work of Wicksell, Hannah Arendt showed that this influence was reciprocal: indeed, the de-privatization of the corporation also led the liberal state to become more involved in social questions. The separation between public space and private space transformed into a separation between the economic space, supposedly left to the corporation and the social space, now supposed to be addressed outside the confines of the corporation. The advent of 'social legislation' had the effect of introducing a new function of the state, no longer merely the guarantor of private property rights, but also the agent for reapportioning these rights – a change that found its culmination in the Welfare State.[10]

Consequently, the more widespread social and working rights took hold, the further the legitimacy of the founder entrepreneur and his/her family as the *sole* arbiter of corporate governance was diminished. Perhaps more than any other change, the battle for the right of workers to unionize symbolized the weakening of familial governance and the entry of *political* themes deriving from modern, liberal thinking such as representation of differences of opinion between employees and employers or legal equality for individuals inside the corporation into the economic domain, initially considered to be strictly private. The right to unionize directly contradicted the model of familial governance, because it implied that employees organized to defend their interests *against* the father of the family. Indeed, many heads of family corporations thought that the right to unionize signalled the end of

---

[10] On these questions, see especially the major work of Hannah Arendt, *The Human Condition*, Chicago: University of Chicago Press, 1958.

business; in fact, it merely signalled the impending end of familial governance. As Karl Polanyi has argued, capitalism's separation of activity into an economic sphere and a public political sphere is not a stable arrangement, and developments in the years between 1930 and 1945 largely vindicated this view.[11] The corporation became a locus for social conflict, a part of society that could not ignore the influence of more general political developments. Thus, the unity of familial governance, which had brought together ownership, authority, and the exercise of entrepreneurial direction, was broken up.

It is important to evaluate carefully the overall effect of anti-capitalist criticism on the familial model of corporate governance. It was not a matter of overturning capitalism and replacing economic concerns with purely social concerns. The increasing influence of social concerns on private enterprise was merely a logical consequence of the functioning of modern democratic society built on individual liberty and *social fragmentation*. It was by these principles that the entrepreneur could become emancipated and was enfranchised to go into business. By these same principles, employees of (family) corporations sought to *emancipate* themselves and protect their *individual* rights, calling upon the support of the public political power of the state to bolster their demands. In liberal society, one cannot accord one set of rights to entrepreneurs and another to employees. Free enterprise and the

---

[11] K. Polanyi, *The Great Transformation*, New York: Rinehart and Co., 1944. Although we cannot but pay homage to Polanyi's detailed analysis of the evolution of capitalism, we do not concur with his conclusions. Polanyi hypothesized that liberalism (and market economics) would die with the political social changes of the 1930s and the rise of a managerial technocracy. We will show that the technocratic period is an avatar of modern liberalism adapted to the challenge posed by the large corporation. Clearly, our analysis of liberalism as a political system differs from that of Polanyi – for him, liberalism implied free markets and the *absence* of politics. With the advantage of hindsight, we can see that liberalism persists, not only through managerialism, but also into the post-managerial period, as we will discuss in the following chapters. From this point of view, the era of the Welfare State appears as a necessary stage in the development of liberalism, adapted to the post-war context. More generally, and contrary to Polanyi's postulates, the dialectic interactions that constitute the liberal political economy (as defined in the first part of the book) continue to be important to this day: the opposition between the entrepreneurial force and social fragmentation, resolved by the democratic technique of government. This is why we prefer an analysis grounded in historical continuity (particularly of corporate governance) over an approach that proposes systemic rupture in the manner of Polanyi.

development of social rights go together, even if they wind up confronting each other. We can say that the ideology that made family business possible also contributed to its weakening.

The fragmentation of the family

Modern liberal society also undermined familial governance by undermining the family's status as a role model for society. Of course, even without social pressures, familial governance suffered from the 'natural' problems inherent to the very concept of family: growth, increasing dispersion, and decreasing cohesion over time; family intrigues and disagreements; loss of interest and disconnection to the point that family shareholders start to behave like uninvolved outsiders with no concern beyond the dividend. This course of events is apparently so common that it is referred to as the 'the curse of the third generation' in almost every European language[12] and has been immortalized in literature through Thomas Mann's *Buddenbrooks*: the founders are followed by the empire builders, who in turn are followed by a third generation of rentiers who aspire only to spend the money and live off its fruits (*fructus*). Or in the words of Landes, 'The third generation [of owners], the children of affluence, tired of the tedium of trade and flushed with bucolic aspirations of the country gentleman ... many of them retired and forced the conversion of their firms into joint-stock companies.'[13] Quite naturally, the informal pressure exercised by the family on the entrepreneur relaxed over time, and the equilibrium of familial governance was disturbed. Moreover, with more and more family members as shareholders in the later generations, it became increasingly difficult to *implicate* them in the life of the corporation. The fact that many family shareholders chose to live as rentiers further undermined the family's legitimacy as a counterweight to the power of the entrepreneur. The latter transformation goes a long way towards explaining the political challenge to the familial model of governance, such as we described it in the previous chapter. No longer was property

[12] J. L. Ward, *Perpetuating the Family Business: Fifty Lessons Learned from Long-Lasting, Successful Families in Business*, Basingstoke: Palgrave, 2004.

[13] D. Landes, 'Technological change and industrial development in Western Europe', in H. J. Habakkuk and M. Postan (eds.), *The Cambridge Economic History of Europe*, Vol. VI, Part 1, Cambridge: Cambridge University Press, 1974, pp. 563–4.

necessarily associated with work, the very basis of the legitimacy of the founder entrepreneur and his successors in the liberal spirit.

At a social level, an even more profound consideration affected familial governance. In the preceding chapter, we pointed out that, as an ideal mode of governance for a group of individuals, the (nuclear) family occupied an ambiguous position in the liberal project. The privilege of blood runs counter to the principle of individual equality; inheritance of capital stands against the principle of advancement by merit; adhesion to a clan is incongruous with individual liberty. Going a step further, we can say that the very call for modern liberty, as defined by Benjamin Constant and centrally anchored in the individual's freedom from control, implies the gradual disbanding of clan and family ties and the emancipation of individuals from the family. This is why liberal society has consistently sought to reduce the influence of the family, even though the nuclear family is first and foremost a liberal invention (cf. Chapter 3). For example, obligatory public schooling 'freed' the child from family education (public schooling for children first became compulsory in 1852 in America, in the State of Massachusetts; in 1880 in the United Kingdom; in 1882 in Germany; and in 1884 in France); salaried work 'emancipated' the wife from the authority of the husband and allowed her access to the public sphere; inheritance laws limited intergenerational transfers of property (death duties were levied from 1894 in England, and from 1901 in France), etc.[14] With the maturing of the liberal political project and the full emergence of the socialist counterproject at the end of the nineteenth century, the family began to be considered either as an anti-liberal or as a reactionary form of socialization. From this time onwards, the family has become the object of a systematic process of weakening and fragmentation that continues to this day. From the patriarchal clan still

---

[14] Tocqueville anticipated how the new laws of inheritance (equal treatment of all children) would destroy the spirit of family and then noted: 'when estate law establishes equal partition, it destroys the intimate connection that exists between the spirit of the family and the preservation of the land; the land ceases to represent the family, for, since it cannot fail to be partitioned at the end of one or two generations, it is evident that it must constantly be diminished and in the end disappear entirely ... Whenever the spirit of the family ends, individuals' selfishness re-enters into the reality of its penchants. As the family no longer presents itself to the mind as anything but vague, indeterminate, and uncertain, each concentrates on the comfort of the present; he dreams of the establishment of the generation that is going to follow, and nothing more' (*DA* I, 1, 3, pp. 48–9).

common in the early nineteenth century, the family today has been reduced to a narrow core (father, mother, and children), and with divorce and single-parent families on the rise it appears to be fragmenting even further. Although these developments are slower in Germany than in France, the United Kingdom, and the United States, they concern all of the Western countries.[15]

Although familial governance appeared like an ideal compromise between tradition and modernity, it stood on fragile legs. The founder entrepreneur, or paterfamilias, legitimated his power to direct the corporation on the basis of an institution that was suffering the sustained onslaught of social fragmentation. The contradictions inherent in familial governance also limited its capacity to adapt to changes in the economic context. The corporation was originally conceived of as 'private', that is to say separate from and even in opposition to the public, political sphere. This juxtaposition led to an increasing amount of tension between the new democratic political order of divided power and the concentrated, discretionary power of the father of the family corporation. The tension between a fragmented democratic society and concentrated family, coupled with natural weaknesses in the structure of the family, helped hasten the decline of familial governance and speeded up the search for a new model of governance effectively to serve the emerging large corporation.[16] Thus, the decline of the familial model of governance can be traced, at least in part, to the logic of social fragmentation that is inherent in the liberal ideology. Social fragmentation lies behind the dispersion of private property and undermines the power of the family of the founder entrepreneur over the corporation; it also splits the family and thus weakens the effectiveness

[15] For example, in Europe, the percentage of children born into single-parent households has increased dramatically: in Germany from less than 1% in 1900, to 2.4% in 1965 and 22.1% in 2000; in the United Kingdom from less than 1% in 1900, to 7.3% in 1965 and 39.5% in 2000; and in France, from less than 1% in 1900, to 5.9% in 1965 and 41.7% in 2000.

[16] The tension between fragmented society and concentrated family must also be taken into account in analysing the family business of today. In view of the fragmentation undergone by both the society at large and the institution of the family in particular, in over a hundred years since the heyday of familial governance, the similarity between familial governance as it was practised then and governance in today's family-owned corporation is largely metaphoric (see also Part III). We will not pursue this subject further here, but note that the historical evolution of family business and corporate governance as practised in the family business merits a study of its own.

of the family as the counterweight to the entrepreneur. By the turn of the twentieth century the political unity that gave familial governance its unique force had been largely broken.

Who would inherit the mantle of the entrepreneur?

The economic and political arguments explaining the decline of familial governance contain the seed of a radical transformation in the status of the entrepreneur. Under familial governance, the entrepreneur holding all of the property rights and driving economic activity was a single person or, as head of a family, represented a unified set of interests. The large, modern corporation with multiple shareholders and professional, that is to say non-shareholder, management saw the emergence of two different heirs to the original family entrepreneur: the shareholder who controlled the rights of *fructus* and *abusus*, and the management who controlled the right of *usus*, and, if he/she also owned shares, a small part of the *fructus*. In the large, modern corporation, as it constituted itself in the early twentieth century, the owner rarely fulfilled the role of management anymore, and senior management generally was not an owner. With the advent of management, a new social category appeared, distinct both from the capitalist owners and from the employees because in the position of exercising power over the corporation. In the context of the general challenge to power exclusively based on private property, the emergence of this new class helped establish a separation of the powers of ownership and control in corporate governance. At a more fundamental level, the adoption of this, the second of the principal procedures of democratic governance, implied a redefinition of the legitimate locus of the entrepreneurial force of direction.

As we showed in Chapter 2, modern liberal thought based the legitimacy of property ownership on two different sources: the *work* of the person who works to make the property bear fruit and the *rights* associated with the property. This double source of legitimacy was not a cause for contradiction, as long as the management was also the owner, or the owners were directly involved in the management. Work and right, the two sources of legitimacy were united in one individual who held all three elements of property rights (*usus, fructus,* and *abusus*). However, with shareholders less and less involved in the management of the corporation, the question of who legitimately exercises the entrepreneurial force became central to all considerations of corporate governance. Who is the entrepreneur: the directors (management) who work but do not own, or the shareholders, who own but do not work? The governance of the modern corporation became a subject of intense debate in the 1920s, a debate which continued until the end of the Second World War. In fact, it was a battle over the mantle of the entrepreneur; with the demise of familial governance, the two potential heirs of the founder entrepreneur, the shareholder and the manager, both aspired to that mantle.

The majority of observers of that period saw legitimate authority over the large corporation now vested in the executive management (who work *even if they do not own*) and not in the shareholders (who own, *even if they do not work*). Indeed, in the tradition of modern liberal thought, work, not ownership, is the privileged source of legitimacy, because work reaffirms individual liberty and equality whereas ownership can be inherited and can therefore contribute to sustaining inequality. In the order of legitimacy which it confers, *usus* must precede *abusus*. Based on this interpretation of the liberal heritage, management took over the entrepreneur's mantle of legitimacy. Although management rarely owned shares in the early twentieth century, it worked for the corporation, was both able and talented, and was seen to put this talent in the service of the general interest. Thus, management could be considered as the true torchbearer of capitalism's entrepreneurial spirit. Shareholders, on the other hand, were for the most part still considered to be mere providers of funds, far removed from the corporation and its concerns, and so interested in the return on capital as to engage in speculation, with potentially serious adverse consequences for business. From 1900 onwards, repeated financial crises intensified the negative aspects of this picture of the shareholders, until the crash of 1929 appeared to confirm everyone's worst fears.[17]

In America, management's claim to legitimacy received support from a wide variety of sources. The father of American institutionalism,

---

[17] See Walter Rathenau, *Gesammelte Schriften: Die neue Wirtschaft*, Vol. V, Berlin, 1918, pp. 179–261, or Thorstein Veblen, *The Theory of Business Enterprise*, New York: Transaction, 1904, but also Chandler's review (1977) of the literature of the period and our discussion in Chapter 7 (*The Visible Hand: The Managerial Revolution in American Business*, Cambridge, MA: Harvard University Press, 1977).

Thorstein Veblen, argued that modern capitalist enterprise should be directed by a 'soviet of engineers'.[18] Berle and Means drew considerable inspiration from Veblen. Contrary to a widely held opinion, Adolf Berle and Gardiner Means were not nostalgic for an idyllic time when shareholders exercised more power, for, as we saw in the previous chapter, such a time had never existed; they observed that in the modern corporation managers were the new entrepreneurs, with full powers, and worried about how the non-owner managers could be stimulated to achieve economic performance.[19] At the same time, James Burnham composed a very polemical but influential treatise on the new managerial technocracy's rise to power. A real managerial revolution was under way, and it affected many countries and multiple spheres of activity. In Burnham's view, the source of the problems experienced in those years was traceable to a system of governance that sought to unite in the same person two sources of legitimacy – work and ownership. For him, technical expertise represented the only acceptable source of legitimacy for governing human beings. Technocracy, or governance by elites distinguished by superior knowledge, became *en vogue*.

In Europe, the debate between the Wars was influenced by the menacing presence of two political ideologies that were strongly influenced by the technocratic ethos: Nazism in Germany and Communism in Russia. Although the technocratic movement found fertile ground in the engineering tradition in Germany, and in the rational school of thought in France and the United Kingdom as well as in Germany, it was dangerously perched between the economic need to replace the family model generally judged to be outmoded and the political danger represented by a totalitarian technocracy.[20] It is important to take this historical context into account when comparing the evolution of the European and the American viewpoints on managerialism. The European spirit, although naturally favourable to technocratic ideals, is marked with a lasting, ambiguous suspicion of technocracy; it is both

---

[18] See T. Veblen, *The Engineers and the Price System*, New York: Viking, 1921.
[19] This judgement is very clearly enunciated in the epilogue of A. A. Berle and G. C. Means' famous book, *The Modern Corporation and Private Property* (New York: Macmillan, 1934). We will come back to this point and provide a more detailed treatment of their ideas in Chapter 7.
[20] A good example of the contemporary French intelligentsia's difficulty in dealing with managerialism can be found in the work of G. Gurvitch (ed.), *Industrialisation et technocratie*, Paris: Armand Colin, 1949.

desired, in the name of reason, and feared, in the name of liberty. Schumpeter's gloomy last study reflects these misgivings, questioning whether or not the new technocracy could fully assume the 'spirit of the entrepreneur' and concluding with serious doubts. In Schumpeter's eyes, the process of turning the entrepreneur into a 'routine' implied in the technocratic approach would erode the entrepreneurial spirit, a spirit which he associated with a single individual who had almost heroic capacities. At the end of his analysis, he was left to speculate, in the same vein as Berle and Means, about a possible degradation of long-term economic performance due to a lack of entrepreneurs.[21]

Such well-placed doubts about the new model's sustainability notwithstanding, scholars agreed that a new era of governance based on managerial work had been inaugurated. During the following thirty years (c. 1940–70), shareholders played a relatively small role, at best that of an economic actor who was necessary but passive (cf. Berle and Means, Schumpeter), at worst that of a simple speculator (Veblen). By the time the world had emerged from the Second World War, there could no longer be any doubt about who had inherited the mantle of the entrepreneur: management was the new pillar of capitalism, and the era of managerial governance was under way.

2 Power to the experts: managerial governance

Technocracy: the legitimacy of knowledge[22]

The rise to power of the new managerial class coincided with the industrial restructuring of the end of the nineteenth century. New

[21] Clearly, Schumpeter's ideal picture of the entrepreneur was based on the image of the founder and father of the family. His point of reference was the golden age of capitalism of the nineteenth century, a time when innovating entrepreneurs drove economic progress, and this does not facilitate his effort to understand the emerging technocracy. Still, Schumpeter remains a splendid analyst of the fragmenting impact of democracy on the legitimate use of entrepreneurial power. See especially Chapter 12 of J. Schumpeter, *Capitalism, Socialism, and Democracy*, New York: HarperPerennial, (1987 [1942]).

[22] For this section, we draw on the classic works of A. Chandler, *The Visible Hand: The Managerial Revolution in American Business*, Cambridge, MA: Harvard University Press, 1977, and 'The United States: evolution of entreprise', in P. Mathias and M. M. Postan (eds.), *The Cambridge Economic History of Europe*, Vol. VII, Part 2, Cambridge: Cambridge University Press, 1974, pp. 70–133.

types of knowledge and new skills became necessary in the organization of the corporation (the work of Taylor, Fayol, and scientific management provides an early technocratic response to the challenges). In the United States, the number of engineers increased from 7000 to 135,000 in the space of just forty years (1880–1920).[23] By the 1920s/1930s, methods of mass production based on the insights of Henry Ford had made a triumphant entry into scores of industries, and experts trained in the techniques of management were firmly installed as executives. Of course, this new reliance on expert management was a direct consequence of the increasing complexity of the large corporation and the division of labour such complexity entailed. The technical logic of this justification notwithstanding, it was important from a sociological point of view that the superiority of managerial work over share ownership be reaffirmed. In the preceding chapter, we saw that managerial expertise was originally not considered as a body of knowledge that could be separated from experience acquired in the family corporation. By building up a body of managerial knowledge that had to be mastered, management was able to assure itself of the possibility of having its capacity to organize the corporation identified and evaluated, and hence to lay a basis for the legitimacy to direct. In this way, (managerial) work could be considered more legitimate than ownership.

Max Weber had already established the basis for the legitimacy of the modern bureaucracy, by showing how its power was based on knowledge, with rationality as the grammar of action. Weber essentially described public administration and the state bureaucracy, but he proposed a theory that could be applied to the de-privatized organization that the modern corporation was to become. From the early 1900s onwards, a base of bureaucratic knowledge began to develop, aimed at discovering rules of 'rational' human government, particularly in the corporation. It was in this spirit that the period saw the beginnings of a new 'science' that defined the specificity of management knowledge. In the beginning, it was often managers themselves who drove the process (e.g. Barnard, McKinsey, and experienced practitioners as lecturers at the Harvard Business School, or in conferences around the United

[23] S. M. Jacoby, *Employing Bureaucracy: Managers, Unions, and the Transformation of Work in American Industry, 1900–1945*, New York: Columbia University Press, 1985, p. 40.

States). When Joseph Wharton founded a business school at the University of Pennsylvania in 1881, there was not a single professor of management on the faculty (early business schools were Chicago, 1898, Tuck, 1900, and Harvard, 1908). Picking up great speed after the Second World War, and with the co-optation of specialists from other academic disciplines, the science of management developed to constitute an original combination of economics, sociology, and psychology. As the science of management took off, it ventured beyond its original confines of factory organization, sales management, accounting, and executive experience, giving birth to its own disciplinary children: human resource management, marketing, finance, and finally strategy.[24] By the 1970s, the whole corpus of study was complete, supported by specialized *business* schools typically integrated into universities, with their own hierarchies of prestige, distinctive curricula, and increasingly numerous alumni. The alumni of the business schools and their European equivalents,[25] in turn, controlled networks of influence and thus came to constitute a veritable technocratic class covering both the private and the public sectors.[26]

As Foucault has shown, the creation of a specific body of knowledge ensures the position of those who exercise power in the name of such knowledge, in management as much as in other professions.[27] The new knowledge allowed for those who knew to be distinguished from those

---

[24] Cf. P.-Y. Gomez, *La république des actionnaires*, Paris: Syros, 2001, p. 42.

[25] Although business schools as such were still rare in Europe until the 1970s, studies in management became available in universities from the 1960s onwards, as faculties of management emerged out of the fields of economics and law; the elite French Grandes Écoles, as well as Oxford and Cambridge in the United Kingdom, for a long time resisted (or still resist) jumping on the business school bandwagon, but individual courses in management were and are offered. For a detailed study of business schools' development in Europe, see M.-L. Djelic, *Exporting the American Model: The Post-war Transformation of European Business*, Oxford: Oxford University Press, 1998.

[26] P. Stanworth and A. Giddens, 'An economic elite: a demographic profile of company chairmen', in P. Stanworth and A. Giddens (eds.), *Elites and Power in British Society*, Cambridge: Cambridge University Press, 1974, pp. 81–101; P. Bourdieu, *State Nobility: Elite Schools in the Field of Power*, Stanford: Stanford University Press, 1998[1989]; G. F. Davis and H. R. Greve, 'Corporate elite networks and governance changes in the 1980s', *American Journal of Sociology* 103(1)(1997): 1–37.

[27] Following a line of reasoning established by Weber in his sociological examination of bureaucracy, Badie and Birnbaum emphasized that 'the great instrument of bureaucratic administration's superiority is specialized

who did not know and hence for establishing the legitimacy of those who governed the corporation over those who were governed by it, employees and other stakeholders.[28] The ongoing professionalization of the management function was accompanied by research studies, academic papers, scientific colloquia, new standards for work, and novel job categories (such as that of the consultant). Sociologically speaking, these all constituted elements of a movement to confirm the existence of a distinctive competence in management based on a rational body of professional knowledge and serving the twin causes of economic and social progress.

The group of individuals qualified in this manner formed a system – the techno-structure. Post-familial governance was conducted in line with Weberian principles of administration, according to a hierarchy that grew in complexity with the size and scope of the corporation. Control was assured by a system of experts who shared a common background in management. The techniques of management developed with the large corporation did not only represent means for specifying knowledge and hence legitimizing power. They were also instruments for exercising the entrepreneurial force and driving economic innovation, making entrepreneurship into a routine and permitting management collectively to embody the entrepreneur: reporting, management control, planning, strategy, etc. were all as much instruments for making the entrepreneurial force now vested in the collectivity of managers coherent as they were instruments of oversight and direction. Alfred Sloan, *salaried* director of General Motors from 1923 to 1956, became the emblematic figure of the new management by technocrats. Under his watch, General Motors installed the 'Super-Factory System',[29] an organization that appeared to work mechanically, built around divisions that were autonomous enough to react

---

knowledge, the absolute need for which is determined by ... the economics of production' (B. Badie and P. Birnbaum, *Sociologie de l'état*, Paris: Grasset, 1975, p. 47, our translation). In his classic *The Economic Theory of Managerial Capitalism* (London: Macmillan, 1964), R. L. Marris strikes a similar chord.

[28] On the intellectual and therefore ideological foundation of managerial power, three classic works must be cited: C. I. Barnard, *The Functions of the Executive*, Cambridge, MA: Harvard University Press, 1968[1938]; R. Bendix, *Work and Authority in Industry: Ideologies of Management in the Course of Industrialization*, New York: Wiley, 1956; and H. Simon, *Administrative Behavior*, New York: The Free Press, 1976.

[29] Editorial in *New York Times*, 19 September 1926.

directly to markets, but tightly controlled by the hierarchical flow of information directed by a central body of management technicians.[30] At the top of the corporation could be found the supreme organ of direction and control which was the executive committee. The executive committee created strategy, stimulated innovation, and made the decisions that the board of directors then ratified. Rather than a single person, it was the body of senior managers ensconced in the executive committee that took over the entrepreneur's position. The legitimate right to direct the corporation had passed from an individual, the entrepreneur owner, to a group, professional management.

The role of shareholders under post-familial governance[31]

The separation between managers and shareholders, and management's appropriation of the mantle of the entrepreneur, was institutionalized by the rise of the limited liability joint stock company. As a legal form, the joint stock company had existed since the beginnings of capitalism, but, as described in Chapter 3, it was not widely used; the partnership with unlimited liability was by far the most common form of incorporation. In fact, the joint stock company ran counter to the spirit of family business – rather than bearing the *family name* it was *anonymous*. Moreover, since the joint stock company allowed for raising capital from individuals without engaging the personal liability of the directors, the joint stock company was at the time considered to be an especially risky proposition. Indeed, it was only in the second half of the nineteenth century that the limited liability joint stock company was freed from onerous requirements for state approval and started to become more common (United Kingdom 1856; France 1867; Germany 1870).

As the nineteenth century drew to a close and the need for investments associated with the large corporation engaged in mass production and mass distribution became very great, the unlimited partnership generally implied too heavy a risk to the fortunes of a family (and its associates, if present). This is why, at least in Europe, the joint stock company which

---

[30] Gomez, *La république des actionnaires*, p. 39.

[31] For further documentation concerning this period, see P. Frentrop, *A History of Corporate Governance*, Amsterdam: Deminor, 2003, pp. 219–301, on oligarchy.

had existed in most of the legal texts for over sixty years only really took off after the turn of the century. The listed corporation remained in the minority, and it was the non-listed corporations that accounted for most of the growth. By a large majority, corporations chose a non-public form of capital, a manner of financing that allowed a group of owners to remain in control of the capital without requiring them to exercise the power of direction: the Gesellschaft mit beschränkter Haftung (GmbH) in Germany (1892), the Private Limited Company (Plc) in the United Kingdom (1907), or the Société à Responsabilité Limitée (SARL) in France (1925). In 1885, limited stock companies represented a mere 5 to 10% of the larger corporations in the United Kingdom, primarily in weapons, steel, and cotton.[32] In 1938, for the first time, they outnumbered the unlimited partnerships. According to Ripert, in France in 1900 there were 6000 stock companies and 7200 unlimited partnerships, while by 1930 there were 45,000 of the former and only 12,800 of the latter.[33] With the rise of anonymous capital, the paths of the founder entrepreneur and the corporation were definitely separated. The corporation became an individual in its own right, and one can say that the corporation emancipated itself from its founder and from its owners.

The rise to domination of the limited liability joint stock company legally sealed the separation of power between managers and shareholders and put management firmly in control of the corporation. In the new technocratic enterprise guided by managerial knowledge, the owning families and other shareholders would be inexorably marginalized. As Payne notes for England, this process of marginalizing shareholders started relatively early: 'a growing lack of interest on the part of those shareholders who were slowly building up diversified equity portfolios or were geographically dispersed was reported to the Select Committee on the Company Acts of 1862 and 1867. The increasing practice of "proxy" voting too was encouraging a loosening of ownership control.'[34] By the 1930s, by which time publicly listed companies had become more common, the shareholder (particularly the small, anonymous shareholder) had come to be considered in a very

[32] P. Payne, 'Industrial entrepreneurship and management in Great Britain', in P. Mathias and M. Postan (eds.), *The Cambridge Economic History of Europe* Vol. VII, Part 1, Cambridge: Cambridge University Press, 1974, p. 195.

[33] G. Ripert, *Aspects juridiques du capitalisme moderne*, Paris: Pichon and Durand-Auzias, 1951.

[34] Payne, 'Industrial entrepreneurship', p. 204.

condescending manner. One of the most famous gadflies of American business history, Lewis Gilbert, liked to relate the story of how he first had the idea of asserting shareholder rights while attending a stockholders meeting in 1933 with the intention of discussing company problems. When he rose to ask a question, he was ignored by the chairman who, instead, invited stockholders to a buffet. As Gilbert put it in 1956, 'I had been publicly humiliated by my own employees. I was a partner in the business but I was treated like a tramp who could be put off with a handout.'[35] Shareholder rights were practically non-existent until the New Deal, when, under the influence of Berle and Means' work, the *Securities and Exchange Act* (1934) was passed and the Securities and Exchange Commission (SEC) was established. Shareholder rights that seem basic to us today – such as the right of the shareholder to be heard at the General Meeting or the right of the shareholder to be informed – are explicitly called for by the text of the Act. Putting the specifications of the Act into practice, however, was a long and onerous process. Thus, even in the United States, the liberal society par excellence, the influence of shareholders over the General Meeting for many years remained very weak.[36] Both the right of expression and the right to information were to become focal points of an extended struggle between a few heroic shareholder activists on the one hand (Lewis and John Gilbert, Wilma Soss, founder of the Federation of Women Shareholders, and James Peck) and management on the other. Contrary to received wisdom, there was no tradition of 'shareholder power' in the capitalist system: under familial governance, the General Assembly was not the legitimate forum for the exercise of a counterweight to the power of the entrepreneur. The General Assembly fared little better under post-familial governance.

[35] As quoted in, R. Marens, 'Evolution du gouvernement des entreprises: l'émergence au milieu du siècle de l'activisme actionnarial', *Finance, Contrôle, Stratégie* 6 (2003), 4.

[36] For more detailed treatment of these questions, one can refer to E. M. Dodd, *American Business Corporations until 1860, with Special Reference to Massachusetts*, Cambridge, MA: Harvard University Press, 1954; W. Roy, *Socializing Capital: The Rise of the Large Industrial Corporation in America*, Princeton, NJ: Princeton University Press, 1997; L. Gilbert, *Dividends and Democracy*, Larchmont, NY: American Research Council, 1956; F. Emerson and F. C. Latcham, *Shareholder Democracy: A Broader Outlook for Corporations*, Cleveland, OH: Press of Western Reserve University, 1954.

Indeed, shareholders no longer had any *justification* for getting involved in the direction of the corporation. On the one hand, they were seen as technically incompetent, unable to comprehend the complexity of the new industrial organizations. The professionalization of management implied that non-professionals, including shareholders, did not have the ability or the time to immerse themselves sufficiently in the problems of the corporation to have a legitimate say. On the other hand, shareholders typically possessed too few shares of any particular corporation to make the extra cost of controlling management worthwhile. However, the dispersion of ownership was merely an aggravating circumstance, not an independent explanation for new governance and certainly not its defining characteristic, as some have argued, interpreting the pioneering work of Berle and Means in excessively narrow fashion.[37] Managerialism was the product of a fundamental change in corporate governance whereby expert management took over legitimacy from the owner director. Shareholders did not have the competence to control the large corporation, and this inability showed most clearly in the cases of dispersed ownership, where shareholders could not have an interest in paying for the cost of control, and,

---

[37] Berle and Means documented the transition to dispersed ownership in the largest American companies over the first thirty years of the twentieth century and presented this dispersion of ownership as a contextual account of the rise of the managerial model. However, the primary concern of Berle and Means was the relationship between ownership and management, that is to say the relative strength of management and the relative weakness of ownership, not with the dispersion of ownership per se. In other words, in Berle and Means' discussion, the dispersion of ownership contextually explains its weakness, but it is not the *only possible* explanation for the lack of involvement by ownership. It is erroneous to consider that what was one element of the American context in the 1930s (dispersed ownership) is the defining characteristic of managerialism. Evidence from the French and German research literatures (F. Bourgignon and M. Lévy-Leboyer, *L'économie française au XIXème siècle*, Paris: Economica, 1988; V. Berghahn, *Unternehmer und Politick in der Bundesrepublik*, Frankfurt am Main: Suhrkamp, 1985; Payne, 'Industrial entrepreneurship') shows that the managerial model (strong management, uninvolved ownership) also obtains under conditions of concentrated shareholdings. In France and Germany, the most typical case has been that of large (block) holdings that do not exert their influence, either because the individual firm is only one of many holdings in a vast portfolio from which the owners only expect a financial result, or because the owners have no competence or interest in the management of the companies they hold. The corporations owned by the French state are characteristic examples of the latter case, with the state delegating full entrepreneurial powers to the managers it had appointed throughout most of the post-war period.

hence, could only be interested in the corporation in as much as they stood to obtain the profits, like retirees waiting for dividend coupons. This explains 'the passivity of … the lower-middle-class investors – increasingly numbered among the shareholders of the public companies – whose desire for knowledge concerning the companies in which they had been advised to invest hardly extended beyond the names of the firms'.[38] As Berle and Means wrote:

[the shareholder's] power to participate in management has, in large measure, been lost to him, and has become vested in the 'control'. He becomes simply a supplier of capital on terms less definite than those customarily given or demanded by bondholders; and the thinking about position must be qualified by the realization that he is, in a highly modified sense, not dissimilar in kind from the bondholder or lender of money.[39]

It was in the economic context of the large corporation and the ideological setting of managerialism that the idea of shareholders being interested *only* in profits came to the fore. This idea is so familiar to us today that we think of it as a law of *nature*: in fact, it appeared as a proposition in the 1930s, with the first treatises of finance.[40] The originality of this idea lay not in the suggestion that shareholders cared about profits, but rather in the emphasis on profits *alone*. Such an idea would have been entirely foreign to the entrepreneur owners and the fathers of industrial families of the nineteenth century and would also not have been taken seriously by the first liberal economists who insisted that the entrepreneur owner had a quasi-aristocratic responsibility for the general good.[41]

The idea of shareholders being interested *only* in profits appeared with the advent of a new model of governance, because the shareholder of the large, modern corporation was considered to be so far removed from the complex realities of the corporation that he/she could only

---

[38] Payne, 'Industrial entrepreneurship', p. 205.

[39] Berle and Means, *The Modern Corporation*, p. 245.

[40] On the use of accounting and the 'invention of profitability' as a means of disciplining individuals, see the brilliant thesis of A. Tinker, B. Merino, and M. Neimark, 'The normative origins of positive theories: ideology and accounting thought', *Accounting, Organizations and Society* 7(2) (1982), 167–200. This work shows how, in the 1930s, the emerging discipline of finance chose to focus on the calculation of individuals rather than on economic institutions.

[41] See Part I, Chapter 1.

understand a very simple and condensed amount of information, as incorporated in the profit figures. The dogma of the shareholder's exclusive focus on profits is a manifestation of the transformation of the shareholder from involved owner to uninvolved coupon clipper. The idea was coherent with the new order, as it confirmed the authority of management over the corporation: management was to hold the legitimate power of direction; shareholders had the right to claim the profits, and *only* this right. Governance by managerial technocracy limited the sovereignty of shareholders to a bare minimum, as management controlled not only the level of profitability, but also the system of information whereby the level of profitability was communicated. Shareholders could not be anything but passive, with the absolute authority of the entrepreneur to define and realize all the principal choices facing the corporation in the hands of management. The passivity of shareholders was even written into law in some countries. Thus, in France, for example, the law recognizes the existence of non-voting shares (with higher dividend, law of 1966), in direct contradiction of the original principles of shareholding property whereby 'every shareholder has a right to vote' (code commercial, art. 1844, al. 1). By depriving the shareholder of the right to vote, public policy actually confined him/her to the status of a coupon clipper and thus contributed to reinforcing the power of management over shareholders. Under these circumstances, modern political economy naturally became concerned with finding a legitimate counterweight to managerial power and a check on its eventual excesses. When Berle and Means wondered about the economic efficiency of management's discretionary power in the modern corporation, they were in fact foreshadowing this question.

3 Limiting the powers of management: technocracy under social control

In the United States as well as in Europe, the technocracy rose to power and firmly established a new model of governance in the years following the Second World War. On the one hand, the technocracy now controlled the institutions of the state, as liberalism's reaction to the social critique led to a new and expanded role for the public powers in defending private interests for the good of the whole. Thus the Welfare State emerged – a necessary but paradoxical stage of development in the liberal project that offered political support to those who had been dispossessed by the progress of liberalism. Technocratic power in the state was exercised in the name of knowledge and expertise. Drawing on the same logic, the technocracy appropriated for itself the entrepreneurial force of direction in large corporations, brushing aside owners (both the successors of founders and the simple shareholders) and building their own basis of legitimate power on rational and efficient economic management. As discussed in the preceding chapter, in a political sense, power cannot be accorded and subsist without a counterweight that constrains its scope and, by the very limitations imposed, renders power acceptable. A superficial reading, or a reading that is too strongly influenced by today's context, might lead one to believe that there was little counterweight to management in the period under discussion – the formal institutions of governance were either inefficient or simply non-existent. Upon closer examination, it becomes clear that a counterweight was indeed exercised, namely by the unions, an institution that grew to great importance during the managerial period. By assuring the legitimacy of social action, the unions limited the domain of management to that which was purely economic, and, in this manner, acted as a robust constraint on power.

The weakness of formal governance regulation

As we have seen, the shareholding body of the modern corporation could be characterized as a unified and uninvolved group of coupon clippers who patiently awaited the profits paid out by the corporation. In the face of expert managers, this group had neither the means nor the legitimacy to impose its views. Moreover, financial markets were still rather poorly developed and could not fully serve the financing needs of the corporation. This assessment held true not only for Europe, but also for the United States, where, although institutional conditions were favourable to relying on the investing public for financing, markets for a long time lacked an adequate number of professional intermediaries and remained of minor importance.[42] In the United Kingdom, the 1935

---

[42] Berle and Means, *The Modern Corporation*; Roe, *Strong Managers*. Although shareholders in the 1930s were more numerous than ever before, they did not yet constitute a mass; even in the 1950s, they numbered less than a million in France, and no more than 6 million in the USA, in other words some 4% of the American population as compared with 25% in 2000 (Source, *NYSE Fact Book*, 1995). See the seminal work of Roe, *Strong Managers*.

House of Lords decision in *Shaw and Sons (Salford) Ltd v. Shaw* clearly circumscribed the institutional position of shareholders: 'If powers of management are vested in the directors, they and they alone can exercise these powers. The only way in which the general body of shareholders can control the exercise of powers by the articles in the directors is by altering the articles, or, if opportunity arises under the articles, by refusing to re-elect the directors of whose actions they disapprove.'[43]

The role played by the board of directors well reflected the balance of power under managerial governance. From the 1920s onwards, the law started to impose stricter rules for the board. The idea that the board should represent and thus define the interests of the shareholders and (or) of the company in general stems from this time (for example, it became compulsory in France in 1940), and the separation of powers between shareholders and managers received its first institutional articulation. In fact, for the entirety of the managerial period, the board did little to assert itself against the executive committee. Boards were composed essentially of managers of the corporation (executive directors), ex-directors, and managers of other corporations (non-executive directors), belonging to the same social and professional networks as the executive committee. The directors effectively controlled themselves. Boards could not exercise critical control over the corporation, and nobody really asked them to do so. The board was an assembly of peers, a kind of registry office in which decisions got ratified, but it was not a body of oversight.[44] Thus, in the 1930s, the National Resources Committee found that 225 of the 250 largest US corporations had at least one director who sat on the board of at least one other of the largest corporations. What is more, 106 of these corporations belonged to eight more or less clearly defined interest groups.[45] Under managerial governance, executive management was the sole master of the corporate ship. Such a system of co-optation and auto-regulation established itself in all of the Western economies,

---

[43] L. Gower, *Principles of Company Law*, London: Sweet and Maxwell, 5th edition, 1992, p. 185.

[44] For more detail on this question, see P. -Y. Gomez, 'On the discretionary power of top executives', *International Studies of Management and Organization* 34 (2) (2004), 37–62.

[45] P. Dooley, 'The interlocking directorate', *American Economic Review* 59 (3) (1969), 314–23.

constituting what Useem calls an 'inner circle' and Frentrop refers to as an 'oligarchic' regime.[46]

Although this system came under severe and sometimes populistic criticism at the end of the twentieth century, it is important to note that its workings are entirely coherent with the managerial organization of power: who but other experts could be fit to control and hold experts accountable? This logic is also compatible with rationalist liberal thought. Since the assumption of the entrepreneur's mantle – indeed the superiority of management over shareholders – had been based on management's special knowledge (the science of management) and work, any higher instance, such as the board, could only be composed of people who had at least equivalent qualifications and involvement in business as the executive. To profess surprise about this state of affairs, in referring to current, twenty-first-century conditions, is to misunderstand the inner logic of the managerial model. The apparent weakness of the board was merely an expression of the notion that technocracy could regulate itself, a notion founded on the primacy of reason in liberal thought. As a result, management and board constituted a homogeneous body. Only actors from the outside, who questioned managerial expertise itself, could provide any counterweight to this system.

External counterweight: the role of the social organizations and unions

It was not the shareholding body but rather the union that appeared as the principal and legitimate counterweight to managerial power. Especially after the Second World War, the Western societies which professed liberalism built upon an increasingly well defined opposition of two spheres of regulation: the economic sphere which was the province of the corporation, and the social sphere which became the domain of labour unions. In different countries with different cultures and histories, this opposition played out in different ways, but whatever the local shadings, it can be taken as a defining characteristic of the period we are describing here. Between the economic and the social

---

[46] M. Useem, *The Inner Circle: Large Corporations at the Rise of Business Political Activity in the U.S. and U.K.*, Oxford: Oxford University Press, 1984; Frentrop, *History of Corporate Governance*, p. 219ff.

spheres, the state intervened as an arbiter, sometimes in the interests of economic growth, at other times in the interests of social equality. Thus, we have the golden triangle of post-war cooperation: the corporation in charge of economic well-being and the unions in charge of social well-being, with the state acting as an arbiter in the general interest.

The economic sphere belonged to the rationality of management, the rationality of production and growth. This sphere was governed by specialists, in the name of organizational reason. As we have seen, executives considered themselves and were also considered by others to be experts in management, and more broadly in all things economic. The managerial literature idealized the vision of the manager who was responsible for economic progress and had to defend the interests of business in negotiation with social forces. The social sphere included consideration of general living standards, equality, and justice, and was firmly in the grip of another group of specialists: social workers, union leaders, politicians, and ideologues whose mission it was to propose social reforms that might improve the general conditions of life. In all of the Western countries, the percentage of the workforce that was unionized and the influence of unions, particularly in the form of strikes, reached new peaks during this period. The great unions appeared at the end of the nineteenth century and became major players in the general spread of Fordism. Thus, we can list the birth of the Trade Union Congress (TUC) in the United Kingdom in 1867, the American Federation of Labor (AFL) in 1886, the German Union League (ADGB) in 1892, and the French Confédération Générale du Travail (CGT) in 1895. A half-century later, in the 1950s, 25% of French employees and 35% of American employees were unionized. By the 1970s, the percentage of union members in the United Kingdom had risen to 55%, or 13 million employees. Against the functioning of the corporation as a private property, the social movement is mobilized to give the counterweight of union power real influence. Among the actions of the social movement, the strike, that is to say the public refusal to do private work (often accompanied by demonstrations and political demands), is the most powerful tool for pressure, because it accentuates the rupture between the social and economic spheres. Over the course of the period of managerial governance, strikes were very frequent. According to OECD calculations, the Western countries lost an average of 15% of annual days worked to strike between 1948 and 1952, 18% between 1953 and 1957, 14% between 1958 and 1962, and 16% between 1963 and 1967; the absolute peak of strike losses was reached between 1968 and 1972, with 32%.[47]

The separation of economic and social spheres is not an inherent characteristic of capitalism, as it is sometimes presented to be.[48] In the period preceding the managerial, this separation was not established; paternalistic entrepreneurs and their extended families were often very concerned about social questions as they touched their corporations (education, hygiene, living standards, etc.). Also, during the familial period, social reformers could be as interested in raising living standards as in the means of achieving their goals (i.e. nationalizations, creation of national industries). Even if society was politically divided into public and private spheres, the corporation was thought of (and considered itself) as a socio-economic unit, albeit totally contained in the private sphere. This unity between the economic and the social in the private sphere broke down under managerialism, for three principal reasons: first, management based its legitimacy on economic rationality and subordinated other dimensions such as the social to this type of rationality. The social movement represented by the unions then rose to influence by establishing itself as a counterweight to managerial power, sometimes in ways that complemented economic reasoning, other times in opposition to such reasoning. Second, the post-war world was divided into two blocs, one claiming a liberal ideology, the other a socialist ideology. This global split created an intense amount of pressure on national systems of regulation. In effect, liberal society internalized the global tensions and found an equilibrium between the competing ideologies – as a means of assuring its own survival. Finally, over and above the interests that oppose different economic actors, a social system cannot last unless the powers that drive the system mutually set some limits on themselves. By opposing the economic and the social spheres and forcing both to deal continuously with the limits placed on it by the other, the West of the post-war period found a way of achieving both outstanding economic growth and rising living standards.[49]

[47] T. Cusack, *Politics and Macroeconomic Performance in the OECD Countries*, OCDE Discussion Paper FS I 95–315, 1995, p. 10.

[48] See H. Arendt, *The Human Condition*, Chicago: University of Chicago Press, 1958.

[49] For a critical but refined analysis of this question as it played out in the United States, see N. Lichtenstein, *State of the Union: A Century of American Labor*, Princeton, NJ: Princeton University Press, 2002.

Corporate governance, in the strict sense of the term defined in the introduction, can only be fully understood in light of its economic and social context, as described in the preceding paragraphs. The democratic separation of powers of ownership and control that characterized managerial governance and differentiated it from familial governance concerned not only the partition of property rights between shareholders and executives, but also the new distinction between the economic and social spheres. Having achieved the upper hand over the shareholder, the executive was still not all-powerful, for he/she had to contend with the unions and the social movements they represented. Informally, the unions did, in most Western countries, participate in corporate governance, trying to orient the entrepreneurial force in their favour. In Britain, France, and Germany, the law institutionalized this influence: thus, the creation of work councils in the United Kingdom (without specific legislation), *comités d'entreprise* in France (legalized in 1945), or *Betriebsräte* in Germany (1952) allowed for the employees (or rather the unions representing employees) to be informed about the strategic decisions of the corporation and to give an advisory opinion.[50] These councils constituted a real source of influence. Of course, the obligation to inform employees was regularly avoided in practice: there would have been an 'official' board meeting with employee representatives and (internally) public voting and a de facto board restricted to management that discussed issues in depth and made strategic decisions. Nonetheless, although the official board was more a theatrical forum for venting opposition, without real decision-making power, the very fact that employee representatives could voice their views provided some measure of balance.

Of course, it was in what is improperly called the German form of governance that the legal institutionalization of the opposition between the economic and social spheres took its most distinct shape. We noted earlier that the law of 1870 (completed in 1884) made it obligatory for corporations in Germany to separate governance bodies into a supervisory board (*Aufsichtsrat*) and a management board (*Vorstand*), with the stipulation that a third of the members of the supervisory board could not be shareholders. In 1951, under the threat of a general strike,

---

[50] See J. Rogers and W. Streeck, 'Workplace representation overseas: the works council story', in R. Freeman (ed.), *Working under Different Rules*, New York: Sage, pp. 97–156.

the federal government enacted a law which assured employees in the coal, iron, and steel businesses a number of seats on the supervisory board equal to the number held by shareholders (*Montanmitbestimmung*). For all other corporations with more than 500 employees, the law of 1952 (*Betriebsverfassungsgesetz*) reserved a third of the seats to the employees. In 1976, towards the end of the managerial period, the law provided for employee/shareholder parity in the number of supervisory board seats to all corporations with more than 2000 employees. This form of board representation is often presented in rather exaggerated tones, as especially typical of the German tradition of concerted action (*Mitbestimmung*). Of course, one cannot deny the cultural idiosyncrasies that made this form of representation possible – especially in comparison with other countries that were also heavily affected by social conflict, particularly the United Kingdom and France, but also, to some extent, the United States. However, an approach which is too narrowly focused on culture tends to obscure an important part of the historical reality: after the destruction of the Second World War, Germany designed its system of governance for large corporations upon the managerial model dominant at that time. In fact, the 'German' model very accurately reflects the double separation of powers we have described as characteristic of the period: between the shareholders and the executive (separation between *Aufsichtsrat* and *Vorstand*), but also between the shareholders and the employees, to great effect institutionalizing the considerable counterweight to managerial power represented by the German unions (separation internal to the *Aufsichtsrat*, with different members representing the different stakeholders). The German approach best translates the counterweight represented by the power of the unions into the highest institutions of the corporation: in this sense, it is perhaps the most coherent with the spirit of managerial governance.[51] Thus, with

---

[51] If our analysis is correct, the crisis of the German or Rhine River form that has been discussed since the 1990s represents not so much the difficulty of a particular social culture, but more a problem of the managerial model in general, a model that the German form mirrors especially closely. In this sense, the famous opposition between Anglo-Saxon and Rhine River capitalisms, such as it has been suggested by Albert appears to have been a thing of the past, even at the time it was announced (early 1990s). See M. Albert, *Capitalisme contre capitalisme*, Paris: Seuil, 1991. Further reference to this deceptive opposition is also made in the following chapters.

the help of our analysis, it is not surprising to note that Germany proved an exception in the use of strikes as a manner of exercising public pressure on the private corporation. Between 1955 and 1977, statistics show 445 days of work lost annually to strike for every 1000 workers in the United States, 265 in the United Kingdom, 151 in France, and only 23 in Germany. In Germany, the social movement was and is channelled through institutions and can exercise its role as a counterweight to power from within the corporation.[52]

4 Equilibrium and threats to managerial governance

After the decline of the familial model owing to the fragmentation of ownership and also to the fragmentation of the family under the pressure of modern, liberal society, corporate governance found a new equilibrium compatible with the tenets of modern society. The *management as entrepreneur* represented the new guarantor of economic rationality, innovation, and progress. For the next several decades, management dominated corporate governance, with economic reason constrained only by social considerations; management's hold was such that it became practically impossible for anyone but professional managers to occupy the direction of a large corporation. The managerial technocracy had brought forth a new elite. This new equilibrium was based on a golden triangle of confrontation and cooperation among the corporation, the unions, and the state, and the legitimacy of those who governed the corporation rested upon expert work rather than upon property ownership disconnected from business. This solution was compatible with the spirit of modernity, because it drew on the notion of equal opportunity between individuals. The separation of powers between ownership and control differentiated managerial governance from familial governance and marked a step forward in the democratization of corporate governance.

In order to understand why the managerial model of corporate governance could be considered legitimate despite apparently deficient institutions of control and accountability, it is necessary to look at it from a broader perspective – that of social regulation as it was practised at the time. Managerialism was more than a model of corporate governance. Closely tied to Fordism and mass production, managerialism

---

[52] See J. -D. Reynaud, *Sociologie des conflits du travail*, Paris: PUF, 1982, p. 28.

was an integral part of a comprehensive system of social regulation – that is to say that it functioned within a universe of diverse power relationships that, by confronting each other, provided the basis for society as a whole to ensure growth and prosperity.[53] It is therefore necessary to understand the managerial model of governance in the larger context of society as it existed in the years between 1920 and 1970.

Except for revolutionary movements on the fringe of Western society, the unions did not deny the legitimacy of managerial power and entrepreneurial leadership; they focused instead on contesting the *implications* of managerial governance for the lives of stakeholders, namely the employees. By taking responsibility for this dimension of social regulation, the unions defied management's dominance and re-equilibriated, to some extent, the balance of powers. Depending upon which country and which moment in time one considers, this opposition of powers between unions and management could take on a variety of forms: conflict, strike, concerted action, or negotiation. In retrospect, it might seem as if the years between the 1920s and the 1970s were marked by recurrent bouts of social strife and a permanent sense of social malaise, in all of the Western economies. Such an impression would mistakenly underestimate to what extent the clashes between economic and social spheres helped constitute an effective, long-term forum for airing differences and balancing powers. In fact, the maintenance of a productive dialogue between economy and society contributed to a period of remarkable growth in the West, in which the managerial technocracy could fully exercise the force of the entrepreneur. Culturally nuanced, but with clearly defined character-istics, managerial governance became the model of reference in all of the Western countries.

Attacked by socialist criticism and challenged by the Communist countries, subject to fragmentation of its constituent interests, liberal society reacted by breaking the fence around the private enterprise and giving the technocracy (separate from ownership) the responsibility of governing and ensuring the maintenance of private freedoms. In this sense, technocratic managerial governance represents a step of progress

---

[53] R. Boyer, 'The convergence hypothesis revisited: globalization but still the century of nations?' in S. Berger and R. Dore (eds.), *National Diversity and Global Capitalism*, Ithaca, NY: Cornell University Press, 1996, pp. 29–32.

in the application of democratic technique, compared to familial governance that was unitary and entirely private. Far from being a rupture of the liberal ideology, the advent of managerial governance represents one of the 'tricks played by history' (Hegel) that permit the liberal society to find a new equilibrium between an acceptable use of entrepreneurial force and social fragmentation.

However, from the 1960s onwards, even while it was still receiving many deserved accolades for its part in the West's impressive post-war performance, managerial governance started to come in for an increasing amount of economic and political criticism – a general questioning that culminated in protest movements that ranged in inspiration from the radical to the ultra-liberal. Two factors intrinsic to managerial governance threatened the established equilibrium of power and counterweight. The first of these was the ambiguous status of shareholders in the managerial model. Even if the shareholding body was passive, as Berle and Means among others had underlined, it still existed and had a function to fulfil in the capitalist system. In the confrontation between capitalism and socialism, the inactivity of the liberal political project's characteristic actor, who, as an owner, represented the ideal of the free man, appeared as a problematic contradiction. If shareholders were passive, what *purpose did they serve*? How did they participate in the performance of the capitalist economy? Were they even needed? Defining the shareholder's place in the equilibrium of corporate governance became a critical concern in the 1970s, with the growth of the number of shareholders fuelled by changes in retirement systems. The managerial model was considerably weakened by its inability to find ways to address this new reality. The second factor threatening the equilibrium of managerial governance concerned the nature of oversight in the model. By the 1970s, it had become apparent that the technocracy could and often did resemble an oligarchy, a state that allowed a small number of individuals to hold a great deal of power over the entire economic system – the corporation, the state, and even the unions. From its origins as a protector of individual liberties against the excesses of private property, the technocracy seemed to have evolved into a dangerous Leviathan. The presence of such an oligarchy, apparently beyond control, was not compatible with the liberal principle of equality and represented a threat to individual liberties. The 1970s and their economic crises carried the seeds of change and led to a revival of the liberal project. Managerial expertise, the ultimate source of the legitimacy of managerial governance, began to lose its halo of (rational) infallibility. As we will show in the following chapters, the internal fragility of the managerial model would prevent it from withstanding the neo-liberal critique and the accelerated social fragmentation that accompanied economic and financial globalization. Corporate governance would evolve with the new reality and change shape once again.

5 | Post-managerial governance (from c.1970): ownership of the large corporation reaches unprecedented mass and fragments into multiple poles

Managerial governance was based on a clear separation of powers, between management on the one hand and shareholders on the other, with unions playing the role of external counterweight. Management was strong and united by the ties of shared expertise, professional standards, schooling, and social convention; shareholders were weak, but united in the passive stance generally adopted towards management (control) and the narrowly focused interest in the profits of the corporation. From the 1970s onwards, with the shareholding bodies of large corporations spreading ever more widely in the population and thereby gaining unprecedented mass, the managerial model started to unravel. Governance by managerial expertise was severely challenged by the resultant change in the balance of power between management and shareholders and came under sustained attack (1). Shareholders fragmented into multiple poles of interest, each demanding that the corporation satisfy different criteria: in other words, the unity of the shareholding body dissolved. As a consequence, corporate governance also underwent a major change, and the function of the entrepreneur was reinterpreted to accord a significant role to investors in the financial markets and long-term shareowners. A new model of governance has emerged, a model that we call *public governance*, to stress the critical role played by the larger public (2). Unlike the transition from familial governance to managerial governance which took place many years ago, the transition from managerial governance to public governance is not yet complete. Many of the developments we will describe in the following pages are fresh, and reversals are still possible. We therefore need to be careful in discussing the reasons for the decline of managerial governance, in full knowledge of the fact that we are, at the time of writing, living through a period of change in which managerial governance and a new model of governance exist side by side.

1 Managerial governance comes under attack

Even in its heyday, in a liberal social context, managerial governance's strength was tempered by structural fragility. Its strength derived from a distribution of power that furthered rational, highly efficient decision-making; a system of governance based on work and expertise was coherent with the rationalist values of modern society. Its fragility stemmed from the fact that with power concentrated in management, managerial governance could take on the characteristics of an oligarchy that no longer respected the individual liberty of employees, shareholders, and societal stakeholders and was open to suspicions of individual excess and abuse. As long as economic prosperity prevailed, namely during the thirty years following the end of the Second World War, debate between management and the other stakeholders of the corporation focused primarily on the allocation of wealth, as expressed by the external counterweight of the unions, and only in small measure on the legitimacy of managerial power, so apparently efficient. In other words, during these years the debate did not touch upon corporate governance per se: what discussion did take place was aimed at finding ways of enlarging the circle of managers to include a greater percentage of the workforce, rather than at questioning the logic of basing the exercise of the entrepreneurial force on rationality and managerial expertise. Since the legitimacy of management was based on the claim of superior expertise, positive economic results during the long period of post-war prosperity only reinforced the political status quo.

The tone changed with the economic shocks of the 1970s. Increasing unemployment, poor corporate profits, and recurring economic restructurings put a dent in managerial claims to superior knowledge. The weaknesses of managerial governance became more visible during this time, and the first sharp criticisms were articulated, most notably from neo-liberal thinkers in the United States and Great Britain, but later also from Continental Europe. Again, it is useful to distinguish between the contextual reasons and the systemically inherent reasons driving this evolution.

Contextual reasons: globalization and the new financing of the corporation

The structural modifications the world economy underwent over the last quarter of the twentieth century have been well documented in the literature. We will therefore limit our description to a general outline of these changes, in so far as they pertain to the subject of this book.[1] The 1970s saw the beginnings of a dramatic move towards the globalization of the corporation. Globalization (business without borders) eventually had an impact on every link in the value chain,[2] and, consequently, also fundamentally affected the financing of the corporation. At the start of the period, a significant economic slowdown made the poor profitability of traditional industries painfully obvious and revealed the need for massive new investments, both in older industries that needed to be modernized to face global competition and in newer, emerging sources of value creation that needed fresh capital to grow. With profits low, it was impossible for corporations to finance their needs on their own, and it became necessary to seek significant outside funding, either by means of borrowing from banks or by raising capital from the financial markets and thereby increasing the size of the shareholding body.

The system of financing in the United States still differed significantly from most of the rest of the world at this time: for reasons of institutional history and legislation, corporate financing relied essentially on the financial markets and only marginally on the intermediation of banks.[3] The American corporation's demand for new capital in the 1970s therefore quite naturally turned to the stock and bond markets. In order to allow corporate growth to take off again, however, the savings side also had to be ready to play its part. The American system of retirement is managed by public and private pension funds which invest the savings of their members both in tangible assets such as land and buildings and in intangible assets such as debt instruments. The

---

[1] The ideas presented here were initially sketched in P. -Y. Gomez, *La république des actionnaires*, Paris: Syros, 2002. Although there is an abundant literature in economics on this topic, few observers have sought analytically to draw out the consequences of these developments on the evolution of the corporation. The enlightening work of Monks and of Fligstein deserves special mention here: R. Monks, *The New Global Investors: How Shareowners Can Unlock Sustainable Prosperity Worldwide*, Oxford: Capstone, 2001; R. Monks, *The Emperor's Nightingale: Restoring the Integrity of the Corporation in the Age of Shareholder Activism*, Oxford: Capstone, 1998; N. Fligstein, *The Transformation of Corporate Control*, Cambridge, MA: Harvard University Press, 1990.

[2] On this question, see H. Korine and P.-Y. Gomez, *The Leap to Globalization*, San Francisco: Jossey-Bass, 2002.

[3] M. J. Roe, *Strong Managers, Weak Owners: The Political Roots of American Corporate Finance*, Princeton, NJ: Princeton University Press, 1994.

primary challenge of this highly regulated system[4] has always been to anticipate and provide for significantly increasing pension commitments. Under pressure to address this challenge while transitioning from a defined benefits regime to a defined contributions regime, the American pension funds received legislative support in the form of new rules relaxing the limits placed on pension fund investments. Thus, they were authorized to invest in a broader variety of financial instruments by the Employee Retirement Income Security Act legislation of 1974, and further encouraged to move into equities by the Tax Reform Act of 1986. As a result, they started to diversify their portfolios and invest a greater proportion of their members' contributions in the financial markets.

From one side, therefore, there was an enormous appetite for new capital from business, from the other side a great afflux of savings, captured by the pension funds. When the two fuses touched, the American financial markets exploded: from 1970 to 2000, the stock portfolio of pension funds grew in size from 172 billion to 1,892 trillion dollars,[5] and the market capitalization of the New York Stock Exchange increased from 704 billion to 21 trillion dollars.[6]

From the point of view of the corporation, the method of gaining access to capital through the issue of fresh shares is particularly convenient, because it does not imply any short-term obligation to repay. Unlike Germany and Japan which conserved their bank-based system of financing until the late 1990s, countries with high levels of inflation like Great Britain (deregulation of financial markets in 1986, the Big Bang) and France (banking law of 1984 and deregulation in 1988) made the decision to finance the restructuring and globalization of their corporations by means of the financial markets; the high rate of local currency interest to be paid at the time would have made bank financing too expensive and put their corporations at a disadvantage. As a consequence, these countries and later Spain and Italy also saw an explosion of equity financing comparable to that of the United States. The market capitalization of London increased from 86 billion

---

[4] Private pensions come under the provisions of the Social Security Act (1935) and the Employee Retirement Act (ERISA, 1974). Public pension funds are run under the regulation of the State in which they are domiciled.

[5] Sources: *Federal Reserve Board Flow of Funds Accounts* and *American Council of Life Insurance*.

[6] Source: *NYSE*, March 2000.

dollars in 1975 to 1.711 trillion in 1995 and 2.7 trillion in 2006; for Paris the pattern is similar: 35 billion dollars in 1975, 586 billion in 1995, and with the merger of Paris, Brussels, and Amsterdam to form Euronext, 2.558 trillion in 2005.

Countries with low inflation and correspondingly lower interest rates like Germany and Japan did not need to develop financial markets as quickly, an element of the historical context that helps explain why managerial governance has been able to resist adaptation for longer in these countries. Whatever the pace, different for each country, equity-based financing has enjoyed unprecedented growth during the last thirty years. Not only has this changed the financial structure of the corporation, giving increased weight to equity, it has also changed the domain of those with a claim on the ownership of the corporation, from national (a small number of local shareholders and banks) to global. The modern corporation described by Berle and Means may have had some international production, but the capital base was national; for the new global corporation, both production and capital are increasingly global. Thus, in 2000, the percentage of total corporate equity held by foreign nationals amounted to 26.6% in France, 14.8% in Germany, 11.4% in the United States, and 37.2% in the United Kingdom. If one restricts consideration to publicly quoted corporations, the percentages of foreign ownership are as follows: 36.6% in France, 25.5% in Germany, 7.5% in the United States, and 22.4% in the United Kingdom. Clearly, the capital of American corporations is the least international – the retirement system gives them a formidable financing base, and the size of the market is still enormous compared to the other countries. Still, the opening of financial markets has also exposed the American corporation to foreign takeover – for example, Daimler's merger with Chrysler in 1998.[7]

Towards a shareholding body of unprecedented mass
Corporations' substantial demand for fresh capital in order to restructure and meet the challenge of globalization has had an important side effect: it has greatly increased the number of shareholders in the world, either indirectly by the intermediary of funds, or directly as stock

---

[7] Source: Banque de France and Caisse des Dépôts et Consignations, Rapport Dietsch, *Mondialisation et récomposition des entreprises européennes*, Paris: Commissariat Général du Plan, 2003, pp. 22–3.

markets have developed and become more liquid. In the space of twenty years, the number of individuals holding shares in one form or another has grown from some 30 million to over 200 million: today, 65 million Americans, 6.2 million French, and 12 million Germans directly hold shares. The changing structure of American savings (see above) and the rash of privatizations in Europe have contributed to accelerating the process of ownership dispersion. Thus, 2.5 million British purchased the shares of privatizing water distributors at the end of the 1980s (e.g. Thames Water), 2 million Germans became shareholders of Deutsche Telekom in 1995, and 6 million French of Edf (Electricité de France). In 2000, the French held an average of 38.4% of their savings in equities, Germans 16.7%, British 17.8%, and Americans 25.1%. Another way of looking at it is to note that American household savings in equities amount to 3.4 times the GNP (with the holdings of financial institutions and all other investors joined together in a third category 3.45 times the GNP and 1.68 times the GNP, respectively). In France, households own 2.37 times the GNP, financial institutions 4.43, and other investors 4.7 times the GNP.[8]

From the point of view of the large corporation, the change in capital structure has been just as far-reaching. For example, the automobile builders we discussed in the preceding chapter in the context of their importance to the beginning of the managerial era are today at the forefront of the redistribution of the large corporation's ownership structure. Founded in 1903 by twelve partners and initially 25% owned by Henry Ford (100% from 1919 onwards), the Ford Motor Company went public in 1956, with some 350,000 shareholders. Fifty years later, in 2005, the capital of the corporation is held by more than 700,000 individuals (the Ford family still retains 40% of the voting rights). Founded in 1899 by two brothers, Renault was nationalized in 1945.[9] Its status reverted to that of a joint stock company in 1990, and it was quoted on the French stock exchange in 1994. By 2005, the French state held only 15.7% of the capital, with Nissan Finance Ltd.

---

[8] J. Byrne and P. Davis, NIESR and statistical year books of the OECD. Given the great practical difficulty inherent in comparing figures of financial structure across countries, the numbers presented in this chapter are to be read more as indications of trends that experts agree upon than as absolutely reliable measures.

[9] Louis Renault was condemned for collaborating with the enemy in 1945. The Renault family, which held 96% of the shares, was expropriated without any compensation.

accounting for 15%, and the employees for 3.3%; 62.2% is dispersed among hundreds of thousands of institutional investors and individual shareholders. There are many more examples of this kind: many if not all of the large, publicly quoted corporations around the world have seen their capital become very broadly dispersed.

The growth in the mass of the shareholding body is an entirely new phenomenon in capitalism, comparable to the development of mass consumption in the first half of the twentieth century. Indeed, never before have there been so many citizens of Western countries so strongly implicated in the capital of corporations. One household out of two in Europe and two out of three in the United States have a more or less strong financial interest in the corporations quoted on the stock markets. Ownership of shares often represents an investment for retirement, an essential way of preparing the future for a population that has a growing life expectancy and hence needs to provide for an income outside the workforce over a longer period of time. The great variety of financial instruments that has become available to the retail sector has also changed traditional savings habits. The degree to which households became banked (established banking relationships) grew relatively slowly over the first three quarters of the twentieth century, but eventually reached 95 to 99% in the principal Western countries; today, these households' savings are oriented towards financial products that are based on the capital of the publicly quoted corporation: as a result, a systemic link between corporate profitability and household investment has become apparent.

Of course, this phenomenon has not touched the entirety of the population, but between 10 and 25%, the middle and upper classes in particular. This has given rise to a new sociology of financial interests – and to a modification of the logic of political action: increasingly, the interests of the middle and upper classes converge with those of the corporation in the support of improved economic performance, to the partial exclusion, at least, of the other classes. This focus on accumulation carries considerable risks of social rift. Even if the evolution towards mass shareholdings does not imply that everyone becomes a shareholder in a 'nation of shareholders', it does signify an important change in the structure of capitalism. With the greater dispersion of share ownership in the largest corporations, much closer and more complex links between the political space of the citizen and the economic space of the shareholder become established. In this sense, the dispersion of ownership is a new political phenomenon that fundamentally challenges the traditional separation between the economic and the social.

The unprecedented mass of shareholders necessarily changes the relationship between the corporation and society. Although originally conceived of and in fact still a *private institution* under the law, the global corporation today has a pronounced *public impact*, not only in terms of its actions, but also in terms of its economic performance. However, not only the performance but also the fluctuation of share prices now directly concerns the savings of a very large proportion of upper- and middle-class households in the West. In terms of the structure of the shareholding body, the interests of (all the) workers and owners can no longer be strictly separated, a new fact that clouds the old ideological arguments opposing shareholders (capitalists) to workers (proletariat) who are deprived of the ownership of the means of production. In an unprecedented way, workers have become owners of shares, particularly but by no means only of the shares of the corporations that they work for, and the classical critical discourse needs to be rethought.[10]

Increased distance between the shareholders and the corporation

In order to provide for the efficient allocation of household savings in the financial markets, a new industry for the placement of shares has been created. The relationship between savers and corporations is increasingly intermediated by a great many different organizations charged with collecting savings and choosing the best placement for them. To illustrate the growth of intermediaries, a few figures: first of all, in the space of thirty years (from 1970 to 2000), the proportion of equities in the portfolios of institutional investors reported on by the OECD rose from 7% to 18%; by 2000, pension funds and life insurances accounted for 23.9% of French household savings, 24% of German household savings, 40% of household savings in the United States, and 52.6% of household savings in the United Kingdom; mutual funds also had a significant part of these savings: 9% in France, 12.1% in Germany, 11% in the United States, and 8.1% in the United Kingdom. The growth of mutual funds, in particular, is largely a feature of the 1990s: whereas mutual funds savings investments were already large in France in 1990 (14%), they accounted for only 4.5% in

---

[10] See Chapter 3, Section 3.

Germany, 4% in the United States, and a mere 0.6 % in the United Kingdom.[11]

In search of the best returns, thousands of competing intermediaries have come to bridge the space between the shareholding body and corporations. These intermediaries are global and search for profitable placements around the world, without concern for the national origin of their investments. Owners of shares, represented by intermediary financial institutions and corporations, operate at a great distance from each other, incomparable with the situation that prevailed for most of the twentieth century. This is a second important element in the transformation of the nature of the ownership of the public corporation: for many funds, attachment to a particular corporation as an *owner* is no longer the primary motivation for holding shares. Today's shareholder can be an *investor* who diversifies his/her portfolio sufficiently to minimize risk and cares little about the *raison d'être* or fate of any individual corporation; he/she is primarily interested not even in a corporation's profits, but in a rise in its share price to improve the performance of the investment portfolio. By implication, the share itself becomes a commodity of exchange that obeys its own laws of supply and demand, to a certain degree independent of the long-term profit expectations of the underlying corporation. What counts in this market for property rights is the possibility of immediate gain by global arbitrage between *different* shares. Fundamentally, the intermediation of ownership changes the manner in which the right of *abusus* is used: buying or selling a share becomes an act of trading that focuses on the logic of price, influenced as much by the whims of traders, the liquidity needs of the market, and speculation in other shares, as by long-term corporate profit expectations. For as long as it has existed, intermediation has drawn the concern of those for whom the private entrepreneur is the only viable basis of capitalism. Concern about the possible negative effects of intermediation takes on broader meaning today, in

---

[11] J. Byrne and P. Davis, NIESR, and statistical yearbooks of the OECD. The apparent difference in the evolution of French savings does not undermine our reasoning. In the absence of pension funds, French household savings already focused on mutual funds in the 1980s (OPCVM in French). During the 1990s, the privatization of a number of large state enterprises led to a sharp increase in the percentage of equities in French household savings (more than 38%, the highest rate among the four countries we examine). As a mechanical result, the percentage held in mutual funds declined slightly.

a world of mass shareholdings, where there are disconnects and some-times deep divides between the interests of global intermediaries with no strong ties to any particular location, corporations that are rooted in international markets, and states accountable to national stakeholders. Each one of these actors, the intermediary, the corporation, and the state, faces a different set of temporal and spatial considerations. This set of disconnects poses a radical and as yet unresolved challenge to capitalism.

In a little over two decades, globalization and the growth of finan-cial markets have combined to change completely the financial context of the large corporation: with their mass, with their direct concern for share price performance, and with the help of professional intermedia-tion, the shareholders' weight as a body vis-à-vis the corporation, as well as their individual motivations with respect to holding shares, has undergone fundamental transformation. This represents a new state of affairs for modern liberal society. However, as important as these changes in the economic environment are, they do not fully explain why managerial governance is facing questioning that goes to the heart of its claim to legitimate authority. Indeed, why has the managerial model not been able to resist these new pressures? Why has manage-rialism never really recovered from the economic shocks of the 1970s? To understand the depth of the crisis faced by managerial governance, it is necessary also to discuss those challenges to the equilibrium represented by the managerial model that are inherent in the system itself.

The general crisis of expertise

Under managerial governance, the legitimacy of directors was based on their expertise and competence as professional managers: this author-ized them to exercise the function of entrepreneurial direction in the name of the corporation. The onset of economic crisis and the transi-tion to globalization cast doubt on the claim of unique expertise and weakened the legitimacy of management as entrepreneur. As a by-product of the changes to the economic system, unions also found themselves weakened to the point that they were no longer able fully to exercise the function of legitimate external counterweight to man-agerial power; this further destabilized the general equilibrium sup-porting managerial governance.

Questioning managerial expertise

From the 1970s onwards, the socio-political landscape began to change in ways that contributed to undermining the legitimacy of managerial governance and raised questions about management's ability to fulfil the entrepreneurial function. First of all, globalization posed a major challenge to management's ability to do what it was supposed to be best at doing, namely coordinate complex organization. On the one hand, globalization called for new competences – transfer of best practices across borders, multi-country production, but also intercultural management, knowledge of multiple legal regimes, and language and computer skills. Management had to be able flexibly to take large investment decisions, act both globally and locally, and change competitive course at speed.[12] In this difficult context of adaptation to complexity, the managerial hierarchies in place since the Second World War often turned out to be too bureaucratic, too slow, and thus inefficient. This assessment represented a revolution in the definition of what constitutes efficient technocratic structure, and a very real questioning of the value of expert knowledge. Indeed, since 1980, a considerable literature in management has made a speciality of calling for radical change, a flattening of hierarchical structures, decentralization, re-engineering, and a focus on excellence.[13] Although this literature is of uneven quality and relies more on example than on sustained analysis, one should not underestimate the ideological importance of works which, in their desire to bring about change in practice, express a strong voice of dissidence towards the dominant managerial bureaucracy. The calls for change, as articulated so well by Hammer and Champy in their *Manifesto for Business Revolution*, collectively represent a desire to transform the established bureaucratic order, frequently including the suggestion to build good practice on an evaluation by market measures. Symptomatically, an important literature has

---

[12] For a basic understanding of this vast literature, we refer to the now classic work of C. Bartlett and S. Ghoshal, *Managing across Borders: The Transnational Solution*, Cambridge, MA: Harvard Business School Press, 1989. Further discussion is provided in our essay, Korine and Gomez, *The Leap to Globalization*.

[13] Two influential bestsellers stand for many other books written along the same lines: T. Peters and R. Waterman, *In Search of Excellence: Lessons from America's Best Run Companies*, New York: Harper and Row, 1982; and M. Hammer and J. Champy, *Reengineering the Corporation: A Manifesto for Business Revolution*, New York: Harper Business Books, 1993.

emerged on the topic of intrapreneurship, a term originally coined by Pinchot,[14] that is to say the development of entrepreneurial activity inside the corporation. The title of the Pinchots' 1993 book, *The End of Bureaucracy and the Rise of the Intelligent Organization*, is in itself a very good indicator of the political challenge to management-as-usual implied in this rethinking of traditional approaches.[15] The stress placed on change, flatter structure, and intrapreneurship can be read as a strong indication of how management is struggling to recapture the lost spirit of entrepreneurship, and, with that spirit, the legitimate right to exercise the entrepreneurial function. In marked contrast to the previous era, cumbersome management structures are being pointed to as the prime reasons for poor corporate performance, and the legitimacy of bureaucratic management to govern the corporation is being called into question.

A second socio-political factor behind the decline of managerial governance can no doubt be found in the wide public diffusion of management expertise. With the rise in the general level of education in the West and the spread of business schools, management knowledge is no longer restricted to a small, elite group; on the contrary, it can be considered as increasingly banal, in some aspects even as a part of popular culture. According to the OECD, today in the large Western countries one employee in five has a university degree (bachelor or higher), with the proportion rising to one in three for younger employees. Management education has seen particularly spectacular growth. Every year, hundreds of universities and business schools around the world produce hundreds of thousands of MBAs, all 'experts' in management. MBAs can now be found not only in corporations but also in banks, investment funds, and financial intermediaries of all kinds, and even public bodies, as representatives of the interests of shareholders and stakeholders. As a result there has been a broad dispersal of the sources of management knowledge and a proliferation of legitimate

---

[14] G. Pinchot, *Intrepreneuring*, New York: Harper and Row, 1985. The related notions of corporate entrepreneurship and internal corporate venturing have also attracted significant attention, both in practice and in the literature. For a review, see P. Sharma and J. J. Chrisman, 'Toward a reconciliation of the definitional issues in the field of corporate entrepreneurship', *Entrepreneurship Theory and Practice* 23 (3) (1999), 11–27.

[15] G. Pinchot and E. Pinchot, *The End of Bureaucracy and the Rise of the Intelligent Organization*, San Francisco: Barrett Koehler Publishers, 1993.

actors to draw upon in referring to management skill. Where expertise is so widely diffused, it is only natural that sceptical and contradictory voices start to be heard: why should a manager know any better what is good for the corporation than the outside analysts who have enjoyed the same or perhaps an even more up-to-date version of management training? Management decisions become a legitimate topic of discussion. Rare management knowledge had formed the basis of management's claim to legitimate authority for decades. Now that that knowledge has become so widely diffused, arguing for distinctive expertise as the source of legitimacy in corporate governance becomes increasingly problematic, albeit not impossible.

Technocracy against individual liberty

The third and perhaps the most important factor in the debate over managerial power has its roots in considerations particular to the liberal political project. As we pointed out earlier, the rise of managerial bureaucracy coincided with the spread of technocratic norms, both in the corporation and in the public sphere. In the evolution of the liberal project, these technocratic norms played the important role of circumscribing the political and social effects of exclusively private direction. However, by the 1960s, the economic power of the technocracy had become enormous and appeared to reign unchecked. Even if it was constrained by the counterweight of the unions' social concerns, management maintained exclusive say in the strategic decision-making of the corporation, limited only by the boundaries of rationality as determined by managers themselves. This kind of exclusive authority was out of step with the broader development of modern Western society. In the logic of the liberal project, any and all sources of social authority that appeared to constrain individual liberty have at one time or another come under attack: no institution – not the state, not the churches, not the schools or the family, not even the military – has escaped this criticism: a criticism that is characteristic of social fragmentation. In its turn, the technocratic leadership of the economy also became the target of protest *in the name of modern liberty*; this was nothing more than a particular projection of a larger movement of general dissent. This dissent derived in part from the liberal suspicion that too much power leads to misuse and in part from a politically motivated questioning of the power of the technocracy and the technology it controls.

From the 1970s onwards, liberal thinking has made a marked come-back, both in politics and in economics, where a new 'economic approach' to property rights has given it a particularly strong expression (Part III discusses the latter development in considerable detail). With its individualistic logic – private interest is the supposed engine of all human activity – this line of thinking has lent itself to popularization as a doctrine of systematic suspicion towards selfish interest as the driver of managerial action. In times of crisis and poor economic growth, this angle of attack has been particularly effective. Popularization aside, we should not forget that this approach marks a return to the basics of the liberal political project and in this sense is justifiably called a neo-liberal approach: it represents a defence of individual liberty and a strict limitation of any technocratic power that might constrain such liberty. This approach, however economic in appearance, merely stands as a pretext for providing a political solution for the dismantling of a modern Leviathan: social fragmentation by means of 'the market' renders the Leviathan powerless, and it matters little whether he appears in the shape of the state or in the shape of the managerial bureaucracy.

In parallel to the liberal resurgence, a different current of thought, based on a political critique, has attacked the danger posed to society by technocracy and technology. It has questioned the uncontrolled power of those who base their authority on the control (or, often, the impossibility of control) of technology. Indeed, for this line of thinking, technology has its own internal logic of development, a logic that creates a path dependency which political regulation cannot rein in. The radical technological and industrial transformations of the late twentieth century are a case in point and show how revealing this critique can be. The influential figures of this powerful movement of anti-technological protest range from Hannah Arendt, who criticized the loss of autonomy suffered by the corps of people subject to technology, to John Kenneth Galbraith, who with a mixture of fascination and dread described the all-powerful techno-structure that, in reality, masks a lack of real power, to C. Wright Mills, who questioned the power of intellectual elites, to Herbert Marcuse, who protested the destruction of culture by technology, or to Noam Chomsky. In France, Jacques Ellul and Piotr Illich theorized about the autonomy of technological development, a power that apparently has no ties to political society. In Germany, Jürgen Habermas demonstrated the anti-democratic character of scientific reason.[16] In one way or another, for all of these thinkers, technocrats represent the danger, because they stand for the autonomization of technology, the severing of its link with politics. The influence of this anti-technological critique was at its strongest in the 1970s and early 1980s, initially through the cultural and intellectual elites, but progressively also felt in systems of education, politics, and finally also management.[17] Without going into any further depth, we wish to underline that opposition to managerialism was not limited to the neo-liberal critique, but has also found very well argued support in radical circles.

With multiple sources of inspiration to draw upon, criticism of the bureaucratic technocracy eventually has taken the shape of a systematic discourse. Aided and abetted by the ambient anti-technological suspicion, the neo-liberal approach has come to dominate ideologically much of the economic literature on the corporation and has imposed a systematic questioning of the managerial model on the study of corporate governance.[18] This questioning started in America, in the 1970s, because the United States was the first country to experience very rapid growth in the number and weight of shareholders, as described above. The alternative conception of governance proposed by the neo-liberals – based on agency theory – is based on a strong form of individual interest and puts a lot of emphasis on the power of shareholders to counter management. It might thus appear typically American, especially to the eyes of sceptical Europeans, but this is an error of perspective: the neo-liberal critique may have adopted culturally fitting clothes in the United States and later on in Europe, but it is a

---

[16] H. Arendt, *The Human Condition*, Chicago: University of Chicago Press, 1958; J. K. Galbraith, *The New Industrial State*, Boston: Houghton Mifflin, 1967; Noam Chomsky, *American Power and the New Mandarins*, New York: Pantheon, 1967; W. Mills, *The Power Elite*, New York: Oxford University Press, 1956; J. Ellul, *Le système technicien*, Paris: Calmann-Lévy, 1977; J. Ellul, *L'empire du non-sens*, Paris: Presses Universitaires de France, 1980; H. Marcuse, *The One-Dimensional Man*, Boston: Beacon Press, 1964; J. Habermas, *Technik und Wissenschaft als Ideologie*, Frankfurt: Suhrkamp, 1968.

[17] Michel Foucault would pick up some of these themes again and popularize them in his 1975 book on the history of punishment, *Surveiller et punir* (Paris: Gallimard), a work of scholarship that was to have considerable influence over the years, expressed in currents of thought critical to management. For a remarkable overview of the latter, see S. Clegg, C. Hardy, and W. Nord (eds.), *Handbook of Organization Studies*, Thousand Oaks, CA: Sage, 1996.

[18] See Part III.

general critique. Indeed, everywhere in the Western world, the classic Fordist manager has come to be seen as a conservative bureaucrat, the very opposite of the 'authentic' entrepreneurs who create new business and the antithesis of those who risk their own capital.[19]

Crisis of the unions and weakening of the external counterweight to managerial power

In parallel to the questioning of management's claim to entrepreneurial power, the 1970s saw the beginning of a general decline in the ability of the unions to act as an effective counterweight. In the case of the decline of the unions also, the historical story has been well documented, and we do not need to belabour the facts.[20] Thus, in the United Kingdom, the percentage of unionized workers decreased from 56% in 1978, to 39% in 1989, and 32% in 1995, from 13.7 million adherents to 6.5 million. In France, the evolution of the most powerful union, the CGT (Confédération Générale des Travailleurs) was characteristic of the general trend: from 4 million adherents in 1948, to 2.4 million in 1975 and fewer than 650,000 by 2000. With less than 5%, France is today the least unionized country in Europe. In the United States, the percentage of unionized workers has gone from close to 50% in the 1940s to 13.5% today. Thanks to *Mitbestimmung* (co-determination), unions have fared better in Germany, where large unions like IG Metall remain relatively powerful today, even if the confederation of German unions (DGB Deutscher Gewerkschaftsbund), the only interindustrial grouping, did lose 4 million members between 1975 and 1995. On the whole, it is clear that the last quarter of the twentieth century has brought about a rapid decline in the power of the unions and in their ability to represent a social balance to the interests of management. Again, the reasons for this evolution have been the subject of much

---

[19] This topic would become very fashionable in the 1980s, yielding an interesting literature of entrepreneurial legends built around such heroic figures as Steve Jobs in the United States, Bernard Tapie in France, or Richard Branson in the United Kingdom. The later Internet entrepreneurs have come in for a similar treatment.

[20] For this section, we refer primarily to the interpretations of M. Launay, *Le syndicalisme en Europe*, Paris: Imprimerie Nationale Editions, 1990, and W. Galenson, *The American Labor Movement, 1955–1995*, Westport, CT: Greenwood Press, 1996.

specialist discussion, and we therefore choose to highlight only those factors that also derive from the crisis of the techno-structure described in the preceding pages.

The first reason for the decline of the unions is to be found in the economic context: economic developments have led to major changes in the structure of the working population. In less than twenty years, the part of the GDP attributable to services has grown to double the size of the part of the GDP attributable to industry in all of the large Western countries: according to the OECD, in 1998 the service sector represented 70.1% of employment in France, 62.3% in Germany, 71% in the United Kingdom, and 73% in the United States. Unions grew to their full strength in the context of industrial economy: at its peak, in the 1950s, the unions' organizations, as well as their capacities of influence and mobilization, were closely tied to the Fordist mode of production. The collective struggle was rendered much more efficient by the fact that work was divided but still concentrated in one place – this is what made strikes so terribly effective in interrupting the production process in those days. A few actors were enough to block the line, and this made it easier to mobilize a large number of employees in a short time. The organization of production in the service sector does not follow the same rules, as it is considerably more spread out geographically and atomized, with independent teams providing much of the value added. Mobilizing such a dispersed and independent workforce requires new methods of collective action, and the unions have generally not been good at adapting to this new context, what with the transition from a manufacturing economy to a service economy occurring over a very short period. Nonetheless, it is remarkable that one had to wait until 1995 to see a member of the service federation (John Sweeny) head up the most powerful American union, the AFL-CIO, for the first time. In France, the industrial unions and the unions of the employees of the state continue to be the most influential into the twenty-first century, even though almost 70% of the working population is now employed in the private service sector. Whether American or French, the unions appear to be characterized by a kind of cultural inertia that has kept them tied to the industrial-age strike as the dominant form of public expression of opposition to economic decisions and prevented them from adapting flexibly to economic and social change.

These structural reasons for the unions' decline have been exacerbated by the effects of globalization. Unions historically grew out of national political, legal, and cultural contexts. Managerial governance also developed in contexts that were proper to national laws and regulations, and so the equilibrium of forces in which unions had their legitimate place as a counterweight to management for the social interest of employees was national in character. Globalization upset this equilibrium: the employees of any one particular corporation today are more and more spread out over the world and hence refer to different rules and laws, and also different cultures. It is not a simple matter for a national union to represent social interests globally, especially because the interests of employees in one country may run counter to the interests of employees in another. The union's expertise in social matters is called into question: if the union defends the advantages acquired by the national employees which constitute their original base, at a cost to foreign employees of the same corporation, it will be accused of parochialism and conservatism; if, on the other hand, the union accepts the differential evolution of salaries and benefits in the same corporation, even if these differences contradict advantages acquired elsewhere, it will be labelled as inconsistent. Defining just what constitutes a union's competence in a borderless world is a highly complex question, and there can be no doubt that this difficulty has reduced the credibility of unions as a counterweight to management.[21]

Finally, the ideological crisis of technocratic expertise that affected the Western world from the 1970s onwards also had an effect on the *technocracy* incarnated by the unions. As Roberto Michels had anticipated in his prescient essay of 1915[22] (an essay that was rediscovered in the 1980s), the unions, by virtue of their role as an institutional counterweight, had themselves become bureaucracies to which the 'law of oligarchy' which the German sociologist had developed to characterize political parties could be applied: they had developed their own specific expertise and their own elites, supported in all of the countries in this study by specific schools, publications, recruitment policies, promotion systems, professional languages, and internal management practices.

---

[21] We will not discuss the efforts undertaken by some unions to internationalize their actions (cooperation agreements between unions at the European level, for example). We would simply note that, in the new race for seizing power in the corporation, the unions have not been able to act as quickly or as flexibly as the large multinational corporations.

[22] R. Michels, *Political Parties: A Sociological Study of the Oligarchical Tendencies of Modern Democracy*, New York: The Free Press, 1962 [1915].

As a bureaucracy, the management of the unions was also vulnerable to the anti-technocratic critique, a critique that took place in all of the Western countries, including Germany. As a consequence of this crisis of confidence, the 1980s witnessed the emergence of new forms of social mobilization, forms that often competed with the established unions: so-called 'autonomous' unions, non-governmental organizations, anti-globalization and ecologist movements, to name just a few of the different forms of organization that now pretended to represent the social interests that had heretofore been the exclusive province of the unions. These new forms of 'organization' were all the more influential because their structures proved to be supple, typically not overly formalized, and their zones of action global, just like the modern economy. Thus, the decline of the unions cannot be understood as a historically isolated phenomenon: rather, this decline forms an integral part of the tendency of social fragmentation in a liberal context that we describe in this book and represents a corollary of questioning management's legitimate right to wield the entrepreneurial power of direction.

In sum, the decline of the unions goes hand in hand with the questioning of management. One cannot isolate one from the other, because it is not possible to separate the legitimate exercise of power in the managerial model from the presence of a credible counterweight – management and the unions together constituted an equilibrium of forces in the managerial model of corporate governance. The economic shocks of the 1970s brought with them a set of contextual and systemically inherent factors that combined in a self-reinforcing manner to weaken decisively the system of corporate governance in place. Managerial governance could not survive globalization unscathed, because the force of social fragmentation was at work to simultaneously undermine the legitimacy of managerial power and its union counterweight.

The great increase in the holdings and in the numbers of shareholders and their own fragmentation into multiple, intermediated groups, on the one hand, and management's failure to perform, loss of exclusive claim to knowledge, and oligarchic holding on to power, in the context of weakening unions who could no longer function as an effective counterweight, on the other hand, challenged managerial governance and management as entrepreneur to a battle that management would fight, but could ultimately only lose. In this new world of borderless competition, who had the legitimate right to exercise the entrepreneurial force of direction? If management could no longer lay undisputed claim to the right to direct economic growth in the service of the general interest, once again the heritage of the entrepreneur was up for grabs.

2 From managerial governance to public governance: two new poles of entrepreneurial power

It is more difficult to describe an emerging model of governance than to comment on past developments for which we can draw on significant amounts of data and considerable distance from the ups and downs of contemporary debate. Today, we find ourselves in the same situation as Berle and Means, Schumpeter, and Polanyi in the 1930s, observing the existing model of corporate governance under great stress and ready to break, and attempting to formulate hypotheses concerning the future. Not only does the genius of our illustrious predecessors force us to remain modest in our own analyses; the diversity and even the contradictions apparent in their conclusions also suggest that we must remain prudent. The difficulty we face lies in the fact that our descriptions have not been purified by enough time and experience to avoid the contamination of commonplaces that have come down to us from seventy years of managerial governance – commonplaces that are no longer valid. For example, many contemporary observers see a conflict between management power and shareholder counterpower as the defining characteristic of corporate governance, and suggest that this state of affairs constitutes a return to normal in the capitalist system. In our view, this is precisely the kind of projection from the past that masks the true significance of the political changes currently faced by the system.

Indeed, a closer analysis imposes a more nuanced view: for one thing, as we have shown in the historical description above, shareholders have never in history functioned as a real counterweight to the force of entrepreneurial direction: in the familial model, capital and management were unified, and thus shareholders participated in the exercise of power – rather, it was the family and its values that served as a counterweight to entrepreneurial power. In the managerial model, power was separated between ownership and control, but shareholders had little influence on the corporation and in no way provided a counterweight to management – this was the role played by the union.

If it does indeed exist, the exercise of shareholder power as a counterweight therefore needs to be thought of as a *new* phenomenon in corporate governance. This becomes very clear if we consider that the advent of mass shareholdings makes it impossible to consider the shareholder in the same way as defined in the nineteenth century or even in most of the twentieth century. The size of financial markets, their lack of borders (globalization), and the physical and emotional distance that separates a shareholder from the corporation all force us to reconsider what it means today to exercise property rights over a corporation. This is the task that we will attack first, distinguishing two distinct kinds of behaviour among shareholders: that of the investor and that of the shareowner. We will show that confusing these two prevents a correct analysis of contemporary corporate governance. With this point established, we will then proceed to develop our main hypothesis, namely that contemporary corporate governance in the publicly listed corporation is less about the opposition between management and shareholders than about the juxtaposition and interplay of investors and shareowners. Both investors and shareowners lay claim to the mantle of the entrepreneur and both fulfil this role in different ways, depending on the structure of the capital of the corporation and the institutions of governance chosen.

The general confusion between the functions of investors and shareowners

It is very important to understand the difference between investors and shareowners under mass shareholding: whereas the investor is focused on the value of a *portfolio of investments* and trades shares to optimize this portfolio, the shareowner's focus is on the *individual corporation*, as an owner. For the investor, a shareholding represents one means, among others, of generating wealth; for the shareowner, a shareholding represents the means whereby he/she can exercise influence over a particular corporation. The philosophy of the two actors and hence also their behaviours differ in clearly definable ways. Whereas the investor cares little about the fate of any individual corporation, the shareowner is tied to the individual corporation, either as a long-term owner (i.e. family, large pension fund), as an employee owner, or as a partner.

Both investors and shareowners share the legal status of *shareholders* in the corporation. However, they differ fundamentally in how they make use of their property rights. In Chapter 1, we pointed out that ownership of an asset gives rise to the rights of control (*usus*), benefit from profits (*fructus*), and sale or destruction (*abusus*). The investor who temporarily owns a fraction of a corporation's shares and compares the yield of this investment to the yields of all other shares to reach decisions about buying and selling essentially uses only the rights of *fructus* (the profit to be extracted from the corporation) and *abusus* (the ability to buy and sell shares in the corporation as a function of the share price). By contrast, the shareowner who intervenes to ensure the survival of the corporation also uses the right of *usus*, truly exercising a function of control over the corporation, and obtaining remuneration by the right of *fructus*. The shareowner uses the right of *abusus* (sale of shares) only in exceptional cases, either because the engagement has come to a contractual end or because the shareowner no longer has any value to add. Both investor and shareowner benefit from the *fructus* (profit), and this is what often leads to confusion; although the investor and the shareowner are both interested in the profit maximization of the corporation, it is not *for the same reasons* and hence not with the same perspectives: the former expects profit (real or anticipated) in order to maximize the share price and hence improve return on the overall portfolio, whereas the latter looks for profit in order to maximize the corporation's chances for survival and hence preserve the asset. Thus, the fragmentation of ownership that has accompanied the massive growth in the shareholding body since the 1970s implies not only a dispersion of capital, but also a partition of property rights, with different actors using their different rights completely or partially, resulting in two very different types of behaviour.

The two types of behavior necessarily exist side by side. Thus for a corporation owned by its founder or for the traditional family business, investor behaviour is negligible or non-existent. To pretend to be the owner of a corporation while considering only the rights of *fructus–abusus* (that is to say, obtaining profit in order to maximize the value of resale) is a position that runs counter to the very basics of familial governance and the legitimacy of the founder owner as we have described it in Chapter 3. Conversely, a global corporation with a highly diluted capital base can well be the property of numerous investors who do not see the corporation except as one financial placement among many others – destined to be valorized without consideration of the social objective of the corporation. In this case, the function of the investor is typically more important than that of the shareowner.

On the side of investors, we would put shareholders with mandates for portfolio management from individuals and institutions, as well as the multitude of different public investment and arbitrage funds. This capital can justifiably be termed floating or speculative. As share-owners one can consider strategic shareholders (and among those many of the shareholding families), some larger pension funds, certain activist funds, most of the private equity players who work as partners of the corporation with contractually determined length of engagement, employee shareholders and government shareholders. Shareowner capital can be characterized as relatively stable. As rough as this opposition might appear, it has the advantage of highlighting the necessity of identifying, among the vast mass of shareholdings, those who follow a more fickle investor logic and those who follow a more stable shareowner logic. The proportion of investors to shareowners varies, by country, by sector, and by corporation, and it is critical to specify the impact of the two types of behaviour at these different levels to understand the evolution of corporate governance in any one particular case.

The financial industry has itself integrated this opposition into its structure. Thus, the investment and share-owning functions are carried out by different actors, or, if under one roof, managed separately, with different groups responsible for the overall portfolio on the one hand, and the engagement holdings on the other. This is especially clearly seen in the activities of pension funds such as CalPERS (US) and Hermes Pensions Management (UK), for example, which actively engage with corporations as shareowners in our sense. The two tasks of managing a large, diversified portfolio and actively engaging in the governance and direction of a few specific corporations are functionally not compatible. Professions associated with investment advice (portfolio managers, fund managers, etc.) and professions associated with providing advice on corporate governance (consultants, share-owners' rights associations, governance rating companies, etc.) have followed distinct paths of evolution and today represent two very different tracks with their overlapping but not identical methods of analysis. It is not an exaggeration to say that investors *do not want to be shareowners*: they would be happy to limit their activity to speculation on the price of shares based only on the right of *abusus*, without having to be burdened with the shareowner responsibilities that go along with holding the right of *usus*. Symptomatically, legislation has

been necessary to *oblige* investors to participate in corporate governance, for example to take part in annual general meetings, or at least to
transmit voting rights to the ultimate holders of shares and to make
their own voting record public (in the United States, private pension
funds have had to make their voting policies public since the passage of
ERISA in 1974; mutual funds have been obliged to do so only since
2003; in France, since 2003, the law requires mutual funds to state
publicly the reason for *not* participating in general assembly votes).
This goes to show how unnatural and wasteful the exercise of even
elementary shareowner rights has appeared to shareholders as investors.

Whereas the separation of ownership and control was at the heart of
managerial governance, the distinction between investment and share-
owning constitutes the basis of public governance. We propose to
analyse this new model by describing in greater detail how these *two
types of shareholders* differ, noting that, driven by different logics,
investors and shareowners can have divergent interests. With management increasingly discredited as the legitimate entrepreneur, we need to
understand how investors or shareowners exercise the entrepreneurial
force of direction and orient the activity of the corporation.

It has been our argument throughout this book that the function of
the entrepreneur is critical to liberal society: entrepreneurial action
makes sense out of the multitude of private interests and provides
direction for an increasingly fragmented and atomized society. In
fact, the larger question posed by business to society goes beyond the
mere understanding of a new model of corporate governance: the new
political and social equilibria of the twenty-first century have yet to be
established and the place in these equilibria of the large, global corporation is still to be exactly specified. In order to advance in this
analysis and be able to draw some concrete conclusions, we will now
discuss each of two cases outlined above in greater detail: entrepreneurial direction by investors and entrepreneurial direction by
shareowners.

Pole I: The invisible hand of the investor

Political roots

There is a strong argument to be made that investors in the financial
markets have taken the mantle of the entrepreneur away from management, at least in the case of large, publicly quoted companies with a

widely dispersed shareholding structure. Investors are rational, well-informed actors who understand the opportunities of business well and place the savings that have been entrusted to their care in the shares that promise the best performance. In searching for optimal placements and allocating money accordingly, they help orient the financing of the economy towards the best opportunities, the most promising innovations, and the most effective strategic choices, and in this way play a major role in driving the economic growth of society. This line of reasoning builds on a liberal anthropology of human behaviour refined by microeconomic theory to become the basis of the argument for socially and politically legitimizing the role of investors in the economy.

The publication of the main analyses of the neo-liberal approach outlined above in the leading journals of financial scholarship (Part III discusses these in more detail with extensive citations) ought not to mask the fact that this work is about much more than financial technique: the ambition is to define the political role of investors as actors in corporate governance and as a collective force in the orientation of economic activity. The effort to legitimize the function of investors by the role they play in the working of the financial markets is an integral part of the logic of modern liberal philosophy: because the choices of investors are explicitly based upon their private interests and the maximization of the value of their personal portfolios, they can be seen as the true economic rationalists, far more so than technocratic managers. Investors escape the crisis of technocratic rationality that we described earlier as one of the major dimensions of the critique made of management as entrepreneur. It is precisely because investors *do not have a joint plan* concerning economic activity and do not lay claim to *the planning knowledge of the technocrat* that their individual choices, guided only by anarchical self-interest, paradoxically appear efficient and acceptable. The optimization of the portfolios that they manage serves the needs of savers – in this way their personal interests rejoin the general interest. It can therefore be argued that investors ensure economic progress for all of society, de facto assuming what is defined as the function of the entrepreneur in liberal society.

In fact, the proponents of the investors as entrepreneur argument do not claim that the individual investor is an entrepreneur, but rather that the *market as a collective body* fulfils the function of the entrepreneur. The reasoning is as follows. In liquid financial markets, investors can buy and sell shares easily. Their defection (sale) or the threat of their defection represents an important signal for the corporation and strongly influences its choice of strategy. In effect, the stock market acts as a kind of thermometer of agreement between management and investors and allows the latter to put pressure on the former (see also Part III). The stock price provides the mechanism whereby individual interests are transformed into a general direction and the investor entrepreneur's influence makes itself felt, in what amounts to a continuous referendum on corporate strategy. In the tradition of Adam Smith, thousands, indeed millions, of individual investors in the financial markets constitute an 'invisible hand' that indicates and finally imposes the best choice of strategy on the corporation.

Economic rationality

Far from being a place of personal enrichment to the detriment of the real economy, as some would have it, the financial markets are seen as indispensable to the governance of the global corporation. Thus, significant strategic choices, such as acquisitions or divestitures, diversification and internationalization, offshoring and outsourcing – indeed nearly all the major investments made by large, publicly quoted corporations today – are driven or at least strongly affected by investor appetite and reaction. When chief executives consult with financial market operators in road shows and conference calls, when they refer to what investors will and will not allow in their statements, and when they justify concrete choices (i.e. layoffs) with financial market pressure, they acknowledge that the set of strategic choices is *constrained*, even to a large degree *determined*, by the demands of investors in the financial markets. Supporting this argument, numerous studies have shown empirically that an acquisition or the mere threat of an acquisition – actions made much easier by the existence of liquidity in the financial markets that permits continuous evaluation of corporate performance – exercises a disciplinary effect on executives.[23] Indeed, since the 1980s, the discourse of top management has become more

---

[23] This literature has been critical to establishing the importance and efficiency of financial markets in the modern economies. For the theoretical background, see M. Jensen, 'Takeovers: their causes and consequences', *Journal of Economic Perspectives* 2 (1) (1988), 21–48. For studies by country, one can cite for the United States J. Martin and J. J. McConnell, 'Corporate performance, corporate take-overs and management turnover', *Journal of Finance* 46 (1991), 671; for the United Kingdom J. Franks and C. Mayer, 'Hostile take-overs in the UK and

and more simplified, based on the economic fatalism of the 'invisible hand' of the investor: 'changes are inevitable'; 'the markets impose constraints'; 'globalization is inescapable'. Whatever the objective pertinence of these statements, and some of these statements are made to preserve the power of top management, such a fatalistic discourse represents strong evidence that management has given the function of entrepreneurship into other hands. The entrepreneur chooses the constraints of the business and tries to bend them to suit his/her interests. By giving the impression that there is no other way than to submit to the will of the shareholders, management has in effect transferred its heritage of entrepreneurship to investors. The management of the large publicly quoted corporation relinquishes entrepreneurial power and becomes an *executor* of choices determined by the financial markets. As an executor, the management is reduced to proposing strategies and action plans and waiting for the markets to confirm or reject the proposition by increasing or decreasing the share price.

The economic logic that supports the investor as entrepreneur is built on three principal pillars. First, the globalization of financial markets permits efficient comparisons between countries, sectors, and corporations. Globalization considerably opens up the horizon of comparison between strategic choices and results obtained; thus, the invisible hand of investors is especially well suited to orienting financial resource allocation towards the best opportunities on the planet. Second, the shareholding body's growth in size to unprecedented mass makes the exercise of the classic participative function of the shareholder illusory – for shareholders who are too many in number, isolated from each other, and far from the corporation, participation is simply too expensive. The marginal cost of participating actively is simply disproportionate to the expected benefit. By entrusting their savings to professional investors, households can maximize their utility. The creation of 'shareholder value' legitimizes the entrepreneurial action of investors, because it is ultimately in the interest of shareholders that investors orient their choices. Third, the financial markets, finally but one service sector among many, have their own proper economic logic for creating value. They generate products of ever increasing

the correction of managerial failure', *Journal of Financial Economics* 40 (1996), 163. Because the national market for quoted stocks is less developed in France and Germany, comparative studies in these countries could not show equally strong effects.

complexity that permit the precise identification of the sources of economic performance. Thus, the financial markets develop according to an autonomous pattern of growth, the objective of which is to maximize the economic value created by global corporations. In this way, the financial sector's own growth is supposed to provide reinforcement to economic development in the world.

Pole II: *The shareowner holds the corporation accountable*

Political roots
In parallel to the emergence of the investor as a full-fledged actor on the stage of corporate governance, what we have called the shareowner – the long-term owner interested in the fate of a particular corporation – also becomes increasingly important. Typically, but not exclusively, in the guise of the pension fund or the family holding, the shareowner generally takes the position that the increased mass of capital also implies an increased need for responsible ownership, namely effective participation in the strategic orientation of corporations and the full exercise of shareholder rights. Under this argument, the shareowner who participates actively in the control of the corporation, and does not rely only on the indirect mechanism of the financial markets to effect change, inherits the mantle of the entrepreneur.

In a book that, ironically, did not receive much attention at the time of its publication, *The Unseen Revolution*, Peter Drucker had already shown in 1976 that the concentration of ownership of the large American corporations in the hands of pension funds was inescapable and would lead to major modifications in corporate governance.[24] The generalized aging of the Western population would orient household savings towards equity capital and bring pension funds into increasingly influential positions with long-term entrepreneurial effects, both on risk-taking and innovation. Although rarely referred to as originally intended,[25] the thesis of Drucker is indicative of a very profound development. Some shareholders cannot be content to manage their

---

[24] P. Drucker, *The Unseen Revolution*, New York: Harper and Row, 1976.

[25] 'None of my books was as on target ... and none of my books was as totally ignored', Drucker writes in the introduction to the 1992 edition. Without a doubt, this work of Drucker suffered from a polemical interpretation of the evolution he so fittingly described. At the beginning of the neo-liberal wave, Drucker's hypothesis of a transformation of the economy towards shareholder

portfolios in a passive manner, without anticipating the evolution of the economy, not only to ensure the value of their investments, but also to make sure that their investments are coherent with their own institutional purpose or *raison d'être*. This is the argument that has given birth to socially responsible investment: savings should not be placed without making sure that the investing institution can trace and verify the use of its funds.

For shareholders who choose to exercise the ownership function in this manner (as a shareowner), managers are no longer entirely credible as entrepreneurs, for the very reasons we have described above. In other words, the activity of the shareowner does not represent a return to managerial governance. Neither does the shareowner accept the financial markets as the only arbiter of entrepreneurship. The 'invisible hand' can err and lead the corporation down a path towards destruction, for example by rewarding risky behaviour, until the corporation fails under the weight of all the risks taken. Of course, according to the principles of financial economics, in the *long term and in general*, the markets are always right. However, the problem of corporate governance from the point of view of the shareowner lies in the particular case: the markets may well correct short-term errors and overshoots *in general*, as they did after the collapse of the Internet bubble, but this cannot satisfy the shareholders of every corporation, taken as a *particular case*. A general correction mechanism cannot guarantee the continued existence of a particular corporation and an error of appreciation can prove fatal, or at least very costly, for that corporation's stakeholders. Whether they are employees, bankers, clients, or shareowners without any special relationship to the corporation, their reason for taking action in any particular case lies in the value they derive from the long-term existence of the focal corporation: the defence of jobs, the securing of credit, the consolidation of good business relationships, the maintenance of adequate diversity in the portfolio (for pension funds), the prevention of ecological risk, etc. For these shareowners, the excesses of the 'invisible hand' are not without danger. Because the ownership of capital has become so massive, and because as a result the financial markets can impose choices on the

socialism was too contrary to be appreciated fully. With hindsight, it certainly merits re-evaluation and also amendment. The 1992 reprint adopted a new title, less polemical and more in line with the data presented, *The Pension Fund Revolution* (New York and London: Transaction Publishers).

corporation that might run counter to the interests of the corporation's stakeholders, some shareholders choose to exercise an entrepreneurial function as *shareowners*.

Holding the management accountable and ensuring the continued existence of the corporation means making sure that the management performs as promised and expected and keeping a wary eye on the information used by the financial markets in evaluating the corporation. The function of the shareowner is not the same as that of the investor. The engagement of shareowners in the affairs of their corporation, their *presence* (as opposed to the absence decried by Berle and Means) is not a mere pleasant decoration, or an unnecessary constraint on the 'free markets': clearly, shareowners can have an important entrepreneurial role to play, stronger or weaker depending on the context. In a certain sense, shareowners of the type described here represent a return to one of the foundational principles of the legitimacy of property in liberal thought: work and the resulting responsibility for the property owned. In the name of defending their long-term assets, shareowners seek to ensure that the choices made by the corporation guarantee its long-term existence. This has the beneficial side effect of serving the general interest of the stakeholders. Much as in the case of investors, but by totally different means, the particular interest (that of shareowners) joins the general interest (that of society).

Shareowners as entrepreneurs
The emergence of shareowners as entrepreneurs does not imply that all individual shareholders have to play this role. By the fact of the dispersion and the fragmentation of ownership capital, it is enough if a minority of active shareholders fully exercise the shareowner function for opinion to be oriented and market expectation to be affected. Joined in associations, supported by pension funds or pressure groups, their expressions of voice inform market operators and are amplified by the mechanics of the free market. In this way pension funds such as CalPERS or Hermes Pensions Management whose positions are large in an absolute sense but merely marginal in comparison to the market, but also individual investors and pressure groups, can become leaders of public opinion. The argument of the relative cost of activism is thus, at least in some cases, turned on its head in favour of active shareowners: with the global market being very fragmented, investors have

an interest in following the opinions of activist shareowners, even if these are few in number relative to the mass of the market, because they are better informed about the particular corporation in which they become engaged. In the situation described here, shareowners and investors interact, with shareowners exercising the true function of the entrepreneur, while investors amplify their views. As Downs has shown in his classical book, a (political) situation such as this, in which active minorities can effectively direct public action by the intermediaries of opinion mobilization and media use, is characteristic of the democratization of a process.[26]

Observing the evolution of activism in the United States, Roberta Romano, in a very detailed synthesis, notes that

before 1986 only a small set of individual investors engaged in such activism: from 1979 to 1983, religious groups and between six or seven individuals, depending on the year, submitted more than half of all proposals, which ranged in the hundreds every year. From 1986 until early 1990's, five institutions (four public pension funds and TIAA CREF, a pension fund primarily for university teachers and administrators) accounted for almost 20 per cent of all proposals. Since 1994, unions have overtaken public pension funds as the most active corporate governance proposal sponsors.[27]

Here again, theory supports observation and allows us to understand the developments. Two principal arguments support the emergence of the active shareowner: the first is based on the objective limitations of the financial markets, the second on the nature of property ownership in liberal society. The number of possible financial operations and the choice of arbitrage dealings among shares are not infinitely large: a secondary effect of the growth to great mass of the shareholding body is that the supply of finance by millions of savers considerably exceeds the demand of some few tens of thousands of publicly quoted corporations in the world. Indeed, the number of international corporations that are leaders in their industries account for the vast bulk of market capitalization, and hence represent inevitable investments for portfolio

---

[26] A. Downs, *An Economic Theory of Democracy*, New York: Harper and Row, 1957.

[27] R. Romano, 'Less is more: making institutional investor activism a valuable mechanism of corporate governance', in J. A. McCahery *et al.* (eds.), *Corporate Governance Regimes: Convergence and Diversity*, Oxford: Oxford University Press, 2002, pp. 507–66. Romano cites numerous references in support of her argument that we omit here.

managers is less than two thousand (Morgan Stanley Capital International index of 1800 corporations). As John Pound showed so convincingly in the 1980s, the financial markets do not enable the systematic resale of shares: either because they have to hold the shares of certain corporations (large blue chips) to match market index performance, or because their holdings are so large that they cannot sell without having a negative effect on the share price, some shareholders are in fact 'stuck with' the shares of these corporations and cannot make use of their right of *abusus* without great caution.[28] Therefore, these shareholders have a clear interest in exercising the shareowner function, that is to intervene in the control of the corporation to ensure the long-term value of their capital. Acting as a shareowner is not necessarily a matter of choice: for some shareholders it is an economic necessity. This conclusion applies to many large pension funds, to family holdings, and to employee ownership. Where markets are not liquid, such as in private equity, the economic need to act as a shareowner is even more pronounced.

The second argument in favour of active shareownership arises out of the liberal theory of property rights. In the first part of the book, we saw that owning shares in a corporation is legitimized by the fact that the shareholder only has a residual claim on corporate profits. Since the shareholder is only remunerated if the corporation makes a profit, the shareholder has a private interest in controlling the corporation and in this way also serves the public interest. Without the risk that ties private interest to public interest, the private ownership of the means of production would be oppressive to individual liberty and hence not acceptable in the liberal system. The theory of residual claims is indispensable for legitimizing the shareholder to have a hand in the direction of the corporation. Now, the shareholder is only constrained by the notion of residual claims if his/her wealth is implicated in a

---

[28] For further discussion of these important questions, see, among others, J. Pound, 'Proxy contests and the efficiency of shareholder oversight', *Journal of Financial Economics* 20 (1988), 237–65; D. Del Guercio and J. Hawkins, 'The motivation and impact of pension fund activism', *Journal of Financial Economics* 52 (1999), 293–340; S. Gillan and L. Starks, 'Corporate governance proposals and shareholder activism: the role of institutional investors', *Journal of Financial Economics* 75 (2000), 275–305; M. Smith, 'Shareholder activism by institutional investors: evidence from CalPER's', *Journal of Finance* 51 (1996), 227–52.

corporation over the long term, so that he/she might suffer negative consequences from failing to exercise his/her obligations as an owner. Without any long-term implication, the shareholder can exit without the risk of suffering losses; even worse, if the shareholder only makes very short-term entries into the capital of corporations, he/she may never be subject to the disciplinary logic of residual claims. In the liberal system, therefore, there is a profound reason for associating property rights with the right to orient the activity of the corporation. The shareholder's obligation of control makes sure that private and public interests *converge*. This argument is often advanced in defence of capitalism and liberal society when experts speculate on how the uncontrolled development of the financial markets (investors), disconnected from the real economy (corporations), might hurt the system.[29] Thus, only the shareowner who fully exercises his/her social function of controlling the corporation and suffers the consequences for failing to do so can pretend to the mantle of entrepreneurial direction in coherence with the principles of liberalism. Put another way and contrary to received wisdom, the orthodox principles of liberalism are not satisfied by an entrepreneurial function that is left to the financial markets alone.

Investors and shareowners: perspectives for analysing corporate governance in a post-managerial world

The disparate descriptions we have sketched here show that the advent of mass shareholding has given rise to two very different types of new actors in corporate governance. A quick read of the current situation could give rise to the erroneous conclusion that the entrepreneurial force is simply exercised by both investors and shareowners, because, legally speaking, both types of actors are shareholders. We have emphasized that this confusion of roles is misleading and prevents an accurate assessment of reality. Investors and shareowners both exercise socially necessary functions, but these contrast markedly and imply different behaviours towards the corporation and its governance. The

[29] See Monks, *The New Global Investors*. In France, Claude Bébéar, Chairman of Axa, the world leader in life insurance, and one of the most influential *parrains* of French capitalism, published a book against investors' dictatorship significantly entitled *They Are Going To Kill Capitalism* (C. Bébéar and P. Manière, *Ils vont tuer le capitalisme*, Paris: Plon, 2003).

investor seeks to be as far removed as possible from the governance of the corporation, so that he/she can continue to look for the best opportunities for the investment portfolio without constraints of responsibility towards the stakeholders of any corporation. The share-owner, on the other hand, seeks, by as efficient a means as possible, to control a particular corporation in order to obtain a return on the capital placed in the corporation's shares, while minimizing the risk of corporate failure.

The way the two actors exercise the entrepreneurial function also differs fundamentally. The investor considers the entire space of business opportunities that are presented to him/her and makes his/her choices independent of the particular interests of the stakeholders of any one corporation. Indeed, the investor can be likened to an anonymous agent of *global natural selection*, contributing to the wealth of the entirety of society, but indifferent to the local consequences of the choices made. The shareowner, by contrast, stands for the long-term health of his/her assets and hence for the particular corporation in which he/she has become engaged. The shareowner is like an agent of *local selective adaptation*, who by generalization over many examples of this type also provides for the economic growth of society. Both of these actors, the investor and the shareowner, contribute to the implementation of the liberal political project, but by radically different means.

Together these two categories of actors make up the mass shareholdings that are characteristic of contemporary capitalism and both play an important role in its economic regulation. Shareholders can play different roles, shareowner or investor depending upon the circumstances, their interests, and their skills. They may also play both roles simultaneously in the management of their portfolio, managing holdings in different companies in one or the other manner. Thus, the two types of actor need not conflict. Quite the contrary, in fact: each one is necessary for the other. Reference to shareowners is indispensable to investors, because shareowners carry the legitimacy of ownership (the sovereign as defined in Chapter 1). Investors cannot ignore the fact that society's acceptance of their influence on the corporation is closely tied to the theory of residual claims and hence to the supposed engagement of the shareholder in the control of the corporation, which, even if this engagement is very volatile and reduced to the fiction of formal sovereignty, is still a doctrinal pillar of liberal society. In this sense, the existence of the shareowner provides the ideological reassurance for the investor. The shareowner, on the other hand, is limited in his/her influence over the corporation by the fragmentation of property ownership and the difficulty of mobilizing a great mass of shareholders. Therefore, the shareowner has to depend on the financial markets as an amplifying circuit for his/her views. The financial markets can give the choices of the shareowner a weight which is decoupled from the actual percentage of shares held. By the mechanism of the financial markets, the investor becomes the spokesperson that the shareowner needs to get his/her views across. There are, then, objective complementarities between the function of the investor and the function of the shareowner, a link that perhaps goes some way to explain the confusion that is sometimes made between the two. However, depending on the context, there is typically, if not always, a hierarchy between the two categories of actors. In the case where shareholdings are highly dispersed and diluted and markets are very liquid, the investor's choices and behaviours have a stronger impact on the corporation and the shareowner is reduced to passivity. In the opposite case, the shareowner plays the critical role, and the financial markets are often little more than a machine for amplifying the shareowner's voice.

Between the two extremes of completely diluted and highly concentrated capital, investors and shareowners interact in multiple ways, according to the balance of power between them and the concrete situation of the corporations concerned. In other words, there is more openness and a greater possibility for contextual evolution than an exclusive consideration of the extremes would suggest. Still, although the two are essential to each other and to the functioning of the system and do interact, it should not be forgotten that investors and shareowners represent very different approaches to regulating capitalism, with their own unique effects on corporate governance.

Both investor and shareowner approaches raise the same question with regard to property rights. The separation of ownership and control, initiated under managerial governance, is further accentuated, to the point that one might ask if investor and shareowner approaches represent a return to a pre-liberal form of governance. As we showed in Chapter 3, in traditional societies property rights were partitioned so that no one individual could own *usus*, *fructus* and *abusus* and, as a result, there was a necessary complementarity between the individuals holding the different rights. In appearance at least, the new role accorded to the shareholder looks similar and certain critics of the financial markets also allude to this point: the power of the shareholder contradicts the liberal political project, because he/she only holds the right of *abusus* but not the right of *usus*; in other words, the shareholder owns, but does not work. As discussed earlier, the right of *usus* is critical in the liberal legitimation of property ownership. The objection to the shareholder's role is valid, if he/she does not seek to intervene in any way in the affairs of the corporation and only considers the stock as a source of rent. In this case, the shareholder resembles the very leisured aristocrat against which liberal ideology revolted. The objection is not valid, if, by one mechanism or another (markets or active engagement), the shareholder does seek to influence the corporation. In this case, the shareholder does exercise at least a part of the right of *usus*. It is clear that the effective exercise of the entrepreneurial function by the share-holder also has a major political implication: it serves to reconcile fragmented property ownership with the liberal political project. The greater the will to exercise the right of *usus* and intervene, the more legitimate is fragmented property ownership by shareholders.

Consideration of property rights and the exercise of the entrepreneurial function by shareholders could also lead to the interpretation that post-managerial governance represents a kind of return to familial governance, in which the entrepreneur was *also* the owner. The difference lies in the *genetic* link that constituted the basis of the familial model, a link that united power (founder father) and its counterweight (family) under familial governance, but is broken under post-managerial governance. Few shareholders today have a genetic link with the corporation in which they hold shares. The exercise of the entrepreneurial function can therefore not be personal and inherited, but must be collective and marketable. A large number of private owners are tied together not by what they have in *common* (as members of a family would be), but by being associated to a *collective* (as participants in a market).

In taking a broader view of these developments, and leaving aside the distinction between investors and shareowners for the moment, it is striking to note how the evolution of the corporation over time tends to involve more and more people in its governance. Today, the entrepre-neurial force is exercised, in one way or another, by thousands, if not millions, of individuals, investors and shareowners. This powerful force is based on the fragmentation of property rights. Our task is to understand according to what institutional mechanisms this force can play out effectively and by what counterweight it is constrained under post-managerial governance. The end of managerial governance implies the modification of the concrete institutions that regulated it (assemblies, boards) and reshuffles the deck. In the two cases described – investor as entrepreneur and shareowner as entrepreneur – who functions as the counterweight and what is the role of management? In the following chapter, we will show that the technique of democracy enables a new model of governance, a model which, by allowing for representation and public debate, exposes the different interests of shareholders and effectively puts them on stage for general consideration. It is in this sense of the word that we refer to the emerging model of corporate governance as *public* governance.

6 | *Interpreting public governance: representation and debate signify a new step towards democratization*

How do contemporary developments in corporate governance fit in with the broader deployment of the ideological and political project of liberalism, such as we have been analysing in this book? More particularly, what new answers arise to the question of 'who has the right to direct the corporation'? It is not enough, from our point of view, merely to describe the growth in the shareholding body and the increasing role of finance in the economy, as set forth in the previous chapter and documented in a large number of studies. We need to interpret the significance of these developments in terms of the general evolution of modern society, in order to understand the emerging model of corporate governance.

The two settings we described in the preceding chapter imply that in the post-managerial model of corporate governance the entrepreneurial force of direction can be held by two different economic actors, investors or shareowners. One might therefore conclude that *two* different models are emerging, one applying to the publicly quoted corporation with widely dispersed capital that is oriented towards the financial markets (the investor as entrepreneur), and one applying to the publicly quoted corporation with closely held, concentrated capital that is oriented towards the activist shareowner (the shareowner as entrepreneur). If true, such a conclusion would be very problematic, both in terms of verisimilitude and in terms of coherence. In terms of verisimilitude, it is clearly not possible to state unequivocally that the two settings are mutually exclusive: on the contrary, as already discussed, the functions of the investor and the shareowner are complementary. Thus, the interesting question is not to ask which actor will dominate corporate governance in different contexts, but rather to discover how the roles of investor and shareowner interact: if the corporation is oriented towards the investor as entrepreneur, what role do shareowners still play in corporate governance? If, on the contrary, the corporation is oriented towards the shareowner as entrepreneur, what function do investors and hence financial markets fulfil?

173

In the contemporary economic context, post-managerial corporate governance invariably implies the presence of both types of actors and can take on *different forms*, depending on whether the investor or the shareowner plays the leading role. By taking both investors and shareowners into account in our description of corporate governance, we are better able to capture the nuances of practice and understand how a corporation may pass from one form to another and indeed back again over the course of its life.

In terms of coherence, it would be difficult to understand why our period of history, of all periods, should be characterized by *two different models of reference* for corporate governance. By definition a *model of reference* reflects the norms of governance that are acceptable in its political and economic context. Hence, the contemporaneous existence of *two* models of reference would represent a contradiction in terms. This methodological point is important, because it suggests that we need to go beyond appearances and look for a *common model of reference*, over and above the differences between the investor and shareowner *forms*. As the succeeding analysis will show, both investor and shareowner forms share a common base, and this base is what we will call 'public governance', to differentiate it from its predecessors, familial governance and managerial governance.

The objective of this chapter is twofold. First, we will attempt to describe the institutional developments that support the growth of the two forms: the ascendancy of investors, on the one hand, and the rise to power of shareowners, on the other. Of course, the two forms are too closely tied together for changes that favour one not also to have favourable consequences for the other, but we must identify the institutional changes that have contributed to building up the *entrepreneurial power* of investors on the one hand and of shareowners on the other. By going back to the 1980s, the time when post-managerial forms of corporate governance began to take shape, and reviewing the major developments that have taken place since then, we will be able to identify which changes in law and in practice contribute to establishing the investor and the shareowner forms, respectively (1).

With the bases of the two forms described and their differences clarified, we can then identify the commonalities between them that define a single *model of reference* for contemporary corporate governance (2). We will show that, in both forms, the importance attributed to information is fundamental and represents a new advance of democratic technique in the regulation of corporate governance. The communication of information induces the actors concerned with corporate governance to manifest and represent their diverging interests. From the moment the corporation includes its shareholders in the power structure, it has to take the diversity of their expectations into account. Whether the diversity of shareholder expectations makes itself felt in the financial markets or in the institutions of governance of the corporation, the expression of this diversity and the consideration given to it in decision-making are characteristic of a post-managerial approach to corporate governance. Building on this argument, we will go on to show that public opinion has become the new *counterweight* to the entrepreneurial force of direction, whatever the form whereby entrepreneurial power is exercised. In describing the locus of the entrepreneurial force, the institutions and procedures supporting its exercise, and the external counterweight, we will have covered all of the elements of public governance, the new model of reference for corporate governance. In conclusion, we will be able to evaluate the extent to which public governance represents a coherent next step in the historical evolution of the liberal political project.

1 Two forms of governance: intrinsic and extrinsic

In a first step, we propose to define the institutional characteristics of the forms of governance that result from the exercise of the entrepreneurial function by the shareholders, acting either as investors or as shareowners. In order to do that, we document the changes in the environment that support the investor as entrepreneur and those that support the shareowner as entrepreneur. In this way, we can show that the institutions of corporate governance can be shaped to direct the information provided by the corporation towards the exterior, so that it can be evaluated by the markets – here we will speak of an *extrinsic* form of governance aimed at investors; alternatively, the institutions of corporate governance can be shaped to direct the information provided by the corporation towards the interior, so that it can be used to make decisions that orient action – here we will speak of an *intrinsic* form of governance aimed at shareowners.[1]

---

[1] We borrow the terms 'extrinsic' and 'intrinsic' from Bruno Frey's subtle analysis of executive motivation, using them in a slightly different sense, institutional rather than behavioural. See B. Frey and M. Osterloh, *Successful Management by*

Evolution of the institutions supporting the investor
as entrepreneur

Putting the entrepreneurial function in the hands of investors implies a system of corporate governance that is based on two kinds of separation: first, the 'entrepreneurs' are outside of the corporation; second, and more subtly, their rational choices are defined not simply in terms of the corporation, but more broadly relative to a universe of investments in which the performances of all corporations (and all asset classes) are compared. The behaviour of investors is guided by the objective of maximizing the value of their portfolios; this leads them to evaluate the strategy and the performance of each individual corporation in relation to the other corporations in the portfolio, on the one hand, and to the opportunity costs of not investing in another, higher performing corporation outside of the portfolio, on the other. For investors to be able to exercise the function of the entrepreneur and guide capital choices towards corporations with higher performance, it is essential that they have the means to compare the performances of the corporations in their portfolios and in the universe of interest to them, in other words to have a sufficient amount and a standardized quality of information on each one of them. Three fundamental developments in the recent history of corporate governance support the investor in exercising the role of the entrepreneur: first, the increase in the number of investors and, consequently, the dilution of corporate capital structure that cuts the direct tie between shareholders and the corporation and gives investors a new kind of power to be used in the financial markets; second, the requirements for transparency and standardization of information in financial communication: and finally, the altered hierarchy of expertise that characterizes the relationship between investors and management: the rise of new management approaches based on 'shareholder value' has the effect of orienting the executive towards controlling the production of the corporation according to *external* criteria of evaluation established by the financial markets.

Motivation: Balancing Intrinsic and Extrinsic Incentives, New York: Springer, 2002. See also B. S. Frey and F. Oberholzer-Gee, 'The cost of price incentives: an empirical analysis of motivation crowding-out', *American Economic Review* 87 (September, 1997), 746–55.

Increase in the number of investors and improvement in their protection

In the preceding chapter, we showed that the post-managerial period is characterized by a great increase in the number of shareholders and by an increasing intermediation of the shareholding function, with the appearance of innumerable funds: pension funds, mutual funds, hedge funds, etc. Since the capital of the largest global corporations has also become widely dispersed over the same time period, ownership itself is now increasingly fragmented. Even in continental Europe, the traditional home of government-controlled (France) or bank-controlled (Germany) corporations with concentrated shareholdings, the situation has changed dramatically since the 1990s: in France, most if not all state-controlled corporations have substantially opened up their capital to the general public; in Germany, banks and insurance companies have been unwinding their large holdings, putting ever larger numbers of shares in the hands of the public.

In order for the invisible hand of the financial markets to work efficiently, the number of market participants needs to be large. Translating the political foundations of liberal society into its own language, microeconomic theory has stipulated the atomicity of markets as one of the canonical conditions of their efficiency. The multiplicity of individual interests that either reinforce each other or cancel each other out results *spontaneously* in a state of equilibrium, as symbolized by the market price. In every other situation, for example in an oligopoly or in a monopoly, the calculations of individuals do not necessarily come together to serve the general interest.

The extent to which the fundamental principles of this liberal political view have been implicitly or explicitly at work in the recent evolution of corporate governance is remarkable. The increase in the number of financial products has been a direct corollary of the shareholding body's growth to substantial mass, and the number of intermediary actors in the markets – mutual funds, pension funds, etc. – alongside the increased number of individuals makes today's financial markets look very much like the atomized battleground described in liberal philosophy, recalling the fragmented society Hobbes described at the outset of the seventeenth century. The development of the markets as a locus for the confrontation of different expectations and interests is further accentuated by changes in capital structure.

With the number of professional intermediaries vying for the savings of households greatly increased and the capital of many corporations much more open than before, management cannot exercise pressure on shareholders in the same way as it used to. In agreement with the pure liberal logic, the fragmentation of ownership implies that only the stock price accurately translates the interplay of individual shareholder interests into the general interest, and provides valid information on the future of the corporation. With investors so atomized, individual owners are not large enough to have any power of influence over others, and the entrepreneurial function devolves to the 'invisible hand of the financial markets', the choices of which are instantly visible in the movement of the stock price. In the liberal logic of individual autonomy, the power of the markets to represent the whole and overcome individual interests arises from the fragmentation of its actors. Following this line of reasoning, the level of fragmentation of a market can be seen as an indicator of the amount of pressure its actors are collectively able to exert on the corporation.

To the extent that shareholding bodies are fragmented and shareholders are of small size, the protection of individual interests requires some form of legal specification. The contemporary focus of policy on laws and regulations to protect the interest of minorities has to be understood in the light of the increasing fragmentation, indeed the atomization, of ownership. The law intervenes to protect minority shareholders, that is to say those who have only a marginal relationship with the corporation, in terms of both the amount of capital invested and the relative importance in the portfolio. Symptomatically, institutional reforms have focused on minority shareholders, making them the veritable focal point of reflections on the nature of the shareholding body. Thus, even in Germany, the country often pointed to as least open to shareholder concerns, the law for 'Unternehmensintegrität und Modernisierung des Anfechtungsrechts' (UMAG) passed in 2005 takes the rights of individual investors as its point of departure. Similar protections have been instituted in France with the Sécurité Financière law of 2003. In the United States also, the Sarbanes-Oxley Act of 2002, although ostensibly focused on auditing, prominently stresses the need 'to protect investors by improving the accuracy and reliability of corporate disclosures made pursuant to the securities laws, and for other purposes'.[2] Even if the capital structure of the

---

[2] H.R.3763, Sarbanes-Oxley Act of 2002.

corporation is not tending towards dispersion in all national settings equally, the legal and cultural superstructures are being put in place to enable investors to influence the corporation in an effective way, not only in theory, but also in practice.

In sum, contrary to widely held opinion, the division and indeed the extreme fragmentation of capital does not necessarily prevent share-holders from taking action. Of course, the power of the *individual* shareholder to act is very limited. However, in the political logic of liberalism, the fact that no single investor is strong enough to have direct influence makes it all the more just, from the point of view of the collective. It is the market as a whole that has the legitimacy to exercise the entrepreneurial force of direction.

Transparency of information and the development of financial communication

Atomized markets cannot fulfil their regulatory function unless inves-tors are correctly, abundantly, and equally informed in order autono-mously to evaluate the strategic options put before them in a rational manner. This is why the diffusion of information has become a central concern in contemporary evolution of corporate governance. Since management has control of corporate information, passing it on to investors has direct consequences for their power, and incentives or even constraints need to be put in place to persuade them to do so.[3] So much so, in fact, that contemporary corporate governance based on regulation by the financial markets makes the provision of information by management a cornerstone of its codes and laws.[4]

Now, the diffusion of information by the corporation is not unpro-blematic. Specifically, the amount and type of information communi-cated must take into account the danger that competitors make use of it to get an edge on the corporation giving out information. This is why a

---

[3] The alignment of information is at the heart of agency theoretic approaches to corporate governance, as discussed in more detail in Chapter 7 below.

[4] The importance of transparency is highlighted in the UK Combined Code (2003) under Section C, 'Accountability and Audit'; in the German Corporate Governance Code (2006) under Section 6, 'Transparenz'; and in the French Bouton Report (2002), under Third Part, 'Financial Information Accounting Standards and Practices'. As mentioned earlier, assuring and maintaining transparency for investors was the focus of Sarbanes-Oxley (2002) in the United States.

certain degree of opacity can be desirable from the point of view of business performance. Here, the *private* nature of business concerns may fundamentally conflict with the *public* quality of information that is to be provided to all investors. Clearly, the strong emphasis on transparency in the recent development of corporate governance and the rigour of new laws enforcing its application are indications that investors are gaining the upper hand on management in the struggle for the right to exercise the entrepreneurial force. Providing as much information as possible to investors means recognizing that they are the ones who collectively will fulfil the function of the entrepreneur.

This evolution towards information transparency has been accompanied by an increasing standardization of the information provided. For investors to be able to do properly their jobs of defining an optimal portfolio and for the invisible hand to exercise adequately the function of the entrepreneur, the performances of corporations need to be compared. Comparison requires information that is substantially identical in form and universally understood. This requirement helps explain why information about the corporation has had the tendency to become increasingly finance oriented. Finance can be seen as a global language that translates the multiplicity of different corporate cases into comparable data. Not only has corporate communication become increasingly financial as a result, but the language of finance, that is to say its key measures and its measurement practices, has also become more standardized, with the emergence and subsequent large-scale imposition of international accounting standards. The work of the IASB (the International Accounting Standards Board) and the influence of the IFRS (the International Financial Reporting Standards) are particularly important here. Under the strong impression that accounting standards need to be harmonized for the benefit of investors, the IASB has succeeded in bringing a high degree of standardization into a profession that has always prided itself on the particularities of national systems. Interestingly, the use of international accounting standards has not stopped at publicly quoted companies, but has come to characterize just about any corporation doing business internationally.[5]

---

[5] See www.iasplus.com/country/useias.htm for a list of countries in which accounting according to IFRS is required of both listed *and* unlisted companies.

As a result of this universal requirement for 'transparency', corporations have set up audit committees and sophisticated internal control systems, charged with extracting information and assuring its correct communication to the financial markets. Public *reporting* such as provided to the markets in the annual report, in quarterly statements, and in regular financial briefings (guidance), all go in the direction of making corporate information freely and continuously available to the markets.[6] At the extreme, the organization for transparency, that is to say the communication of reliable and standardized information, is sometimes considered as the very embodiment of 'good' corporate governance.[7]

However, transparent communication alone is not sufficient. In order to ensure the reliability and quality of the information provided, it is necessary to extract this information as early as possible in the business process. The tendency towards standardized, financial information for the financial markets has had a profound effect on the internal governance of the corporation and on its management. The internal evaluation of value creation has become increasingly aligned with the external evaluation performed by investors, giving rise to a new set of management tools. During the 1990s, the development of systems of audit and evaluation that allow judgement of financial returns (for example EVA, but also various forms of project evaluation based on measures of return on capital invested) has made it possible for corporations to identify those operations in the value chain that promise a high return on capital and thus correspond most closely to the interests of investors. The required transparency of information disciplines the corporation and tends to orient internal practices towards the demands placed on the corporation by external entrepreneurs. In this way, the separation between the governance function

[6] The Sarbanes-Oxley Act, or, by its full name, the Public Company Accounting Reform and Investor Protection Act, of 2002, makes increasingly detailed reporting a legal requirement. Although other countries have not adopted the same stringent requirements, the effect of Sarbanes-Oxley has been broadly felt, as all firms capitalized at more than $150 million and dealing with the US must (since 2006) report on their internal accounting controls and highlight potential flaws.

[7] For an interesting perspective on the negative effects of transparency, see T. C. Welch and E. H. Rotberg, 'Transparency: panacea or Pandora's box', *Journal of Management Development* 25 (10) (2006), 937–41.

(ensuring the legitimacy of decision makers) and the management function (ensuring the efficiency of decisions) is undermined and the corporation as a whole becomes permeable to the demands of the financial
markets. The corporation is no longer a black box, but a transparent
box. In effect, a new managerial bureaucracy is born, one that one might
call a *glass bureaucracy*, whose job it is not to organize the corporation
in such a way that it is *separated from the markets*, but rather to make
sure that internal practices *respond to the expectations of financial
markets*, by making the corporation as transparent as possible.[8]

In sum, we can say that a second series of indicators shows that the
global corporation is increasingly structured by the information that is
required by and aimed at the financial markets. The institutions that
contribute to 'good governance' from this point of view are those that
help align the *internal* creation of value with the *external* interests of
investors. This alignment of orientations reinforces the entrepreneurial
function of the 'invisible hand' of the financial markets.

Management increasingly subordinated to investors

In the preceding chapter we described the reasons why managerial
expertise has come to be questioned. On the one hand, this questioning
has led to a general suspicion of the authority of expertise; it has also
led to an increasing separation of managerial expertise into its specialist components; complexity of the kind encountered by the global
corporation cannot be adequately addressed by the expertise of a single

---

[8] Recently, Courpasson and Clegg have argued that the managerial bureaucracy is
making a 'comeback' (see D. Courpasson and S. Clegg, 'Dissolving the iron cages?
Tocqueville, Michels, bureaucracy and the perpetuation of elite power',
Organization 13 (3) (2006), 319–43). Indeed, the contemporary exercise of
power inside the corporation requires an increasing use of internal procedures and
controls (reporting, standardization, evaluation, etc.). In our view, this does not
equate with a return to a Weberian bureaucracy, founded on reason and
hierarchical organization. The bureaucratization and the standardization of
management have the purpose of improving the process of extracting information
for the markets. This implies a new form of bureaucracy, what we call the
'glass bureaucracy' in order to indicate that its role is not to create a frontier
between the markets and the corporation, such as was the case described by
Weber, but, on the contrary, to make the corporation as transparent as possible to
the financial markets so that they in turn can serve as an external discipline on
internal practices. The meaning of contemporary bureaucracy needs to be
rethought, it seems to us, not in order to deny its existence, but for the purpose of
making its function and real power better understood.

individual or management team, but frequently requires the help of specialists (consultants, technology experts, financial engineers, etc.). This evolution of the technocratic structure serves the logic of the financial markets, made up as they are of investors who are themselves increasingly well trained in the economics of business. Management is no longer the sole repository of managerial knowledge. In the position of arbitraging between different types of investments, the professional investor often has broader knowledge than management concerning the sources of performance. Although it is not part of the investor's mission to realize results, he/she can evaluate and compare them, and, in so doing, judge the quality of management of any particular corporation. This *external position of comparison* gives the investor a decisive advantage in choosing which strategies to favour. In the general atmosphere of doubt towards expertise that characterizes contemporary business, the professional investor's authority appears to stand above the fray – after all, his/her choices are only based on a simple comparison of observed performances. In this scenario, it is up to management to prove that the decisions it proposes are sufficiently well supported by reason and fact.

The frequency of *road shows* and the importance accorded to them, the care taken in financial communication, and the regularity of providing information to the markets all contribute to reducing the perceived authority and the prestige of management, in relation to investors and the financial markets. In the new, post-managerial configuration of corporate governance, management is often considered a priori to be *suspect* and has to defend itself in front of the tribunal of investors in charge of evaluating the best strategic choices. The ultimate sanction accorded to a managerial strategy proposition resides in the *welcome* it receives in the markets, as indicated by the resulting variation in the price of the stock. The importance of this welcome is nowhere more clearly observable than in mergers and acquisitions in which the acquirer has to maintain the price of its shares as a condition for successfully concluding the transaction.[9]

Even indirectly, the price of the share provides a synthesis of how well investors appreciate a strategy proposed by management. For the

---

[9] For example, because it proposed to pay for the 2006 purchase of Arcelor in part with its own shares, it was critical for LNM Steel that the financial markets showed their approval of the proposed merger by maintaining the share price of LNM Steel once the deal was announced.

movement of the share price has an impact on the implementation (or not) of the strategy, an impact which is accentuated even further when internal project evaluation is aligned with external evaluation by the markets. Unsurprisingly, more and more corporations prominently display the price of their shares in their headquarter buildings – updated every five minutes, as if to symbolize the tight connection and perhaps even the subservience of the corporation to investors. As the function of management loses respect, the quality of investor judgement gains even further ground. In this way, we almost can see the force of entrepreneurial direction passing from the visible hands of management to the invisible hand of the markets.

We have seen that the multiplication of investors has made the financial markets sufficiently fragmented to be able 'spontaneously' to exercise their function of selecting the best decisions without being influenced or controlled by the corporation. Transparency of information gives investors the means for autonomously making rational choices and aligns the processes of the corporation with investors' criteria and choices. Finally, management finds itself increasingly subordinated to the markets and has to take investors' reactions into account to define and weigh decisions – investors' reactions legitimize managerial choices. The large global corporations are thus oriented by the game of finance, a game that transforms differences between corporations into a universal algebra of comparison. This is a new situation in the evolution of capitalism; the large quoted corporation with a dispersed capital base (*public company*) is now influenced by the public not only in terms of *production* (by the workings of competition), but also in terms of its *governance*. In the post-managerial period, the committees of audit and financial control, the audits, the public reports, the road shows, the communications with financial institutions, and indeed all of the processes that permit investors to wield the entrepreneurial force in a more fluid manner, become the key institutions and practices of corporate governance. These institutions and practices tend to be structured as 'reliable and neutral' channels for communicating information.

Evolution of the institutions supporting the shareowner as entrepreneur

In chronological parallel to the developments supporting the investor as entrepreneur, we can also observe a movement towards institutions and practice that have made it easier for shareowners to participate directly in corporate governance. In this second movement, shareowners have come to exercise considerable influence on the strategic choices of the particular corporations in which they have taken positions. The shareowner, in our definition, is the shareholder who seeks to intervene actively in the control of the corporation. He/she is not simply waiting for a *return* on his/her investment decisions, but rather takes part in the construction of corporate strategy. In contrast to the setting of the investor as entrepreneur, the influence of the shareowner is not mechanically felt, by the workings of the market and systematic comparison of financial performances alone. The influence of the shareowner makes itself felt through direct participation in the decision-making of those corporations the shareowner seeks to defend, develop, or control more closely. What we now want to do is to provide evidence of those recent changes in corporate governance that have increased shareowners' ability to have a *voice* in corporate decisions. Three basic changes have moved the corporation in this direction: first, the emergence of vocal opinion leaders among shareholders; second, the increase in contradictory, but constructive debate between shareowners and corporations; and third, the growth in the practice of putting 'independent' members on corporate boards.

The emergence of opinion leaders among shareholders[10]

As we have seen, the financial markets have become highly fragmented, with a very large and still increasing number of actors. The fragmentation of the financial markets has, however, also been accompanied by the emergence of opinion leaders among shareholders. These opinion leaders belong to several categories, with reciprocal influences and memberships among the categories: large institutional shareholders; funds for socially responsible investment; shareholders' associations, employee shareholders, and also activist and hedge funds that invest in a focused manner. To some degree independent of their size and their motivation, these shareholders generate collective behaviours of direct

---

[10] For more detailed coverage of these questions, the work based on the personal engagement of Bob Monks as an active shareowner is especially helpful.
R. Monks, *The New Global Investors: How Shareowners can Unlock Sustainable Prosperity Worldwide*, Oxford: Capstone, 2001.

intervention in corporate strategy; in this way, they fulfil the function of shareowners, rather than the function of investors.

As a first indicator of this kind of behaviour we wish to cite those very large shareholders who, for ideological and economic reasons, seek to carry out their perceived responsibilities as shareowners. For some of these institutions, it forms a part of their *social mission* to take on this kind of responsibility – it allows them to reassure their savers or members that shareholdings in the portfolio receive proper care as to the quality of their governance and management. This argument holds for some institutions that represent public employees or formerly public employees, such as CalPERS and TIAA-CREF in the United States, or Hermes Pensions Management in the United Kingdom. These large institutions also have good economic reasons for their activism: their size is such that any decision to buy or sell shares has an effect on the markets, either directly by an effect on the transaction price, or indirectly by encouraging similar actions by smaller funds. This risk of amplification makes a policy of pure investment difficult in those cases in which the institution and the corporation have a disagreement over strategy. In other words, some of the very large funds have an interest in participating in corporate governance in order to assure the long-term value of their holdings.[11]

As a second indicator of the emergence of opinion leaders, we can see that the very multiplication of investment funds has given rise to a subcategory of funds that seek to differentiate themselves on the market for funds by the explicitly stated intention of shaping the social impact of those corporations that they hold shares in. These funds, grouped under the heading 'socially responsible' (SRI), inscribe the exercise of shareholder rights in their codes of conduct. By making their contribution of capital conditional on certain ethical, social, or political criteria and analysing corporate reports and assembly resolutions with these criteria in mind, these funds seek to orient the strategic choices of corporations in ways that concern not only the future economic performance, but also the means of attaining it. In this sense, they go beyond the role of investor to play the role of an active shareowner, and their points of differentiation reflect the social and moral preoccupations of our societies.

---

[11] This phenomenon is treated in more theoretically grounded detail in Chapter 5.

In Europe the integration of non-financial criteria in investment decisions was originally driven by pensions and religious congregations. Almost non-existent in the 1980s, the number of socially responsible investment funds grew steadily in the 1990s, from 60 in 1994 to 160 in 1999, and exploded to 360 in 2004, representing a total of €19 billion invested. In the United States, the phenomenon is older: the first such fund, Pax World, goes back to 1971. In the United States, as well, it was only in the 1990s that growth really took off: in 1994, 60 funds managed $150 billion; by 2004, 200 funds were managing $1400 billion.[12] The question of whether or not socially responsible investment funds have an effect or influence on the orientation of corporations has been the subject of much debate in the literature, but answering it is beyond the scope of this book.[13] Here, it is enough to say that these funds, by the mechanism of imitation that characterizes any fragmented market, but particularly one as fragmented as the global market for equities, have had an effect on the preferences of investors. Thus today investors integrate into their financial valuation of a corporation the risk that it will fall foul of the standards of socially responsible investment and be the subject of a public outcry, for example by excessive pollution, insufficient attention to human rights, or inadequate ethics. Investors favour those corporations that demonstrate up-to-date social responsibility principles, and this mechanically amplifies the impact of statements by activist shareowners that take up the same points in public. In other words, even if they only play a limited role in terms of absolute size (although in toto they constitute a very large block of invested assets), socially responsible investment funds contribute to the markets' preference for strategies that are environmentally and socially 'clean' and go beyond the mere delivery of comparable financial returns.

Third, we can point to the rise in power of shareholder rights organizations. For small shareholders, in particular, representative shareholder rights associations exercise the function of voice, especially through the media. Their capacity of influence appears to be

---

[12] Source: Social Investment Forum: Mutual Funds; Assets under SRI screens.

[13] For an insightful discussion, see S. Hellsten and C. Mallin, 'Are "ethical" or "socially responsible" investments socially responsible?', *Journal of Business Ethics* 66 (4) (2006), 393–406. This discussion is important, but not critical to our argument, for we are interested in shareholders' capacity for direct influence and not in the content or direction of the influence so wielded.

disproportionate to their small size and minuscule real weight. In many Western countries, shareholder associations, such as NASAA and AAII in the United States, ADAM in France, DSW in Germany or UKSA in the United Kingdom, have gained significant power by taking their concerns to the public, sometimes in spectacular fashion, as in the cases of publicizing managerial salary excesses, speaking out for or against takeovers, or calling for clarity in succession planning. They have become sources of pressure on corporations to publicize (disclose) information that, in former times, could stay closely held. However, in contrast to the classical investors that we described earlier, these associations are not primarily after standardized financial information; rather they care about the content of corporate information, the fairness that it implies, and its distributive dimension.

Shareholder rights associations are particularly active and influential when the law authorizes *class actions*, as in the United States, because activism can lead to a date in court, encouraging and multiplying the voices heard in the name of defending collective interests. Thus, it is not surprising that the United States has a large number of shareholder rights associations that have formed to take a class action against a particular company. In Europe, by contrast, it is more typical for one and the same shareholder rights association to work on a large number of cases.

Employee shareholdings represent a fourth source of opinion leadership among shareholders. This category of shareholding has experienced spectacular growth over the last twenty years, as Employee Stock Ownership Plans (ESOPs) have taken on various new forms (stock purchase plans, pension plans, stock options, etc.). From very modest beginnings in the 1950s and still relatively low levels in the mid-1990s (around 5% of employees, according to the Bureau of Labor Statistics), employee stock ownership in the United States today (2006) covers 17.5% of the total workforce.[14] Employee stock ownership plans came to Europe in 1987, with the launch of the UK ESOP. Similar plans (adapted for local tax regulations) have since been set up throughout the EU. By 2001, 19% of European employees in the private sector were shareholders (of their own corporation), with 10% of the capital

[14] Cf. General Social Survey, 2006, as reported by the National Center for Employee Ownership; Bureau of Labor Statistics Report on Employee Compensation, 2001.

of the largest British corporations in the hands of employees and 3% of the capital of the largest French corporations.[15]

The extension of employee ownership plans to more and more employees has allowed corporations to stabilize their capital base and thereby build up some resistance to hostile takeovers. Employee share-holdings can be seen as a particular kind of 'poison pill', one that may or may not support the interest of management.[16] This class of share-owners is still not very well organized, but it constitutes a potentially powerful structuring of the shareholding body, with long-term effects that bear careful observation. Employee shareholdings have a strong interest to participate directly in corporate governance – after all, they represent one of the most important stakeholder groups in the corporation. In France, the privatization of the majority of the great state enterprises in the late 1990s strongly encouraged employee sharehold-ings. These privatizations systematically opened the corporate capital base to employees, but at the same time obliged corporations to create the position of *administrateur salarié* (Giraud Act, 1994) – board members who represent employees as shareowners (as of 2006, twenty-one of the forty corporations on the CAC-40 and all twenty former state enterprises had such 'employee board members'). In Germany, employees were already on the board, in the context of *Mitbestimmung* (co-determination), but the growth in employee share-holdings has begun to change the equation for employee representa-tives on the board. No longer can the pure opposition between

---

[15] For a general survey, see E. Poutsma, *Les tendances récentes de la participation financière des travailleurs dans l'Union européenne*, Report to the European Foundation for the Improvement of Living and Working Conditions, Dublin. http://ec.europa.eu/employment_social/publications/2002/tj3701477_fr.pdf. The difference between British and French figures is due to the absence of pension funds in France. Nonetheless, the recent development of the Fonds Commun de Placement Entreprise (FCPE) has permitted rapid growth in this type of shareholding: by 2004, in seven of the SBF 250 largest French publicly quoted corporations, employees had become the largest single shareholding block (source: France Corporate Governance Institute).

[16] On the role of employee shareholdings in protecting management from hostile raids from the outside, the literature is abundant. See L. Gordon and J. Pound, 'ESOP's and corporate control', *Journal of Financial Economics* 27 (1990), 525–55; S. Chang and D. Mayers, 'Managerial vote ownership and shareholder wealth: evidence from ESOP', *Journal of Financial Economics* 32 (1992), 103–31; J. D. Rauh, 'Own company stock in defined contribution pension plans: a takeover defense?' *Journal of Financial Economics* 81 (2) (2006), 379–410.

shareholder and employee serve as the basis for a balance of power in the supervisory board (see Chapter 5). From the moment that employees also have substantial shareholdings, the frontier between shareholders and employees becomes indistinct and the carefully cultivated balance of power between the two tends to break down. In a general sense, we can say that the emergence of employee shareholdings makes a division of interests among stakeholders based on the classic political opposition between capital and labour problematic. One of the more interesting consequences, from a socio-political point of view, of the massive growth in the size and spread of the shareholding body is the need to rethink this hallowed opposition.

Specialized investment funds (such as Relational Investors in the US and the Hermes Focus Funds in the UK) or hedge funds (such as Icahn, Kerkorian, Laxey, TCF, etc.) and private equity funds that invest in a focused manner in particular corporations, with the avowed purpose of intervening in the governance and strategy of these corporations in order to change their direction and increase their stock price, constitute the fifth and newest source of opinion leadership among shareowners. For these players (some of whom are investors turned shareowners), active shareownership is a market niche and represents their very reason for existence. The spectacular growth experienced in this niche over the last few years and the large amount of capital it now represents show that this has also become a viable approach to shareownership – an approach founded on the idea of the shareowner acting as entrepreneur *in the place of underperforming management.*

The first set of indicators of shareowner activity that we have just described provides some evidence for a movement towards active shareownership. This movement has accompanied the fragmentation of financial markets that gave investors their new entrepreneurial power, but it points in a different direction: whereas investors collectively act as an invisible hand, shareowners act individually and sometimes jointly as a very visible hand and vocal voice in corporate governance. Shareowners make the claim to be exercising their responsibilities as shareholders who wish to intervene on the content of strategies and hence want to have a word to say in the process of decision making, in the choice of management, and in the compensation of the directors. These opinion leaders *interpret* the information corporations communicate to the markets, seek deeper insight in discussing with management, and also bring their own knowledge to bear on the corporation's strategy. In this way, they play an important mediating role between the corporation and the financial markets.

Intensification of debate between shareowners and corporations

The advent of mass shareholdings has led to a reconsideration of the working of the annual general meeting (AGM). With today's number of individual shareholders running into the hundreds of thousands if not millions for the largest corporations, the classic form of the AGM, developed for a very limited number of participants, is no longer viable. If all of a typical large capitalization stock's shareholders decided to attend an AGM, there would be no football stadium large enough to hold them. For the AGM to continue the way it always has, corporations have relied on proxy voting which concentrates shareholder concerns in a few hands and, just as commonly, on non-participation. However, shareholder absenteeism considerably weakens corporate governance, as it deprives governance of one of its most basic sources of legitimacy. After all, governance in capitalism is based on the rights of ownership, even if these rights are only symbolically exercised. If shareholders do not participate in the formal process of evaluating and legitimizing the policies of the corporation at least once a year, there is a risk that the entire system of governance is eventually destabilized.

This is why legislators in some countries and expert reports in others have sought to encourage the practice of participating in the AGM and voting on resolutions. In the United States, the Employee Retirement Income Security Act (ERISA) of 1974 mandated voting by private pension funds, and the Department of Labor has continued to monitor compliance and offer advice over the years, modernizing procedures. Although not formally covered by ERISA, public pension funds in the United States have largely followed private pension funds in adopting proxy voting practices. In the United Kingdom, a series of expert reports has strongly urged shareholders to vote – from the Cadbury Report of 1992 to the Hampel Report of 1998 and the Combined Code of 2003, the vote is highlighted as a responsibility of shareholders.[17] In France, both of the Vienot Reports (1995 and 1999), as well as the Bouton Report of 2002 and the NRE legislation of the same year,

---

[17] Cf. C. Mallin, 'Institutional investors and voting practices: an international comparison', *Corporate Governance: An International Review* 9 (2) (2001), 118–26, for an excellent summary of voting practices in the US and the UK.

underscore the importance of the shareholder vote. In Germany, finally, multiple voting shares have been eliminated (KonTraG, 1998) and the exercise of voting rights facilitated (NaStraG, 2001).

At the same time, shareowners who desire to exercise their owner-ship responsibilities apply pressure directly to ensure themselves of the possibility to express an opinion at the AGM. Thus, the last few years have seen a battle over what constitutes just AGM procedures, with shareowners seeking improvements on several counts. First, there is a need to receive information (including the invitation itself) far enough in advance of the AGM in order to be able to form an opinion; second, the right to express an opinion at the AGM cannot be so strictly regulated that no outside voices are heard, while at the same time, the expression of opinion has to be subject to an order that prevents a cacophony of irrelevant concerns from drowning out serious debate; third, votes need to be controlled and protected from manipulation. Even if shareowners cannot yet point to many AGM victories, this battle over procedures in the effective exercise of the shareowner func-tion has demonstrated that some shareowners, even relatively small ones, have an increasing ability to mobilize shareholder opinion.

The number of resolutions submitted to an AGM vote by share-owners is an indication of this tendency and shows that more and more shareowners would like to participate effectively in debate over the future of the corporations they hold shares in. Although overall numbers and statistics on shareowner resolutions are hard to come by, particularly for the earlier years, the work of Graves, Rehbein, and Waddock sheds considerable light on the recent pattern of evolution.[18] Thus, based on data from the Investor Responsibility Research Center (IRRC) for the period 1988–98 (United States), they report a marked uptick in the number of shareowner resolutions from a relatively steady 200 per year in the 1980s to a relatively constant 300 per year in the 1990s, an increase of almost 50% on average.

A second indicator of shareowners' desire to enter into direct discus-sions with corporations is the increasing prevalence of bilateral meet-ings between management and significant shareowners, over and above the AGM. As we have already pointed out, the requirement to

---

[18] S. B. Graves, K. Rehbein, and S. Waddock, 'Fad and fashion in shareholder activism: the landscape of shareholder resolutions, 1988–1998', *Business and Society Review* 106 (4) (2001), 293–314.

communicate in a transparent fashion has led to the increasing sub-ordination of management to investors; at the same time, the practice of bilateral meetings with selected funds and associations has arisen to give active shareowners relatively more direct influence over the cor-poration than that which can be exercised by the common shareholder. More and more commonly, in fact, influential shareholders of all stripes, but particularly those with stable, long-term holdings, have regular meetings with management to discuss the progress of the busi-ness and consult on major strategic issues.[19]

This practice, now quite common, actually goes against the ideal of absolutely transparent information as favoured by the investor: even if no confidential information can be exchanged in these bilateral meet-ings, the exchanges do favour shareowners who are interested in the content of corporate strategies and not just in the relative price of the share. A kind of quid pro quo for shareholder loyalty in some cases and hence a factor in the stability of the capital base, this form of commu-nication is not strictly public, but still gives shareowners a discrete and real way of influencing the strategic orientation of the corporation.

As a last indicator in the same vein, we observe in some global corporations the recent emergence of a new type of forum, situated between the AGM and the board, namely a shareholders' committee. Here we are talking about consultative bodies constituted of active shareowners, without specific legal powers, but with the vocation of serving as a regular forum of exchange and debate between share-owners and management. An early example is the Shareholder Committee created by Air Liquide (France) in 1987; similar commit-tees exist at Sanofi-Aventis (France) and Drax (UK), to name just a couple. The shareowners who take part in these committees are pri-marily representatives of shareholder rights groups and larger funds (pension or investment). Although this type of consultative body is still rare, its emergence is evidence of a clear need to find new ways of expressing opinions and of making different interests converge in an age of mass shareholding and weakened management power.

---

[19] For a particularly interesting perspective on the impact of such meetings on managerial attitudes and behaviours, see J. Roberts, P. Sanderson, R. Barker, and J. Hendry, 'In the mirror of the market: the disciplinary effects of company/fund manager meetings', *Accounting, Organizations, and Society* 31 (3) (2006), 277–94.

The second set of indicators of shareowner activity that we have described reveals that a variety of forms of representing shareowner interests in corporate governance has arisen over the course of the last decade. These forms of representation have emerged alongside the new relationships between investors and management, and allow shareowners who seek actively to exercise the ownership function to establish links with management that, in contrast to the investor–management link, are more oriented towards debate and deliberation and less concerned with a mere transfer of information.

The drive for independence in the composition of the corporate board
Contemporaneously with the developments towards active share ownership described in the preceding section, the role of the corporate board has also been examined and considerably reinvigorated.[20] The evolution of the corporate board has gone in the direction of making it more independent from management in the way it effectively exercises its function of *oversight* of the corporation and of management. The reform of the corporate board has three convergent demands: the emphasis on independent board members (non-executive directors); the focus on evaluating the activity of board members; and the drive to separate the functions of Chairman and CEO.[21]

These three demands derive from a single purpose: to make the board more autonomous in its dealings with management and hence to turn it into a body of effective oversight and strategic deliberation, as opposed to a body for registering and approving management decisions.[22] On a technical basis, these demands lead to a separation of the function of oversight from the function of direction, not just in principle, as in the

---

[20] In this section, we are interested in the larger significance of the board, not in its detailed workings. For a comprehensive and well-documented contemporary treatment of the workings of the board, we refer the reader to M. Huse, *Boards, Governance, and Value Creation*, Cambridge: Cambridge University Press, 2006.

[21] The board reforms we refer to collectively here are described in detail in the following: for the United States, the Sarbanes-Oxley legislation (2002); for France, the Vienot I (1995), Vienot II (1999), and Bouton (2002) reports; for Germany, the KonTraG (1998) and TransPuG (2002) legislations, and the GCCG (2002) code; and for the United Kingdom, the Cadbury (1993), Turnbull (1999), and Higgs (2003) reports.

[22] For a more detailed discussion of the contemporary conceptual underpinnings of these three demands, see P.-Y. Gomez, *La république des actionnaires*, Paris: Syros, 2001.

managerial model, but in effective practice. Thus, today's boards routinely publicize their number of annual meetings, as an indicator of the effective exercise of their function and as a part of 'good governance' practice. Increasingly, the board acts as the locus of control and mediation between the shareholding body and the corporation. The separation of the functions of Chairman and CEO where it is not required by law further distinguishes the board's role from that of management.

On a more symbolic basis, the increasing autonomy of the board is legitimized in terms of defending the interests of shareholders:

> The senior independent director should attend sufficient of the regular meetings of management with a range of major shareholders to develop a balanced understanding of the themes, issues and concerns of shareholders. The senior independent director should communicate these views to the non-executive directors and, as appropriate, to the board as a whole.[23]

Under managerial governance, management effectively controlled itself, a practice that was justified by the sharing of rare expertise; today, board members are increasingly required to have the necessary personal and professional independence to be able to control management – without being in any way constrained by ties to management. The establishment of audit, nomination, and compensation committees (specifically recommended in the UK's 2003 Combined Code and in Germany's 2002 German Corporate Governance Code), typically to be headed by non-executive directors, accentuates the distinction between the functions of the board and the functions of management and puts a premium on board members with the requisite skills for running such committees.

However, the increasing autonomy of the board also underlines the distinction between shareowners and investors. The latter are interested in the relative performances of the corporations that are in their portfolio (and of those that are outside of the portfolio but could be added at any moment). For the investor, the workings of the board are a black box – only the final effect on performance counts. By opening the black box and involving themselves in the designation of roles in this institution of corporate governance, shareowners make it clear that they are interested in the *process* by which decisions concerning their holdings are reached and not only in final performance numbers. In this

---

[23] Higgs Report, London: Dechert, 2003, pp. 5–6.

sense, active shareowners' still rare requests for a seat on the board can be seen as a further indicator of their increasing desire to take part in critical deliberations and influence the direction of the corporation.[24]

This third series of indicators of shareowner activity points to a two-pronged movement in the contemporary evolution of corporate governance institutions. On the one hand, we can observe the increasing entrenchment of shareowner power with respect to and over management. On the other hand, it is also clear that the institutions of corporate governance are being restructured to allow for more active participation of shareowners, in boards, via independent directors, or through consultative shareholder committees. While the investor as entrepreneur may consider these developments to be of minor significance, or even just costly, and certainly less important than efforts to ensure information transparency, the shareowner as entrepreneur considers them essential to the exercise of ownership rights.

Parallels and overlaps between the investor as entrepreneur and the shareowner as entrepreneur

Opposing forms of governance

The setting favouring the investor as entrepreneur is built on the mechanism of the financial markets, the simplicity of access to these markets, and the sophistication of the financial instruments they offer. Investors exercise the function of the entrepreneur in the global corporation by means of a continuous evaluation of the corporation's market value and the ever present threat of sale. Good direction translates into positive anticipated performance and a high stock price. The post-managerial institutions of corporate governance are focused on the requirement of providing information to the markets. One can speak of *extrinsic* institutions, because it is their vocation to transfer information on the corporation to the anonymous investors (entrepreneurs) who reside outside the corporation. These institutions are legitimized by the principle of *information transparency*, in other words the need to extract information (internal reporting), control it (audit, audit

---

[24] Such requests have started to increase from active hedge funds (e.g. Kerkorian in the case of GM) or private equity players (e.g. Blackstone in the case of Deutsche Telekom). As mentioned earlier, in France and Germany employee shareholdings are legally required to be represented on the board.

committees, and appropriate board responsibility), and transmit it (financial communication, annual report). In this setting, the formal institutions of governance such as the AGM or the board should remain as neutral as possible, in effect to function like an instrument for the exact transfer of information, without bias or inappropriate secrecy (information retention). The frontiers of the corporation as an autonomous economic actor are rendered porous by this transfer of information, and more transparency implies 'better governance', because it allows investors outside the corporation to make rational choices on the sole basis of performances, actual and anticipated. The allocation of global financial resources towards the highest performers is the collective result of multiple individual evaluations by investors. The upshot is a 'spontaneous' direction of the economy and hence also of society, without a central organizer, based on individual interests in the purest liberal logic. The entrepreneur is the market, and the market is a collection of anonymous individuals.

As a contemporaneous development to the rise of the investor as entrepreneur, we observe the exercise of the entrepreneurial function by the shareowner, as evidenced in laws and codes, as well as in the practices of active shareowners. The activity of the shareowner is based on the will of certain shareholders to take on a role of influence in the orientation of the corporation in which they have an ownership interest. From the point of view of the corporation, this development is supported by the need to stabilize the capital base and engage in long-term relationships with owners; from the point of view of shareowners, their engagement is made necessary by their involvement as stakeholders in the corporation and their desire to protect their own medium-to long-term interests. Between the 'invisible hand' of the markets and the very visible role of management, active shareowners play the roles of catalysts and mediators. They intervene in the corporation on the basis of the rights accorded to them as property owners, rights that are at the heart of the logic of capitalism. The formal institutions of corporate governance such as the AGM and the board have evolved in the direction of permitting shareowners to participate effectively in the control of the corporation by interpreting information and using it as a basis for working with management and other stakeholders. In this setting again, the corporation can be called porous, because it integrates considerations from the *outside* in its deliberations and choices. In contrast to the investor as entrepreneur setting, however, the shareowner as entrepreneur gives rise to *intrinsic* institutions, in other words institutions that facilitate the participation of external stake-holders in the governance process of the corporation. Here, the information provided by the corporation is indispensable raw material for presenting different points of view and plays a critical role in the bodies of deliberation. By expressing opinions (*voice*) and by participating in the interpretation of the information provided by the corporation, active shareowners polarize the multiple interpretations existing in the markets into positions that they consider necessary considerations for the corporation. In this way, shareowners exercise the entre-preneurial force, not in general by allocating resources to the highest performers, but in particular, for the corporation in which they have an interest and in which they wish to maintain or improve the perfor-mance. Case by case, active shareowners can thus be said to orient the entire economy, in keeping with the liberal logic which attributes to the entrepreneur the role of a catalyst in ensuring that private individual interests combine to serve the general interest.

The forms of corporate governance respectively dominated by the investor and by the shareowner can thus be placed side by side on the basis of two criteria of comparison: (1) the institutions of corporate governance are extrinsic or intrinsic, according to whether they seek to diffuse information to investors who stay *outside* the corporation, or, on the contrary, they seek to integrate active shareowners in the inter-pretation of information with the purpose of providing direction *inside* the corporation; (2) the global economy is regulated by different means, as described in the previous chapter, either by *natural selection* in the case of the investor as entrepreneur or by *local adaptation* in the case of the shareowner as entrepreneur.

The two forms of governance coexist
The two forms cannot be considered as exclusive of each other, neither in space nor in time. In space, one can observe both simultaneously – in a given economy, some corporations will be primarily oriented by investors, while others are oriented by active shareowners. On all of the major exchanges, we have large corporations with widely dis-persed, diluted capital bases that appear more influenced by investors coexisting with corporations large and small with more concentrated capital bases (i.e. family or fund) that appear to be under stronger influence from shareowners. Contemporary economic developments

do not allow one to speculate on one form disappearing in favour of the other; rather, the continuation of coexistence appears likely. Therefore, it is necessary to determine anew for each exchange and for each corporation *who* effectively exercises the force of entrepreneurial direction, according to the structure of the capital base, the relative powers of investors and shareowners, and the type of corporate governance institutions – extrinsic or intrinsic.

Similarly, the two settings are not exclusive in time. In fact, one and the same corporation can, over the course of its life, change the structure of its capital base: open its capital, go public, or, on the contrary, exit from the financial markets; it can introduce short-term investors into its capital base, but also long-term shareowners; and it can even dilute its capital completely, only to see itself the subject of a hostile takeover by a group of shareowners that has become dominant. The institutions of corporate governance also evolve accordingly, becoming more intrinsic or more extrinsic, with the composition of boards tightened or opened, the debates at the AGM shortened or deepened, the flow of standardized information more or less controlled, etc. There are as many possible configurations as there are financing needs, strategic options, and growth stages. In other words, within a larger model of governance, we find malleable forms.

We would stress that these forms are not bound to a specific culture, contrary to what the cultural literature would suggest: thus, 'Anglo-Saxon' corporations are not necessarily extrinsically governed, and continental corporations are not necessarily intrinsically governed.[25] Rather, it seems more correct to say that both forms can be observed within the same cultural space: both in the United States and in France, one can find large, publicly quoted corporations with a diluted capital base that are clearly investor driven, and hence can be characterized as extrinsically governed, as well as corporations with closely controlled capital that appear more shareowner driven, or intrinsically governed.

---

[25] See, for example, M. Albert, *Capitalism vs. Capitalism*, New York: Four Walls Eight Windows, 1993 [1991]. Again, we do not wish to deny the particular historical and legal characteristics of the different countries. However, we would insist that country specificity cannot be based on different governance forms, for we can find both forms, more or less developed, *within* each national space.

Of course, the historical and structural conditions of a country can lead to a preponderance of one form over another at a given point in time, as a variety of descriptive studies have shown.[26] However, what seems most important to us is to recognize that the investor driven and shareowner driven forms can and do coexist in the same market.

We conclude that the developments described lead not to different models of corporate governance, but rather to different forms within the same model. It is this common model that we now need to characterize more fully in order to understand what are the general traits of post-managerial governance that allow the malleability of forms described above.

2 One model of post-managerial model governance: public governance

The broad movements that we have sketched here give a dominant role in the exercise of the entrepreneurial force of direction to investors and shareowners. Beyond the differences of form that we have described here, there are fundamental commonalities between the two forms; these similarities permit us to argue that the exercise of the entrepreneurial function in the two settings is comparable and that the two forms in fact constitute a single model, a model we call 'public governance'. We will first show that the two forms – investor as entrepreneur and shareowner as entrepreneur – both lend significant weight to information, representation, and debate. This assessment of commonality is further reinforced by the finding that in both cases the counterweight to entrepreneurial power is exercised by *public opinion*, a new actor that is truly omnipresent in the corporate governance of global corporations. On the basis of this argument, we will conclude with a description of the characteristics of the new model of reference in corporate governance, a model that represents the contemporary incarnation of the liberal project.

---

[26] See R. LaPorta, F. Lopez-de-Silanes, and A. Schleifer, 'Corporate ownership around the world', *Journal of Finance* 54 (1999), 471–518; R. Dore, *Stock Market Capitalism: Welfare Capitalism. Japan and Germany versus Anglo-Saxons*, New York: Oxford University Press, 2000. For an overview, C. Mallin, *Corporate Governance*, Oxford: Oxford University Press, 2000, pp. 160–5.

Foundations of public governance: information, de-privatization, and public debate

The observations presented to this point can be boiled down to three characteristics of contemporary corporate governance: the omnipresence of information; the 'de-privatization' of the corporation, meaning the tendency for all things corporate to be considered increasingly a matter of public, rather than private concern; and the role played by debate and the representation of different interests.

Information omnipresent

In both of the forms of public governance we have described, information plays a material role in the process of governing the corporation; if one compares the current era with previous periods, this is a true departure. Under familial governance, the principle of *business secrecy* was paramount, closing off the corporation from the outside and maintaining the authority of the family father as a guarantee for organizational unity. Business secrecy was further reinforced by family secrecy; regulation of the corporation by means of the institution of the family required a strong internal hold on information, because a hold on information implied cohesion – of the organization and of the family – and supported the power of the father of the family.

Under managerial governance, the primacy of management expertise implied that information on the corporation was necessarily controlled by the managers. The legitimacy of the expert rested on his/her ability to extract and interpret information. If the expert communicated a result or an opinion, this was to be considered as an expert's conclusion and not as raw material for debate. As a result, the flow of information to the outside was reduced to the legal minimum (accounting was not generally imposed on corporations until after the Second World War), and shareholders had a great deal of difficulty in getting any kind of supplementary reports from the corporation.[27]

---

[27] See Lewis D. Gilbert, *Dividends and Democracy*, Larchmont, NY: American Research Council, 1956, for numerous examples from the first three decades of managerial governance. A broader summary of early corporate governance activism can be found in R. Marens, 'Inventing corporate governance: the mid-century emergence of shareholder activism', *Journal of Business and Management* 8 (4) (2002), 365–89.

In a significant departure from the practices of familial governance and managerial governance, information plays an important and indeed a systematic role in public governance. In marked contrast to the principles of good governance that had prevailed until recently, the retention of information is today considered to go against good practice, and secrecy is treated as a fault. Rather, good governance in today's world implies the need to assure a permanent and precise flow of information about the corporation. As a consequence, the amount and depth of information support materials has grown tremendously: annual reports, of course, but also reports of specialized committees, reports of experts, financial reports that can be consulted electronically, reports on corporate social responsibility, corporate internet sites, etc. Never before in the history of the corporation has such a mass of information been available.

As a corollary of such widespread dissemination, information has become increasingly standardized. So that it can be rationally interpreted and used by a large number of actors, the elaboration, extraction, and transmission of information has to be tightly controlled, and its neutrality has to be ensured. This is why so much emphasis is put on setting universal standards both by industry groups and by regulators: for the information system to be credible, 'veracity' which can always be debated is less important than *conformity* to rules and procedures.

The very nature of information is modified in the process. No longer is information a mere passive statement of account of the corporation's activities; instead, information has become a means to adapt and even transform the corporation's activities and practices in order to align them with the kind of results that are expected by investors. As mentioned earlier, the information transmitted to the market can and does increasingly serve as a means of internal measurement and management: EVA, return on investment, return on capital, etc. The same thing can be said of the information communicated to shareholders on the functioning of the corporation; for example, the need to publish board composition, today widely accepted, itself can generate changes in practice – changes such as increasing the diversity of the board so as not to appear to lag behind. The information communicated thus becomes a tool by which corporations discipline themselves, in the process ending up organizing their governance structures so that they *can be presented* as 'normal'. The English practice of *comply or explain*, which supposes that the corporation is free to differ from general good practice on the condition of explaining why it differs, is perhaps the most sophisticated form of the disciplinary role attributed to information in contemporary governance.

In sum, we can say that in contemporary governance, information appears as a widely distributed, continuous flow of increasingly standardized material that itself has a standardizing or normalizing effect on the practices it is supposed to be reporting on.

The global corporation is increasingly de-privatized

The changes that we have described clearly demonstrate that today shareholders – investors and shareowners – play a critical role in the exercise of the entrepreneurial force and therefore also in corporate governance. Some commentators have called this new situation 'the return of the shareholder'; as we pointed out earlier in our description of the historical evolution of corporate governance, this kind of assessment is not correct, for shareholders have never before exercised the entrepreneurial function. To see active shareholders who do not actually work inside the corporation, but base their power only on the right of ownership, is a radical departure in the history of capitalism. Under familial governance, the owner was also the director, and the two functions of ownership and control converged; under managerial governance, management based its legitimacy on its expert work and not on ownership. We are therefore in a new configuration: the shareholder as entrepreneur (investor or shareowner) does not work *inside* the corporation. However, the shareholder does work *for* the corporation, in the sense that he/she contributes to orienting the strategy.

The key difference is that today the function of the entrepreneur resides *outside* of the corporation. The entrepreneur intervenes to orient strategy from the point of view of the financial markets, or for the purpose of protecting savings, or based on strategic interests that are not strictly those of the corporation, but may momentarily overlap with them. Investors, but also active shareowners, claim to represent the interests of those individuals (savers) who have entrusted their money to them. With the growth of the shareholding body to great mass, it is as if society as a whole were implicated in the performance and the strategic orientation of corporations. The corporation therefore is constrained to modify its production process so that it can satisfy the external expectations, whether they be financial, economic, or environmental. The objective of contemporary corporate governance

is therefore to align these *external* interests with the productive potential of the corporation. This alignment may take the shape of demands
on results (such as, for example, return on capital) or of demands on
means (such as the cessation of child labour). As we have seen, this can
generate extrinsic institutions which align the corporation with the
markets, or intrinsic institutions that align the corporation with shareowners in the processes of government and control. In both settings, it
is important to realize that contemporary corporate governance has the
particularity of opening the corporation to the social environment
constituted by its shareholders. These shareholders, in turn, are multiple, are more or less loyal, have different interests, and are motivated by
their own visions of the corporation's future.

Corporate governance in the post-managerial period further accentuates the process of 'de-privatization' of the corporation that has
been going on since the beginnings of capitalism. Both the investor
and the shareowner settings described here represent a new step in the
interpenetration of corporation and society, and a weakening of the
structural walls around the corporation that maintain its privacy and
make it a space that is separated from society and governed according
to its own interests and rules. This privacy was once incarnated by the
internal entrepreneur, first the founder owner and then the management. The salient facts of today – the function of the entrepreneur
exercised by investors or active shareowners; the institutions of governance extrinsic or intrinsic but focused on communicating information;
the multiplicity of opinions and individual choices that make up civil
society – have such a strong influence on the corporation that we
consider its governance to be a public matter.

Different interests, representation, and public debate
The process of arguing for diverging interests by shareholders and
corporations alike has taken on great importance. Different interests
are a mechanical consequence of mass shareholding and the diversity of
expectations necessarily present in such a mass. If, for example, both
hedge funds and employees can be shareholders of the same company,
it is clear that the only point they have in common is the right of
ownership – the performance and prospects of the corporation are
likely to be evaluated in very different ways by these two types of
actors. From this context arises a third characteristic of contemporary
corporate governance, namely shareholders' increasing recourse to

debate, often public, as a means of manifesting their specific expectations. Such debate can lead to open opposition with the management of the corporation, for example on the choice of strategy, but it can also result in conflict among shareholders, such as in the case of an acquisition that some might judge to be favourable to their interests, while others see it as prejudicial to theirs.

Such an open, quasi-theatrical debate is a new phenomenon in corporate governance. There was no equivalent under the familial and managerial governance models. Under post-managerial governance, we have public controversy carried out in the media, aggressive disputes in the AGM, contradictory interventions in the corporation by outside experts (i.e. financial analysts), and many other forms of public debate among shareholders. At the same time, various new bodies of representation have appeared (i.e. shareholder rights groups and shareholder committees), along with new locations for carrying out debate (e.g. road shows, bilateral meetings with key shareowners, etc.), to make interactions between shareholders and corporation ever more numerous and more varied.

These developments derive from the advent of mass shareholding and the fragmentation of the shareholding body. The transformation of the private interests of investors and shareowners into a general interest for the corporation is made possible in a process that allows for the (at least apparent) *representation* of different interests. This process of representation takes different points of view into account and can lead to a convergence of interests towards a solution that ends debate and becomes binding for all. Debate and representation can resolve differences as 'spontaneously' as if it were one actor who imposed his/ her interest. This transformation by debate and representation appears unnecessary in the setting of the investor as entrepreneur, because the 'invisible hand' of the financial markets leads to the fixing of a price – the value of the share – that is supposed to integrate all of the different expectations and interests. However, the finding of this price level is invariably preceded by discussion between investors and the corporation, nourished by transparent communication of information, road shows, and expert financial opinions. The positions eventually adopted by shareholders are the result of multiple exchanges that integrate a wide variety of information, from rumours to sophisticated analyses.

The transformation of different interests into a general interest is a more complex process in the setting of the shareowner as entrepreneur;

it may include discordant board meetings and disputed AGMs, and typically requires that the different parties determine ways to express their views and arrange modalities of deliberation. In both settings, the legitimacy of the final decisions taken in the name of the corporation depends to some degree on how they have been *made public* and *discussed*. They are only valid in the sense that they are a product of such discussions. Very far from the familial and managerial models, management has become one of the actors in a collective discussion of the future of the corporation that includes a variety of experts from the outside and requires an explicit consideration of diverging interests.

The post-managerial era thus marks a new step in the extension of the techniques of democracy to corporate governance. The third procedure of democracy – representation of diverging interest and public debate – now extends also to the corporate governance of global corporations. By the creation of new board structures and committees, by the process of formal and informal meetings between management and shareholders, and by the public expression of opinion (voice) in the media and in the AGM, the procedures for validating entrepreneurial actions have been redefined. The legitimacy of power exercised in the corporation depends upon holding advance discussion between the different interests concerned and making this discussion or its contents public. Making differences between shareholders part of a theatre-like debate is today an essential element of corporate governance.

Public opinion as the counterweight to entrepreneurial power in public governance

Throughout the historical description, we have pointed out that the power of the entrepreneur is not stable unless it is opposed by a counterweight that limits its extension and defines its legitimate scope. Based on the remarks in the last two chapters, it seems evident that *public opinion* is the force that stands as a counterweight to the entrepreneur in contemporary corporate governance. By *public opinion* we mean the manifestation via the media of communication of the collective sentiment of broader society that, in the final analysis, establishes what is and what is not acceptable for the governed. Not coincidentally, as Tocqueville showed many years ago in his observations of America's young democracy, the manifestation of public opinion as the criterion of justification for 'good practices' is a characteristic of a democratic regime.[28]

As a counterweight, public opinion represents the opinions and interests of individuals, not as shareholders, but as citizens of the societies in which corporations operate. Public opinion bears witness for the entirety of rules, habits, and general sentiments that determine what is fair or unfair: for example, child labour in multinationals, a variety of environmental concerns, and the question of executive compensation have all been the subject of public discussions that go beyond even the very vast circle of shareholders. What is new here is that public opinion is no longer simply a contextual constraint for corporations, but a counterweight that exercises influence on corporate governance and can lead to director resignations, strategic redirections towards more or less nationalistic interests, or steps to protect the environment that otherwise would not have been considered or emphasized by shareholders.

The mechanism by which the counterweight of public opinion works its influence derives directly from the growth of the shareholding body to great mass. We observe multiple interactions among the mass of consumers, the mass of shareholders, and the mass of citizens in a society. The economy as a whole, and more particularly the businesses of the largest corporations, can no longer be separated into distinct population groups – consumers, owners, workers, etc. Today, more and more, the same actors indifferently assume all of these functions. With mass shareholding, one and the same individual is likely to be an employee of a corporation, a consumer of its products, and an owner of its capital. The dilution of the capital base of corporations has had the effect of enlarging the circle of discussion on the corporation to the whole of society in which citizens are also shareholders.

The effects of this evolution are to be found less in a collective consciousness of the new situation than in the complex, systemic risks that public opinion can imply for the life of a corporation. Thus, the public sentiment of injustice with regard to executive compensation, or immoral conduct, or lack of respect for human rights, can

---

[28] Tocqueville, of course, was well aware that public opinion is a double-edged sword. Cf. Tocqueville, *DA* I, 1, 9 and 10 on the positive power of public opinion as evidenced in the freedom of the press and the freedom of political association (necessary elements of a functioning democracy) and Chapter 12 on the dangers of public opinion when manifested as the tyranny of the majority.

crystallize into negative reactions towards a particular corporation, brand, or product. In this way, questions of corporate governance can have an effect on a corporation's image and thereby also enter into the financial evaluation. This is a state of affairs that cannot be ignored by investors or by shareowners. They have to integrate this dimension into their calculations and have to reckon with it, anticipating the effect that a negative move in public opinion can have on the businesses of the corporation and, hence, on the share price. The counterweight of public opinion, so familiar to us in other fields of Western society such as politics or social affairs, has now also become a force in shaping the equilibrium of post-managerial corporate governance. Two major indicators reinforce this conclusion: first, the increasing degree to which corporate governance has become a subject of the media, and, second, the pedagogical role of 'scandals' in the evolution of corporate governance.

The functions of corporate governance become a favourite subject of the media

One of the most spectacular aspects of contemporary corporate governance must surely be the amount of media attention devoted to what was once considered a dry subject of interest only to a few specialists. The different actors on today's corporate governance stage – investors, shareowners, management, board members, regulators, and sundry experts – all receive an unprecedented amount of media coverage. Even if the techniques of finance and the questions of law involved are complex and tend towards increasing complexity, the actors concerned no longer exercise their functions in secrecy, in the sole company of a *happy few* specialists. Newspapers, television programmes, web sites, all devote an increasing amount of space to issues related to corporate governance.[29] Thus, almost every daily newspaper has a section devoted to the financial markets and comments on the results of the major corporations. An ideology of 'investment for everybody' that vaunts the advantages of universal access to share ownership seems to have taken hold. Clearly this ideology also has a demagogical

---

[29] For a particularly insightful discussion of the role of the financial press in the functioning of contemporary financial markets, see J. Pixley, *Emotions in Finance: Distrust and Uncertainty in Global Markets*, Cambridge: Cambridge University Press, 2004, especially Ch. 3.

side to it, but we will not enter into this discussion here. What is important for our thesis is to point out that once the functions of investor and shareowner are presented as open and available to all, they become part of the domain of public opinion.

While investors today receive regular coverage in the pages devoted to the stock market, shareowners often come in for special treatment when on to a 'big case'. Notable proxy battles at the largest corporations have taken on the importance of major political elections in recent years: for example at HP in the USA (in 2002 over the merger with Compaq), at Eurotunnel in France (in 2004 over the proposals to dismiss senior executives and renew the board), at GlaxoSmithKline in the United Kingdom (in 2003 over executive pay), or at Nestlé in Switzerland (in 2006 over the proposal to combine the CEO and Chairman positions in one and the same individual). These battles and others like them have made the public increasingly aware of the AGM's role in supporting or disavowing managements and strategies. Here again, the media have acted as catalysts, and the topic of 'corporate governance' is now considered to be of general, not just specialized interest.

Certain themes, such as executive compensation and the defence of the national interest in takeover battles, come back again and again. What was once considered to be a secret of business is now the subject of public approval or disapproval and takes on a political dimension; the fairness of the compensation systems of large corporations is seen as an important topic in society, not primarily because large compensation packages seriously diminish corporate profits (although there have been such cases), but because they symbolize in the public eye an unacceptable hierarchy of wealth between executives and employees. It is in this sense that the topic is political and appeals to public opinion. Also for political reasons, the defence of national interests by corporations that have become global has become an important topic for discussion and the application of pressure through public opinion. Examples abound: the purchase of the German Mannesmann by the English Vodafone; the integration of the American Chrysler into the German Daimler; more recently the battle over the European Arcelor and its final purchase by Mittal, or the defensive alliance between the French infrastructure giants GDF and Suez. Each one of these cases has generated considerable *political* debate, publicly carried out in the countries concerned. These debates go beyond the pecuniary interests of shareholders and pose questions about the independence of nations and the defence of specific economic sectors – questions that are further complicated by the fact that shareholders are in many cases also citizens of the countries concerned. Beyond the commonplaces and the populist excesses of some of these debates, it is important to appreciate that the attention given by the media contributes to structuring public opinion and reinforces the perception of a cleavage between shareholder rights and management obligations. Significantly, it is as a consequence of these developments that the CEO finds himself/herself a public figure.

The pedagogy of scandal

It is quite clear that many of the major legal and regulatory modifications to corporate governance in the post-managerial era have come on the heels of scandals. Thus, the fraudulent collapse of Maxwell motivated the Cadbury Commission's broader inquiry and recommendations (1992); the French law on stock options owes a lot to the controversy surrounding Michelin's simultaneous announcement of record profits and substantial layoffs (1999); Enron and Worldcom provided the fertile ground on which Sarbanes-Oxley could take root (2002); and the implication of employee board representatives in corruption at Volkswagen (2005) has led to a general re-examination of the inner workings of the supervisory board, and especially the position of employee representatives, in German corporations. A systematic analysis of the corporate governance rules put in place in response to public scandals shows that the logic of the rules is strongly influenced by the negative effect of dishonest or unseemly corporate behaviour on public opinion.

This relationship provides support for the argument we wish to make here. The events listed in the previous paragraph are less interesting economically than politically; as *scandals*, they are evidence that certain phenomena have a social importance that far outstrips their objective economic impact. Indeed, scandals function as a barometer for the evolution of corporate governance, indicating the degree to which public opinion counts and, by becoming 'scandalized', can generate changes in corporate practices. In other words, such scandals are not simply accidents or contingent elements of history. Rather, they are a manifestation of the role played by public opinion as a symbolic but effective counterweight in contemporary corporate governance. Rules or codes that may appear unnecessarily severe, such as Sarbanes-Oxley, are a response to public opinion. Thus, because certain behaviours are presented and appreciated *as scandals*, they actually contribute to the development of a new model of governance in which public opinion is of paramount importance. Relayed and amplified by the media in the manner we have described, scandals are evidence that public opinion has become an arbiter of what constitutes correct practice and effectively puts boundaries around what is and is not acceptable in corporate governance. As a consequence, the threat of a scandal and its effects acts as a new source of discipline on the different actors in corporate governance. Executives, for example, can be removed from office, if the board has reason to believe that publication of their behaviour might lead to a public scandal that can hurt the corporation, as demonstrated in 2006, in the case of Antoine Zacharias, president of Vinci, the world leader in construction, who was forced to resign from his post following a brief, but intense press campaign. The compensation legally awarded to him by the board appeared *unjustified*, not so much to shareholders, but to public opinion.

In public governance, the scandal plays a similar role to the roles played by bankruptcy under familial governance and the strike under managerial governance, marking an open rupture between power and the counterweight to power. Bankruptcy publicly revealed the director's inability to ensure the survival of the family business, his failure to provide for the extended family; the strike symbolized a break between the economic and social spheres and was typically accompanied by dramatic conflict; the scandal, in turn, appears today to put governance problems between power and counterweight to power on display. The scandal is a symbolic indicator of the counterweight public opinion can bring to bear on the corporation.

In sum, the advent of mass shareholdings and the wide dispersion of ownership have had the effect of broadening the horizon of the corporation. The multiplicity of interests and expectations, and the actions of innumerable investors and a variety of different shareowners, have made the preoccupations of society as a whole enter into the corporation and become corporate preoccupations. Public opinion, with its variations and its capacities for judgement becomes an integral part of the new governance context, the counterweight to entrepreneurial force. In our view, it is not an accident that the themes of responsibility and sustainability, once limited to narrow special interest groups, take on greater importance over the same time that the shareholding body is growing to great mass.[30] These themes echo the preoccupations of a much larger shareholding body, and, beyond that, of public opinion that has come to consider political and social issues of this kind as questions that must also concern corporations. We can therefore say that more and more of the largest corporations cannot be considered as 'private property' anymore and today, perhaps better than ever, truly deserve to be called *public companies*.

3 Synthesis: public governance in the context of liberal society

From the preceding analysis, we can derive the essential characteristics of corporate governance in a post-managerial world, a model of governance we call public governance. In our estimation, the model of public governance is already quite well established in the largest quoted corporations and is in the process of spreading much more broadly in each of the four countries under study in this book (see Figure 2).

The point of departure for this model is a phenomenon radically new to capitalism, namely the shareholding body of great mass and the resultant fragmentation of ownership. The growth of the shareholding body to great mass leads to a multiplication of owners and generates two different types of behaviour: investors, who valorize the corporation from the point of view of their portfolio, and shareowners, who valorize the corporation by participating directly in its control. The entrepreneurial function is performed by the mechanism of the financial markets, in the case of the investor, or by the direct participation in the corporation's bodies of deliberation, in the case of the shareowner. The fact that the ownership *of capital* plays the role of the entrepreneur in both settings represents a historical first.

Nevertheless, according to the type of ownership, the exercise of the entrepreneurial function takes different *forms*. We can speak of *investor driven* corporations and *shareowner driven* corporations. In the first setting, the development of the corporation occurs by the game of natural selection of strategic options as performed by the financial

---

[30] For a complementary view that stresses the societal dynamics behind the growth of socially responsible investment, see L. McCann, A. Solomon, and J. F. Solomon, 'Explaining the growth in UK socially responsible investment', *Journal of General Management* 28 (4) (2003), 15–36.

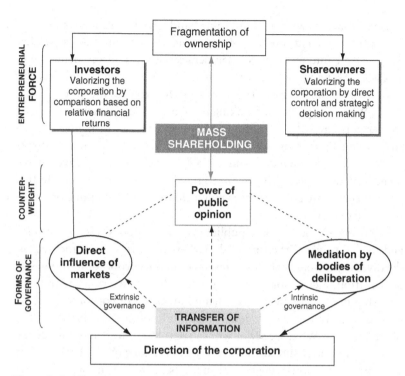

Figure 2 Public governance: two forms for a single model

markets; in the second setting, development of the corporation is the product of voluntary adaptation to the intentions and proposals of active shareowners. In both settings, the entrepreneurial function has *departed* the corporation and is exercised by actors who do not *necessarily* have any particular function within the firm. Entrepreneur and the management are separate; beyond differences of form, this is the defining characteristic of public governance.

Information plays a critical role in this new model, because it provides the means for aligning the production process with the expectations of shareholders who are not inside the corporation. This leads to a new chapter in the *de-privatization* of the corporation and in the socialization of capitalism, that is to say the degree to which capitalism and society overlap. The different interests of multiple shareholders are made to converge in a process of representing and indeed acting out the differences, by the kinds of debate and decision-making process that are typical of the democratic technique of governance. When the financial markets with their 'invisible hand' provide the mechanism for joining the different interests of shareholders, one can draw a parallel with the technique of direct democracy; as in a direct democracy, investors exchange information, make up their minds, and vote by buying or selling shares. The result of this vote is the price of the share. When the process of making the shareholders' different interests converge is carried out in the corporation's bodies of deliberation – AGM, board, shareholder assembly – the differences among shareholders are intermediated and indeed represented by active shareowners whose voices give weight to the differences of opinion. In this setting, corporate governance is much closer to the technique of representative democracy.

Whatever shape or form public governance takes, either extrinsic and turned towards the financial markets or intrinsic and focused on the diversity of shareholder interests within the corporation's bodies of deliberation, a common logic is at work. Public governance implies a new step in the direction of the democratization of corporate governance in the context of the ideological and political evolution of the liberal project. What we see at work here is modern society's tendency to fragment and assure the legitimacy of decisions on the basis of that same fragmentation – whether by markets or by institutions, the technique of democracy gives fragmented property ownership the means to exercise the entrepreneurial force. In effect, property ownership replaces the managerial technocracy, and the techniques of democracy provide the basis for aggregating fragmented, divergent interests. As so many times before in the history of the liberal project, the Leviathan is conquered by the division of individual interests.

In perfect agreement with the logic of liberal thought, the transfer of information that serves the power of ownership also serves the counterweight exercised by public opinion. By its representations (i.e. media) and by its judgements, public opinion puts pressure on corporate governance and needs to be taken into account; investors have to worry about the effect of public opinion on the value of shares, and shareowners have to be concerned about public opinion as it relates to the actions they take in specific corporations. The importance of public opinion is a natural corollary of this new chapter in the democratization of corporate governance. It provides the final link in a new model of governance that arises out of mass ownership and is regulated by the opinion of the masses.

Conclusion to Part II

Corporate governance has changed considerably over two centuries, co-evolving with the transformation of the entrepreneur and the spread of democracy. However, the underlying dialectic opposition for legitimacy between the entrepreneurial force and the liberal fragmentation of society has not changed. The resulting dynamic interplay of forces helps explain the unity of the questions asked and the diversity of responses offered over the history of corporate governance.

With this understanding we can lay to rest one of the most common errors in the field – namely that interest in corporate governance is only of relatively recent vintage, traceable to the 1930s and the work of Berle and Means, or, by some accounts, to the 1980s and the advent of modern finance, or, most preposterously of all, to 2001 and the spate of contemporary corporate scandals. This idea is obviously wrong. Who could reasonably believe that it has taken over two centuries of capitalism before people suddenly began to ask questions about the legitimacy of those who direct corporations? On the contrary, it is clear that these discussions started with the creation of modern enterprise and that criticism questioning the legitimacy of those in power over the corporation has never ceased: diverse political parties of the left and the right, individual lawmakers, philosophers, churches, and business leaders themselves have all at one point in time or another worried about who had the right to direct the corporation, on what basis directors could legitimize their authority, and by which procedures the governing could obtain acceptance from the governed. Every generation likes to think that it is at the start of a new era, and our own generation is no different, pretending to have invented corporate governance. The history that we are living through today is part of a long, dynamic evolution, during which the same difficult questions about what constitutes a just model of corporate governance get posed again by each new generation, according to its context. As we have attempted to show here, the question '*What* gives the right to direct?' can only be satisfactorily answered by referring to the role of the entrepreneur, whoever it may be, within a modern democratic framework that legitimizes the power of the entrepreneur. Our generation has asked the question as it pertains to our context: that of the global corporation with a capital base of great mass. The answers we provide are relevant for our context, and in that sense they represent new answers to what is now a very old, but ageless question.

Dynamics of corporate governance

The historical journey we have undertaken provides evidence of the importance of two different but related oppositions of force in the evolution of corporate governance: opposition, on the one hand, between the entrepreneurial force of direction and the force of social fragmentation; and, on the other hand, between the entrepreneurial force of direction and the external counterweights that limit the entrepreneur. The dynamics of corporate governance arise out of these two oppositions.

The first opposition is a constitutive element of the liberal political project. In a society based on individual liberty, the exercise of entrepreneurial force is necessary in order to bring together private energies, to orient collective action, and, concretely, to give the corporation strategy and direction. As described in Part I, liberalism entrusted private actors, the entrepreneurs, with this mission. In the early days of capitalism, the entrepreneur was the founder and father of the family; in the twentieth century, the function of the entrepreneur was taken over by a group of individuals united by expertise – professional management; today, the function of the entrepreneur in society appears to have devolved to an even larger group, shareholders who are both investors in the financial markets and active shareowners. Of note, the function of the entrepreneur is still private, but as capitalism develops, it is less and less commonly identified with an individual. The function fragments to include multiple actors, supported by technocracy under managerial governance and by the financial markets under public governance. In the name of the same *legitimate rationality* that gave the founder entrepreneur so much power in the early days of capitalism, the entrepreneurs of public governance today follow the logic of the markets in determining the viability of a project and assuring its socio-economic legitimacy. The dynamics of corporate governance cannot be separated from the evolution of the figure of the entrepreneur. As we have seen, the force of social fragmentation, necessary to the liberal political project, acts upon the entrepreneur from the beginnings of capitalism. Every power that might constrain individual liberty is questioned and opposed. This dialectic opposition between entrepreneurial force and social fragmentation is a necessary ingredient for understanding why corporate governance *evolves*.

At each stage in the evolution of corporate governance, the entrepreneurial force of direction finds a counterweight *outside of the corporation*: in the institution of the family for familial governance, then in the union representing social interests for managerial governance, and, finally, in public opinion representing 'the public interest' and taking the shape of media and scandals in what we have called public governance. The juxtaposition of internal power and external counterweight is a recurrent theme in political economy – no power can be defined without defining the limits to power, because, without limits, power is nothing but a constraint. The corporation is a social institution, and, as such, it is society that provides limits and, in so doing, confirms the power of those who direct the corporation. The limits to the acceptable power of the entrepreneur are a function of the cultural, social, and political environments of the corporation. As a consequence, changes in these environments modify the extent and the legitimacy of entrepreneurial power. Each institution acting as a counterweight to the power of the entrepreneur at a particular stage of history has its own place in the liberal political project and is an adjunct to the extension of capitalism and the growth of the corporation. The family acts as a counterweight to the corporation that is locally embedded, the union takes on this role in the large national corporation, and public opinion, borderless, limits the global corporation. Between powers and counterweights acceptable equilibria become established: founder/family; management/union; and shareholders/public opinion. These equilibria between powers and counterweights are maintained by institutions of governance and define models of reference in corporate governance. Thus, we have the familial, managerial, and public models, each with its own context-specific logic of action, legitimacy, and effectiveness.

As Figure 3 below summarizes, the opposition of forces between entrepreneur and social fragmentation defines *who* the actors are with the legitimacy to determine the orientation of the corporation. The opposition between external counterweight and the entrepreneurial

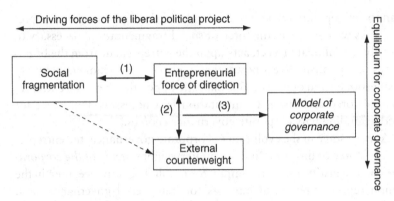

Figure 3 Dynamic model of corporate governance

force of direction defines *how* the function of entrepreneurial direction is exercised in practice, with what kind of control mechanisms and institutional procedures. Out of this double opposition, emerges the model of reference for corporate governance, a model that, at any given point in history represents an acceptable and efficient *equilibrium* among these forces.

The structures of corporate governance tend to become democratized over time

As a result of the dynamics described and as a consequence of the extension of the liberal political project, we have seen an inexorable democratization of corporate governance. By fragmenting power, the political technique of democracy plays an essential role in assuring the fairness of its exercise. Of course, democracy did not immediately hit corporate governance with full force. Instead, the three principal procedures of democracy have been built into corporate governance in distinct stages, over time: first, equality of rights that permitted and initiated the enfranchisement of the entrepreneur and the emergence of private ownership of the means of production; then, separation of powers between owners and management in the large corporation of the early twentieth century; and finally, in our time, representation and public debate as a means of giving the shareholding body effective voice in the direction and oversight of the corporation. As a system of governance that has found general use in modern societies, democracy has also, albeit slowly, extended its reach to include corporate governance (see Table 1).

Table 1 *The evolution of corporate governance and the procedures of democracy*

	Model of reference for corporate governance		
	Nineteenth century to 1920s Familial	1920s to 1970s Managerial	1970s to twenty-first century Public
Techniques of democracy			
Economic enfranchisement	Implementation. Creation of rights to ownership independent of social standing.	Reinforcement. Strengthened by law and corporate practice. Public general meetings become standard.	Reinforcement. Strengthened by new rules on the right to vote; protection of minority interests.
Separation of ownership/control	No.	Implementation. Generalization of the limited liability form, with boards and disclosure requirements.	Reinforcement. Increasing board supervision over managers.
Representation with public debate	No.	No.	Implementation. Mass ownership; stakeholder activism.

Distinguishing between property ownership form and corporate governance model

In interpreting Table 1, it is important to emphasize the distinction between governance model and ownership form. Over the last two hundred years, multiple ownership forms (family, partnership, cooperative, government, listed company, etc.) have coexisted, and they will undoubtedly continue to do so in the future. In fact, family-owned firms far outnumber all the other forms put together. However, the model of reference for corporate governance for all these different ownership forms has changed over time. Thus, for example, the family owned firm of today is not governed in the same way as it was in the nineteenth century. Instead, corporate governance in the (larger) family-owned firm of the twenty-first century is likely to integrate separation of ownership and (non-family) professional management, a board of directors including non-family members, a significant amount of disclosure, and an explicit policy for responsiveness to stakeholders. Thus, even though *ownership* may still be in the family, the *model of reference* for corporate governance today can no longer be called familial. Similar remarks can be made about the managerial model: the separation of ownership and control today no longer operates in the same way as in the times of Berle and Means or even as in the first decades after the Second World War; even in those cases in which management is still seen to exercise the essence of power, mentalities, expectations, and rules concerning transparency of information and quality of debate over strategy have changed considerably, in line with the expectations that have given rise to the *public* model of governance. As our historical summary shows, ownership alone does not explain corporate governance choices: the dialectic opposition between entrepreneurial force and social fragmentation in historical context, and the interplay of power and its counterweight in practice, explain why and how apparently similar types of property ownership can give rise to very different corporate governance models over time.

With this background one can understand that although private property has imposed itself in all of the modern Western societies, the corporation has undergone a process of 'de-privatization' over the last two hundred years. In other words, the corporation is not considered as an object of private property per se anymore, but rather as an institutional title of support for individual private ownership. These titles are more and more numerous and also more fragmented. Entirely in step with the liberal political project, the entrepreneurial force remains in the private domain. However, whereas the familial model assumed a privatization of both entrepreneurial force and counterweight, reinforced by individual control of capital, later models are marked by increasing distance between private individuals and the exercise of power and counterweight. Management and unions both exercise *collective* forces; this trend to the collective exercise of power is further accentuated under public governance with markets and public opinion. The de-privatization of the corporation does not imply that it regresses to fall under the direction of a communal force (such as the king or the state), in contradiction to the liberal political project. On the contrary, in the spirit of liberal fragmentation, the corporation becomes a collective space that fewer and fewer private individuals can hope to control alone but in which more and more people are collectively implicated. As a paradoxical result, the more developed the liberal project becomes, the more difficult it is to speak of the corporation as a unit of private property identified with a *particular* person. This evolution is perfectly compatible with the democratic spirit of modern Western societies: the individualization of property ownership is an essential corollary of the democratic fragmentation of powers and hence also of the preservation of individual liberties.

The missing link: corporate governance and economic performance

The political and historical treatments we have offered in the first two parts of this book cast new light on a topic that has long been the exclusive preserve of lawyers and economists. The legal structures of corporate governance evolve as a function of the (national or international) political environment and represent an almost inexhaustible variety of regulations and corporate governance forms. It cannot be the ambition of a book such as this to delve into the detail of these local adaptations, and we have therefore tried merely to draw the outlines of the general political context that drives legal considerations as capitalism has evolved. We have described this general context as a historical co-evolution between the directing force of the entrepreneur and the opposing force of social fragmentation, but our framework for analysis is still incomplete, because we have not said anything yet about the connection between economic performance and the evolution of corporate governance. In order to prevent the evolutionary analysis from staying at the purely descriptive level, it is imperative to examine this connection.

Why does a certain model of corporate governance become established, while other forms experience only limited adoption or fall by the wayside? Was the appearance first of managerial governance and then of public governance a simple matter of political constraints, or did the process of evolution follow the logic of increased efficiency? If so, what reasons explain why corporations under one model of governance might outperform corporations under another model? The question of economic performance is critical to understanding why certain forms of corporate governance become established and succeed over others, why at every stage in the evolution of corporate governance it was the large corporations that led the way to a new model, and, finally, why corporations that differ in terms of size, activity, and history also often differ in terms of corporate governance. A comprehensive examination of the definition and evolution of corporate governance cannot avoid or make a purely abstract treatment of the question of the *relative performance* of different governance models: that is why the third part of this book focuses on the economics of corporate governance.

Corporate governance and performance: the contribution of economics

Introduction to Part III

In Part I, we argued that stakeholder acceptance of corporate governance needs to be understood as a part of the broader ideology of
modern democratic society built upon the guarantee of individual
liberty. This ideological context defines what is politically acceptable
in society, both in general, and in the particular case of the corporation.
In Part II, we showed that corporate governance has evolved over the
last two hundred years to reflect both a changing definition of the
entrepreneurial function and an increasing fragmentation of society.
Although the dialectic opposition of power between entrepreneurial
concentration and social fragmentation is integrated in corporate governance models to this day, corporate governance procedures, like
governance procedures more generally, have democratized over time.

Our conclusions from Part I and Part II notwithstanding, it would be
wrong to stop at this point and conclude that corporate governance is
nothing more than a special case of political governance in modern
society. The corporation is a political space, but it is also, and above all,
an *economic* space. The political and indeed the broader social legitimacy of the corporation are substantially tied to its ability to create
wealth for society. After all, the corporation's objectives are not to
assure the peace (like the state) or to nourish spiritual well-being (like a
church). As a form of organization, the corporation will only be
accepted by society for as long as it produces wealth for the collective.
In Part I, we showed that the defining characteristic of capitalism is the
privatization of the creation of wealth, under the direction of entrepreneurs. Those who submit to corporate governance (shareholders,
employees, and the broader public alike) do so in order to support
the capitalistic way of driving economic progress. No matter how well
governed according to political requirements, the corporation that is
consistently unprofitable will lose its legitimacy. Because *the creation
of wealth is essential to the political existence of the corporation* and
the legitimacy of entrepreneurial direction, the study of corporate

governance has to address economic performance. One cannot separate society's acceptance of the corporation from the specifically economic vocation of this form of organization.

Efficiency matters. How does the entrepreneurial capacity to give direction, counterbalanced by fragmentation, lead to a level of corporate performance that legitimizes the actions of the entrepreneur? The dialectic opposition of entrepreneur and social fragmentation explains the evolution of corporate governance over time, but it does not clarify how the evolution of corporate governance relates to the performance of the corporation or to the economic growth of society. Has the democratization of corporate governance weakened the entrepreneurial force and, consequently, decreased the economic performance of the corporation? Or, on the contrary, does democratization contribute to improving corporate performance and economic progress?

In the third and final part of the book, we will examine the contribution of economics to the study of corporate governance. Consistent with our methodology of building on past research, we will draw extensively on the results this discipline has already provided to characterize the link between governance and performance. In Chapter 7, we will describe and explain the emergence of a pure economic model of corporate governance, a model that translates political liberalism into a strictly economic relationship between the governing and the governed. This pure economic model, formulated in the language of agency theory but based squarely on the liberal theory of property rights, constitutes an analytic body of work that is both formally elegant and analytically rich. Although the pure economic model remains ideologically dominant in academic circles, current developments in corporate governance have proven difficult to integrate. We will address this point in Chapter 8, arguing that, contrary to received wisdom, the economic model is not *too* liberal, but rather not liberal *enough*. In Chapter 9, we will seek to establish an explanatory framework for the link between corporate governance and economic performance, drawing on economic concepts outside of agency theory. This framework will allow us to understand not only why different governance forms persist despite the emergence of new dominant models, but also in what sense the successive fragmentation of power that follows in the wake of democratization is at least theoretically not incompatible with increases in economic performance.

7 | The Pure Economic Model of corporate governance: an analysis

'*What* gives the right to direct a business corporation?' If this question were posed to academic specialists, business people, and policy makers, nine out of ten would probably answer: 'The pursuit of economic efficiency.' After all, the objective of a business corporation is the creation of wealth. The existence of the corporation as a form of governance is justified by the corporation's ability to optimize the use of the resources at its disposal and, ultimately, to maximize profits. If every corporation optimizes its use of resources, the argument goes, society as a whole obtains the maximum benefits as a result. Therefore, it is the pursuit of economic efficiency that provides a strong basis for the presumption of legitimacy for the direction of the corporation.

The line of reasoning we have traced is so widely accepted that it is only rarely spelled out. The shared belief that individual economic successes enhance collective social justice is a major conceptual building block of modern Western society and has permeated liberal thinking for the better part of the last two centuries. At the heart of this shared belief stands the process of entrepreneurial direction. As discussed in Chapter 1, when we refer to the process of entrepreneurial direction, we mean the process whereby utility maximizing entrepreneurs direct their businesses to maximize their own wealth, and, in so doing, contribute to maximizing the wealth of society as a whole. The private action of entrepreneurs leads to a socially desirable outcome. Experts who argue that corporate profits are the ultimate measure of the quality of corporate governance and are therefore not only legitimate, but also desirable, are implicitly (and often explicitly) referring to the process of entrepreneurial direction.

The two hundred years of economic growth that have followed the industrial revolution and the associated ideology of progress have made the link between private property and economic performance appear incontestable. Since the political philosophy of Locke and the historical emancipation of the entrepreneur, liberalism has led to a freeing up of the economy[1] and legitimized the creation of wealth as proof of good governance. The owner entrepreneur is the soul of this construction, because his/her success (or failure) bears witness to his/her personal involvement in economic growth. Criticism of capitalism focuses on the social cost of this kind of economic performance. Even Karl Marx, the most rigorous of its critics, does not attempt to counter what appears to be self-evident, namely the relationship between entrepreneurship and economic performance, but challenges instead the fairness and social cost of economic performance and hence casts doubt on its permanence. For example, the theory of the pauperization of the proletariat shows that the mechanisms of wealth accumulation lead to an unsupportable level of exploitation that, in the long term, threatens the social and also the economic survival of capitalism. In other words, it is not the economic performance of the private entrepreneur that is denounced, but the excesses of performance and, finally, the sustainability of performance.

The evolution of capitalism has seen increasing fragmentation, on the one hand of the original entrepreneur who has given way, first to a managerial system, then to the financial markets in the form of investors and shareowners, and on the other hand of ownership, which has become further and further removed from the daily reality of the corporation. The figure of the owner director combined economic direction and legitimacy based on the ownership of property and thus represented an ideologically perfect synthesis of the driving forces of liberalism – individual responsibility, individual freedom, and economic performance. As this type of entrepreneur has become increasingly rare (in the larger corporations), the modern liberal society faces a considerable challenge: the majority of stakeholders in corporate governance do not work for the corporation and have different, sometimes divergent interests regarding the pursuit of its activity. Given such a variety of interests, what can ensure that corporate governance is compatible with the economic performance of the corporation and hence also politically legitimate?

In order to resist such a radical questioning, twentieth-century theorists have developed a general economic model that aims to establish

[1] K. Polanyi, *The Great Transformation*, New York: Rinehart & Co., 1944. See also M. Granovetter, 'Economic action and social structure: the problem of embeddedness', *American Journal of Sociology* 91 (3) (1985), 481–510.

the legitimacy of corporate governance in the absence of the individual entrepreneur owner. According to this model, the economic calculations of the different parties in the corporate governance system must converge to maximize corporate profits, *as if* the single entrepreneur were still directing the corporation. Consequently, the historical transformations corporate governance has undergone are not seen to modify in any way the initial logic of the liberal political project; in the reasoning of the model, the relationship between the individual interests of stakeholders and the general interest served by economic performance is strictly maintained. The objective of what we will refer to as the *pure economic model* of corporate governance is to reconcile the twentieth-century reality of shareholders who own but do not work for the corporation with entrepreneurial capitalism, as it was originally intended in the liberal political thought of the eighteenth century.

To describe the content of this model and appreciate its power, we will take the seminal work of Berle and Means (1932) as a starting point. Berle and Means' description of the emergence of the large, managerial corporation with a widely dispersed shareholding body marked the beginning of economics' quest to understand the new reality of managerial governance and represented one of the first attempts to reconcile this new reality with the foundations of the liberal doctrine. *The Modern Corporation* presented a political analysis of corporate governance in essentially economic terms – this was its major innovation. The book pointed out a paradox: the size of large corporations invariably leads to an absence of control, and performance can therefore not be ensured by the quality of corporate governance; this makes public regulation a necessity (1). In reaction to this reformulation of the relationship between governance and performance, from the 1960s onwards a core group of economic thinkers developed a purely economic model of corporate governance (PEM). This group constructed a powerful analytical framework, forming a theory of property and a theory of interest adjustment (agency theory) into a coherent whole whose influence on the academic representation and the practical evolution of corporate governance has been considerable (2).[2] We will show in the conclusion of this chapter that the current of thinking represented by the PEM can be traced back to the

---

[2] Cf. Chapter 5.

foundational principles of liberalism; its appellation as neo-liberal is therefore entirely justified.

1 The paradox of Berle and Means

First published in 1932, *The Modern Corporation and Private Property* has had and continues to have an enormous influence on the analysis of corporate governance, not only in the United States but also around the world. Co-authored by a legal scholar, Adolf Berle, and an economist, Gardiner Means, this book is without a doubt the most frequently cited work in the field.[3] Interestingly, Berle and Means were not the first nor even the most intellectually innovative scholars of their era to have developed an analysis of the new managerial corporation. From the beginning of the twentieth century, in fact, a number of important authors focused on the emergence of a novel type of capitalism in which the owners no longer retained full powers of direction and professional management ran the corporation according to technocratic principles. Writers such as Walter Rathenau (1918) and Thorstein Veblen (1923) or Karl Polanyi (1944) viewed these developments positively, putting faith in the capacity of management experts to direct the corporation in a rational manner. Others, such as Walter Lippman (1914), Thomas Carver (1925), William Ripley (1927), and Maurice Wormser (1931), on the other hand, worried that the separation of capital and entrepreneurial risk-taking represented a fundamental change in the philosophy of capitalism. These reflections on the emergence of the managerial corporation were not limited to the United States, but occurred in Europe as well, where commentators like Ripert in France or Chandler in the United Kingdom also recognized the significance of the separation of ownership and control, as it began emerging in their countries.

In the context of the financial market excesses of the late 1920s and the Great Depression which followed the Crash of 1929 in so many countries, the efficiency and hence also the social legitimacy of capitalism came under intense scrutiny. The greed of financiers and the

---

[3] According to Moore's review in the early 1980s, *The Modern Corporation*, was the sixth most frequently cited work in all of economics, after Keynes, Schumpeter, Morgenstern and Neuman, Hicks and Pigou. T. Moore, 'Introduction', *Journal of Law and Economics* 26 (April, 1983).

mismanagement of industrialists were widely blamed for the economic collapse.[4] Large swathes of public opinion rebelled against the system in place and its representatives, with industrial strikes, social unrest, political instability, mounting protectionism, and the rise of communism on both sides of the Atlantic.

In a situation of general political crisis, many questioned whether the publicly listed corporation, apparently held hostage by greedy financiers and incompetent management, should be allowed to continue to play such an important role in the economy. Around Europe, and even in the United States, the influence of the new Soviet model was felt, and the policy of nationalizing the largest corporations found numerous advocates. The large, managerial corporation appeared to be a new Frankenstein,[5] out of control and apparently beyond control. Such was the context in which *The Modern Corporation* burst on the scene and made its mark.

The qualities of The Modern Corporation

The work of Berle and Means has a number of intrinsic qualities that differentiate it from that of their contemporaries and help explain its lasting impact. First of all, Berle and Means establish a rigorous thesis. They show that the growth in size of major American corporations since the 1890s was accompanied by a change in the capital base; their capital base had grown, split into many parts, and dispersed widely. The new owners of corporations' capital were both far more numerous and much smaller in size than before. As a consequence of this change in the nature of ownership, owners were no longer readily able to exercise the original ownership function of directing or at least guiding the corporation. The fundamental thesis of Berle and Means is that

---

[4] In France, for example, the so-called 'deux cents familles' (two hundred families) that owned the Bank of France at the time (on the Lloyd's of London model) came in for repeated denunciations in the 1930s, representing in the public eye all that was wrong with a capitalism controlled by greedy shareholders. Elsewhere in Europe, and in particular in Germany, a similar way of thinking directed criticism at the Jewish minority, accused of controlling the world of finance. See also Chapter 5.

[5] *Frankenstein, Incorporated* is the title of I. M. Wormser's book (New York: McGraw-Hill, 1931); the same phrase appears as a chapter title in a book by the French scholar Ripert (G. Ripert, *Aspects juridiques du capitalisme moderne*, Paris: LGDJ, 1945).

large, public corporations are characterized by an increasing separation of the ownership of property from the control of property. As corporations grow in size and the number of owner directors declines, ownership tends to become passive, in other words without real influence on management, and a class of professional managers emerges to exercise the function of control. The tight link drawn between general economic developments and specific changes in the nature of ownership is what gives the argument of Berle and Means its unique force.

The second outstanding quality of the work of Berle and Means is the strong empirical grounding – every point of the argument is carefully supported with statistical evidence, and numerous examples from American economic history provide contextual richness. The empirical grounding of the work was contributed by the economist, Means, and it is the emphasis on evidence that ensures the durable impact of *The Modern Corporation*. Unlike other authors of their era who present a similar thesis (e.g. Wormser, 1931) or articulate the implications of the managerial revolution (e.g. Burnham, 1941, 1943), Berle and Means are not content with assertion and criticism;[6] in the institutionalist tradition, they accumulate documentation and provide what we today appreciate as hard data. Perhaps just as important to their method is the use of a measured, scientific tone of discourse. Rather than denouncing the failings of the system, as so many of their contemporaries chose to do during the crisis of the 1930s, Berle and Means offered a straightforward exposé of the facts. The question of tone is not merely of academic interest. Although the question of what constitutes 'good' corporate governance had already been discussed long before the 1930s, the work of Berle and Means inaugurated a new way of addressing the topic – an approach based on the logic and methodology of economics. By focusing on economic evidence and presenting this evidence in the apparently value-neutral language of economics, Berle and Means opened the door for generations of scholars to address ideological questions of corporate governance and indeed capitalism

---

[6] Building on the same thesis as Berle and Means, but taking it to radical conclusions, James Burnham (1905–87) published two bestsellers: *The Managerial Revolution: What Is Happening in the World* (Bloomington and Indiana: Indiana University Press, 1941) and *Machiavellians: Defenders of Freedom* (New York: John Day, 1943), books that denounced all colours of the technocratic rise to power – capitalist, communist, or fascist.

itself not in moral or social terms, as until then established practice, but in economic terms.

An economic approach to the study of corporate governance

Berle and Means point out that the characteristics of the capital base of the large, public corporation make it very difficult to exercise one of the original functions of ownership, the function of control. In the historical case, where the owner was also the director of the corporation, he/she controlled the corporation and maximized its profits of personal necessity: the profits of the owner and the profits of the corporation were one and the same. This is the process of entrepreneurial direction, as described earlier, and Berle and Means consider this basic process as a point of reference in thinking through the question of whether or not the large, public corporation fulfils its social function – maximizing profits.

Where the individual owner holds only a small percentage of the corporation's capital, however, he/she will not be a director and will not be able to exercise his/her sovereign right of control. Berle and Means argue that, under these conditions, the profits of the owner and the profits of the corporation do not coincide and corporate profit maximization can no longer be assured. Like their contemporaries, Berle and Means too diagnose a crisis in capitalism, but instead of framing the analysis in terms of social justice like the socialists or the institutional theorists (e.g. Veblen) they change the terms of the argument by framing the analysis of capitalism and corporate governance in terms of *performance*. This is the major contribution of *The Modern Corporation*: in the case of the large corporation with a diluted capital base, corporate governance is first and foremost an *economic* issue.

The separation of ownership and control implies an inability on the part of the owners effectively to check the management of the corporation and threatens economic efficiency. In the logic of Berle and Means, management unchecked will seek to maximize their personal utilities, to the detriment of maximizing corporate profits. This is an essential point in appreciating the originality of their reasoning, because it turns on its head the existing criticism of the large corporation. The essential contrast in Berle and Means is that which opposes the profit maximizing entrepreneur and self-seeking management. Their criticism of the large, public corporation does not blame the economic underperformance of their time on the greed of those who own shares, but rather on the *passivity* of the shareholding body and its failure to check management. Managerial self-seeking has no counter-weight.[7] If the economy as a whole is not doing well (as was the case in the 1930s), this is not because of an *excess* of capitalism, as so many people at the time argued, but because of a *lack* of capitalism when ownership no longer exercises its role of ensuring profit maximization. Unlike radical and anti-capitalist critics of the system, Berle and Means do not reject the process of entrepreneurial direction; rather, they draw on the characteristics of this process to expose the new problems created by managerial capitalism.

The dilemma of size: a challenge for liberal (pure market) economics

Framing the analysis of corporate governance in economic terms is not without ambiguities. For the thesis of Berle and Means poses an essen-tial dilemma: on the one hand, growth and size are necessary for achieving economies of scale and thereby increasing efficiency; on the other hand, growth and size lead to an enlarged, dispersed capital base with passive ownership, diminished pressure for profit maximization, and hence declining efficiency. In other words, size has conflicting effects on economic efficiency, and difficulty arises from the fact that the entrepreneurial function has been split between two parties (manage-ment and shareholders) that do not necessarily have identical interests.

How can this dilemma be resolved? Without a single, legitimate entrepreneur, is capitalism condemned to sub-optimal performance? For Berle and Means, the developments described are irreversible; there can be no return to the small company and the owner director of the nineteenth century, no reunion of ownership and control. History does not move backwards, and mass production as incarnated in the large corporation has become a necessary ingredient of economic perfor-mance. The gains of returning to the previous owner director form of corporate governance would be lost in reduced economies of scale. In

---

[7] It is remarkable to note that Berle and Means never once in *The Modern Corporation* mention the question of unions and their capacity to act as a veritable counterweight to management, in spite of historical evidence to this effect (cf. Chapter 4).

other words, owners cannot hope to regain all of their original entrepreneurial power.

The worst solution to the dilemma, according to Berle and Means,
would be to put all of this power in the hands of management. As
institutionalists themselves, the authors do recognize that management
possesses indispensable expertise and needs a certain amount of power
to run the corporation. On the other hand, they are sure that management, if left to its own devices, will not maximize corporate profit in
the manner of the entrepreneur owner. Just as disconcerting for Berle
and Means, the importance of management deprives the owner of control over private property. Nevertheless, the authors believe that institutions can help reduce the negative effects of managerialism and alleviate
the large, public corporation's problem of sub-optimality.[8] Between
'strict property rights' and 'a set of uncurbed powers in the hands of
control' (p. 311), they propose a median way that would give those who
control the corporation a mission to work for the general good:

The control groups have, rather, cleared the way for claims of a group far
wider than either the owners or control. They have placed the community in a
position to demand that modern corporations serve not alone the owners or
the control but all the society ... should the corporate leaders, for example,
set forth a program comprising fair wages, security to employees, reasonable
service to their public, and stabilization of business, all of which would divert
a portion of the profits from the owners of passive property ... courts would
almost of necessity be forced to recognize the result, justifying it by whatever
of the many legal theory they might choose. (p. 312)

This visionary median way supposes that the 'control groups' address
the conflicts of interest between the different parties to corporate governance and work to seek satisfactory solutions that can gain broad-
based support. In what is a very political conclusion to an economic
analysis, Berle and Means posit economic actors as coordinators of
multiple interests for the good of society as a whole. It is not insignificant
that the authors recognize the courts of justice (cf. p. 312, supra) as the
ultimate arbitrators of the legitimacy of a corporation that is to maximize not shareholder profits but the general interest. In other words, in
the final instance, the corporation and its governance should be evaluated by a public institution and not by the owners or the markets.

---

[8] All citations of *The Modern Corporation* are drawn from the 1968 edition,
London: Transaction Publishers.

Although it offers only the outline of a resolution to the central management–shareholder problematic raised in the book, the conclusion of *The Modern Corporation* clearly calls for the protection of those parties who are disadvantaged or at risk in the new world they describe and, even more significantly, suggests that influential players in corporate governance develop a higher or more noble conception of their responsibility to serve the 'paramount interests of the community' (p. 312, supra). 'It is conceivable, – indeed it seems almost essential if the corporate system is to survive – that the "control" of the great corporations should develop into a purely neutral technocracy, balancing a variety of claims by various groups in the community and assigning to each a portion of the income stream on the basis of public policy rather than private cupidity' (pp. 312–13).

Again, Berle and Means do not want to leave corporate governance up to the purely individualistic logic of economics. The vague term 'neutral technocracy' is another attempt to bring institutions and the public interest into play. And yet, the righteousness of the authors' intentions cannot mask the fact that the conclusion remains rather vague. The thrust of the conclusion appears to be in conflict with the reasoning developed in *The Modern Corporation*: whereas the argument of the book is based on the confrontation of private interests, namely those of shareholders and management, the conclusion calls for virtuous behaviour on the part of managers. Of course, this does not occur by accident – Berle and Means are fundamentally critical of liberal society and draw heavily on the American institutionalist tradition (see below and note 12). If Berle and Means' book can be reasonably faulted from today's vantage point, it is in this: the economic analysis of the issues arising from the split between management and shareholders is much more powerful than the attempted institutionalist resolution.

However problematic, this lack of rigour in the final analysis is also an indicator of the coherence of Berle and Means' conclusions with their approach to corporate governance. That approach is based on considerations of economic efficiency, but they are convinced that economic efficiency cannot be attained by the pure play of market forces alone. In the absence of shareholder action, they argue, politics has to propose rules of control. Democrats of the New Deal, Berle and Means believe in the need to support market forces with political intervention. It is up to public regulation, in the final instance, to provide a basis for entrepreneurial direction. Their concluding argument is consistent with the policies of Roosevelt and the economics of Keynes. In fact, *The Modern Corporation* has been called the 'Economic Bible' of the New Deal.[9] Although finally political, their analysis is firmly anchored in economic reasoning and has had a much stronger long-term impact on scholarship than on policy making. Nevertheless, we should not lose sight of the fact that, with the paradox of the modern corporation, Berle and Means posed a major problem to liberal thought; the profundity of the problem is what led to the opening of a new way of theorizing about corporate governance.

2 Reaction to Berle and Means: a Pure Economic Model of corporate governance

Berle and Means formulate corporate governance as an economic question; as a direct result of their work, corporate governance becomes a central topic in the field of economics. For economics, the integration of corporate governance marks an important step in its path to ideological dominance of the social sciences and strengthens its hold on the regulation of society. However, the apparent victory of economics due to Berle and Means contains an important irony. For the authors, the market mechanisms that economics champions are not sufficient to regulate properly the challenges raised by the separation of ownership and control. On the contrary, Berle and Means argue for public intervention and institutional regulations (laws, codes, etc.) to limit the powers of control.

The conclusions offered by Berle and Means are not to the liking of the defenders of liberal thought who believe that markets in which individual interests can freely clash and play out ensure a sufficient level of self-regulation in the system. Those who hearken back to the process of entrepreneurial direction and would therefore base the

[9] *Time* Magazine, 24 April 1933. Berle was a member of the Roosevelt Administration and contributed to two major new pieces of legislation, the Security Act of 1933 and the Security Exchange Act of 1934, both of which put limits on managerial discretion. Means continued his career as an institutional economist, publishing work on the administration of price controls from 1935 onwards. See, Gardiner C. Means, 'Industrial prices and their relative inflexibility', S.Doc. 13, 74 Congress 1 Session Washington, DC: Government Printing Office, 1935.

legitimacy of good governance exclusively on economic performance are equally disturbed by the paradox of *The Modern Corporation*. In other words, while they endorse the authors' pioneering economic analysis of corporate governance, the majority of the economists who follow in the footsteps of Berle and Means cannot accept their conclusions.

Instead, over the fifty years which follow the original publication of *The Modern Corporation* a systematic body of economic work develops to address the challenge of overcoming the inherent inefficiency of separating ownership and control by relying only on market forces, that is to say *without political or institutional regulation*. The objective of this research has been to return to the roots of the liberal tradition and found a 'pure' theory of corporate governance, that is to say a theory that is 'purified' of the need for any kind of public intervention and is focused solely on profit maximization.

This body of work, ideologically dominant in the discipline of economics from the 1970s onward, is built on two theoretical foundations – a theory of the economic function of property rights and a theory of the relationship between the owner of property rights and his agent, the management who makes use of those rights in the owner's name.[10] Let us examine how these two theories allow economists to overcome the dilemma of Berle and Means and establish a pure economic model (PEM) of corporate governance.

Private property: foundations of an economic theory of governance

The first step in resolving the dilemma posed by Berle and Means consists of articulating the precise content of property rights. In fact, Berle and Means themselves do not specify what exactly ownership of

---

[10] In the economic theory of property rights, the seminal works are those of S. N. S. Cheung, 'Transaction costs, risk aversion and the choice of contractual arrangements', *Journal of Law and Economics* 12 (1) (1969), 23–42; H. Demsetz, 'Some aspects of property rights', *Journal of Law and Economics* 9 (October) (1966), 61–70; H. Demsetz, 'Toward a theory of property rights', *American Economic Review* 57 (2) (1967), 347–59; A. A. Alchian and H. Demsetz, 'The property right paradigm', *Journal of Economic History* 33 (1973), 16–27; E. Furubotn and S. Pejovich, *The Economics of Property Rights*, Cambridge, MA: Ballinger Publishing, 1974; H. Demsetz, 'The structure of ownership and the theory of the firm', *Journal of Law and Economics* 26 (2) (1983), 375–90.

shares gives rights to. Recall that private property has three dimensions: *usus, fructus,* and *abusus* (see Part I). The formal articulation of property rights reveals what Berle and Means do not see, or at least do not state clearly: the advent of the modern corporation does not completely change the nature of ownership; rather, it merely alters one of its dimensions, namely the dimension of *usus*. Although shareholders do not exercise the right of control in the modern corporation, they still exercise the rights of *fructus* and *abusus*. In other words, shareholders still benefit from profits as remuneration for their ownership (*fructus*), and still can buy and sell shares (*abusus*), as they please. The emergence of passive ownership does not represent as radical a change in the nature of ownership as Berle and Means would have us believe. Certainly, shareholders no longer exercise *usus* in the manner of the classical owner director *directly* to orient the corporation towards profit maximization, but they are not without the means of action – shareholders can *indirectly* act to maximize corporate profits.[11]

The second step in reinventing the role of shareholders is to show how their indirect action to maximize corporate profits is motivated. Does capitalism really need shareholders as a separate class? If they do nothing more than supply capital, like a financier or a bank, it is not clear in what sense shareholders have a socially useful and hence legitimate right to property over the corporation. Indeed, an influential current of thinking in Europe and America has argued that the very existence of shareholders remunerated by profits was unjust (why should shareholders be treated any differently from traditional savers?) and joined Keynes in demanding the '*euthanasia of the rentiers*' (by inflation).[12] By resurrecting the age-old notion of *residual claims*, the

---

[11] Pure market economists do not draw a distinction between portfolio oriented investors and shareowners focused on individual corporations (see Part II). In the pure economic formulation of the problem, shareholders are all alike, and we will adhere to this simplification in discussing the PEM, speaking only in the general terms of shareholders and share-holding. As we have already seen, and the following pages will deepen the argument, this is a non-trivial simplification with wide-ranging consequences for both theory and practice.

[12] J. M. Keynes, *The General Theory of Employment Interest and Money*, Cambridge: Macmillan and Cambridge University Press, 1935, chapter 26, II. This approach finds support in the United States from institutionalists like Veblen and, later, radicals like Marglin. It is more explicitly inspired by Marxism in Europe. On both sides of the Atlantic, the critique is characterized by a negative view of financial markets and speculative shareholding.

theory of property rights as developed by economics turns this argument on its head and hypothesizes a unique position for shareholders. Shareholders, unlike all the other suppliers of capital, are only remunerated in case of success, if the corporation makes a profit. As residual claimants in theory, shareholders *resemble* ideal entrepreneurs – they too only become wealthy if the corporation succeeds.

Their hypothesized position as residual claimants forces shareholders to *watch* the business of the corporations they invest in. Shareholders cannot be completely indifferent to the well-being of the corporation, because their remuneration depends on the results obtained by the corporation's management. If they want their property to bear fruit, shareholders are *obliged* to verify that the corporation is well managed. Like any economic actor, shareholders are interested in increasing the utility to be had from their property and hence will seek to maximize its *fructus*. Since they are residual claimants, the maximization of their interests coincides with the maximization of corporate profits. Even though shareholders are not 'entrepreneurs', in the strict sense of the term, they need to act to maximize corporate profits if they want to maximize their own profit. Shareholders can therefore be expected to act *as if* they were entrepreneurs.

Having reinvented the role of the shareholder in the likeness of the entrepreneur, economic theory still needs to show *how* shareholders can act to ensure that management will maximize corporate profits.[13] When the capital base is diluted (or when the capital base is concentrated,

---

[13] It is important to underline that this does not reflect the views of Berle and Means: in their view, the passivity of shareholders excludes them from acting as residual claimants: 'the owners of passive property, by surrendering control and responsibility over the active property, have surrendered the right that the corporation should be operated in their sole interest' (Berle and Means, *The Modern Corporation*, p. 312). For the same reasons, Alchian and Demsetz point out that 'the residual claim on earnings enjoyed by shareholders does not serve the function of enhancing their efficiency as monitors in the general situation. The stockholders are "merely" the less risk-averse or the more optimistic members of the group that finances the firm' (A. A. Alchian and H. Demsetz, 'Production, information costs and economic organization', *American Economic Review* 62 (5) (1972), 777–95, at note 14, p. 789). It is only with the development of agency theory and the work of Jensen and Meckling and of Fama that the shareholder is endowed with the status of residual claimant by the PEM (M. C. Jensen and W. H. Meckling, 'Theory of the firm: managerial behavior, agency costs and ownership structure', *Journal of Financial Economics* 3 (4) (1976), 305–60; E. F. Fama, 'Agency problems and the theory of the firm', *Journal of Political Economy* 88 (2) (1980), 288–307).

but major shareholders are disinterested in management), shareholders do not act directly to keep management in check. The passivity described by Berle and Means is thus a necessary outcome. Economics addresses the question of how shareholders can act by referring to the market for property rights. By the threat of sale and the incentive of purchase, the markets give shareholders the power to exert the force of entrepreneurial direction.

The role of the financial markets

It is fundamental to the reasoning of the PEM that shareholders do not have to hold on to their shares. By definition, the property rights of shareholders include *usus* (although this right is emasculated in the managerial corporation, it still exists in theory), *fructus*, and *abusus*, and hence they are free to buy and sell shares. Financial markets (stock markets) permit these actions; the more developed these markets are, the more precisely the forces of supply and demand are brought to bear on shares of the corporation. The share price then stands for equilibrium: as a function of the expectations and calculations of the shareholders, the prices of the shares of the more profitable corporations will appreciate (and the prices of the shares of less profitable corporations will depreciate). The financial (stock) markets are in fact markets for property rights.

The shareholder can exert real influence on the corporation through the financial markets. By buying and selling shares, shareholders designate those corporations that are more efficient and those that are less efficient, and in so doing they orient the flow of capital. Viewed from this perspective, ownership can only be characterized as passive where the free exercise of the right of *abusus* is restricted – in other words, in those markets where shareholders cannot easily sell their shares. This conceptual result is very significant in relation to the thesis of Berle and Means: to property rights economists, the problem of ownership losing control in the managerial corporation is only really worth considering in those contexts in which shareholders are dispossessed of the right of *abusus* (and *not* in contexts in which owners are only dispossessed of the right of *usus* – the original concern of Berle and Means).

This is why supporters of the PEM of corporate governance insist on the importance of the financial markets. The financial markets are indispensable to reconciling shareholders with entrepreneurial direction, not, *nota bene*, in directly controlling the corporation, but in indirectly influencing the corporation through the valuation given to its plans and activities. Contrary to the expectations of Berle and Means, therefore, a dilution of the capital base need not have a negative effect on economic efficiency in the pure economic model, *as long as* property rights are easily bought and sold in financial markets. By contrast, (national) financial systems that prevent or encumber the free entry and exit of shareholders are castigated as inefficient in the PEM: in poorly developed financial markets, corporations can avoid the indirect control of shareholders and are therefore likely to underperform. In this precise case only, the PEM matches the conclusions of Berle and Means.

It is worth noting that, after the change of focus (from *usus* to *abusus*) achieved by the PEM, the dilemma of Berle and Means (passive ownership) applies in particular to those corporations whose capital base is *not* diluted: publicly quoted corporations with large shareholders such as families, financial houses, cooperatives, and states.[14] In practice, a diluted capital base can only come about in the presence of fluid financial markets, and concentration often signifies a financial market that is not fluid. Whereas Berle and Means worry that the dilution of the capital base poses problems, contemporary property rights theorists find that the *absence of dilution* (resulting in illiquid markets) is problematic.[15] The 'lack of capitalism' bemoaned by Berle and Means (see above) is thus transformed into a 'lack of liberalism' by the economists of the PEM.

Economics has built on the original insight of Berle and Means and the theory of property rights to construct a model of corporate governance that apparently resolves the problem of inefficiency Berle and Means saw as an inevitable consequence of a widely dispersed shareholding body. The model consists of four basic elements, with one building on the other: (1) Property rights have three distinct dimensions, *usus*,

---

[14] This restatement of the dilemma has led to numerous studies, see especially E. G. Furubotn and S. Pejovich, 'Property rights and economic theory: a survey of recent literature', *Journal of Economic Literature* 10 (December, 1972), 1137–62.

[15] This inconsistency between Berle and Means and the PEM is often poorly understood, to the point that many have drawn a one to one link between the *dilution* of the capital base and managerialism. See Chapter 4, note 37.

fructus, and *abusus*; (2) the managerial corporation changes the nature of the right of *usus*, but does not change the other rights; (3) the dividend on profits (*fructus*) represents a residual claim on the corporation, and, as residual claimants, shareholders must exercise influence to ensure profit maximization; (4) to the extent that the share is easily bought and sold (right of *abusus* protected), shareholders have an indirect means of directing the corporation: the freer and more liquid the market for property rights, the more strongly shareholders can make their influence felt. The PEM proposes a theory of *indirect control* by shareholders: shareholders are the guarantors of corporate profit maximization. They have the capacity to exercise the entrepreneurial force, and there is no need for external political intervention or institutional regulation, as conjectured by Berle and Means. The economic system can regulate itself – this is the conclusion of the PEM, the pure economic model of corporate governance.

Agency theory: aligning private interests

Our description of the pure economic model of corporate governance (PEM) is still incomplete in one respect: we have not explained how indirect control by shareholders actually has an effect on how management runs corporations. In other words, even if shareholders wanted to maximize their remuneration (*fructus*) by means of financial market pressure (*abusus*), it is not clear why management would respond to this pressure by exercising their function of *usus* in the interests of the shareholders. In practice, management could be indifferent to the share price, as Berle and Means in fact supposed. By contrast, if it could be shown that management has an interest in adjusting its behaviours in order to maximize corporate profits, then the PEM has succeeded in demonstrating that the couple of shareholders and management can have the same beneficial effect on the economy as the original individual owner director and is therefore of equal social legitimacy. If the couple of shareholders and management can in fact work towards a common interest, then the large corporation with a diluted capital base is the most efficient of all forms: incorporating massive economies of scale not available to the individual entrepreneur for the unique, legitimate purpose of corporate profit maximization.

The body of work which describes the ties between managerial behaviour and shareholder profit is called agency theory, or, more generally, theory of incentives in principal–agent relations.[16] Agency theory provides a framework for describing how a principal, P, who owns a property but does not manage it, can ensure that an agent, A, who manages the property but does not own it, works for the maximization of the profit of P. In terms of property rights, we could restate the relationship as a question: how can the owner of the right of *abusus* ensure that the management who has the right of *usus* maximizes the *fructus* of the property? Or, more narrowly, how can the incentive of buying and the threat of selling shares force management to maximize the profit of the corporation? The relationship between agency theory and the theory of property rights is very well articulated in the literature,[17] and together the two theories form a coherent whole that provides a powerful means of analysis. We will not enter into the details of the formal developments made in this area. For our purposes, a demonstration of what agency theory contributes to the PEM and hence to the economic legitimization of corporate governance has to suffice.

For the PEM to prevail as a theory of corporate governance, it is essential that a satisfactory explanation of the behaviour of shareholders and of management can be stated in purely economic terms, without recourse to ethical or moral considerations and independent of political and institutional conditions. For shareholders, the economic calculation is quite straightforward: as residual claimants, they can only maximize their remuneration if the corporation(s) they invest in maximizes its profits. Management, on the other hand, maximizes its personal utilities. The challenge of agency theory in the PEM is to *align* shareholder and management interests. In the extreme case where the manager is *also* the owner, the interests of the manager and the shareholder coincide, and corporate profits will be maximized. This is the original process of entrepreneurial direction, where *usus*, *fructus*, and *abusus* of property rights are perfectly aligned. At the other extreme,

[16] The seminal articles in this line of thinking are those of Jensen and Meckling, 'Theory of the firm'; Fama, 'Agency problems and the theory of the firm'; E. F. Fama and M. C. Jensen, 'Separation of ownership and control', *Journal of Law and Economics* 26 (2), (1983), 301–26; and E. F. Fama and M. C. Jensen, 'Agency problems and residual claims', *Journal of Law and Economics* 26 (2) (1983), 327–50.

[17] See L. de Alessi, 'Property rights, transaction costs and X-efficiency, an essay in economic theory', *American Economic Review* 73 (1) (1983), 64–81.

one can posit the case in which management has no interest whatsoever in maximizing corporate profits, because shareholders have no means of influencing the corporation. In this case, managers can act against the interest of shareholders, choosing strategies that maximize their salaries or ensure social peace or result in unjustified profits for their friends at the expense of creating value.[18] Underperformance is the consequence, *usus* and *abusus* are not aligned, and authority based on ownership has no clear economic legitimacy. This is precisely the case which economists seek to refute.

In the effort to align *usus* and *abusus*, *fructus* assumes the critical linking role. Let I be the maximum economic profit to be achieved by a corporation, and let I_u be the personal gain obtained by management in directing the corporation for the purpose of maximizing their personal utilities; the *fructus* due to shareholders will be $I - I_u$. We note that I_u will never be zero: in the managerial corporation the shareholders inevitably lose a part of the *fructus* to the management. *Ceteris paribus*, the managerial corporation performs less well than the corporation owned by its director.[19] Nonetheless, agency theorists argue that it is an error to stop at this point, as do Berle and Means, and conclude that the managerial corporation tends towards sub-optimization of corporate profits. The real challenge is not to minimize I_u, but to maximize $I - I_u$. Economic logic proposes that the loss of part of the profits to management is not important, if total profits accrue *even if this growth is owed to the fact that managers take out a part for themselves.*

In fact, profits for managers can lead either to a decrease in profits for shareholders, if I is constant and I_u grows, or to an increase in profits for shareholders, if $I - I_u$ grows faster than I_u. It is this second scenario that needs to be encouraged. The critical task, therefore, lies in setting up a system of incentives for the managerial corporation such that management can maximize I_u only if $I - I_u$ is also maximized. Under such a system, management has a personal interest in maximizing the interest of the shareholder, because their interests are aligned. In

---

[18] See A. Shleifer and R. W. Vishny, 'Manager entrenchment: the case of manager specific investment', *Journal of Financial Economics* 52 (1989), 737–83.

[19] Of course, the size of the managerial corporation and the inherent economies of scale allow for a much greater economic profit than would be possible in the small, entrepreneurial firm. In general equilibrium terms, the part of the profit cut off by managers for themselves must be largely compensated by the increase in profit due to size.

setting up such an alignment of interests, the financial markets typically play the major role. The share price provides the bridge between management and shareholders: based on the reasoning that markets are efficient and that the future price of the share will therefore perfectly reflect the profits realized, systems are set up to remunerate management on the basis of the future price of the share (e.g. bonus tied to absolute share price development; bonus tied to sector-relative share price development; stock options; etc.), so as to motivate them to maximize I_u and maximize $I - I_u$.

It is also possible to align the interests of shareholders and management via the market for takeovers (corporate control):[20] by the same reasoning as above and the threat of job loss with a change of ownership (where $I_u \rightarrow 0$, for incumbent management), all restrictions on takeovers (e.g. poison pills, restrictions on non-voting shares, etc.) are removed, so as to motivate management to maintain the highest possible share price and maximize $I - I_u$.

Clearly, the mechanisms described above represent only the tip of the iceberg. Research in agency theory has been particularly creative in the development of instruments for interest alignment, and these developments have had a profound impact on practice. We simply wish to show here that incentive alignment mechanisms and their formal justifications – however sophisticated they have become – rely on very simple reasoning: to ensure that management maximizes corporate profits, management needs to be evaluated in terms of the selective pressure applied by financial markets. The disciplinary dimension of the financial markets is essential to the economic model of corporate governance. It is not possible to count only on the good will, the loyalty, or the sense of honour of the management. Therefore, in the tradition of modern liberal political thought, one has to appeal to individual self-interest. Incentive mechanisms force management to make the 'right choices', in other words choices that maximize corporate profits rather than managerial utility. Thanks to these market-driven incentive mechanisms, shareholders are in a position to check the quality of management.

---

[20] A. Shleifer and R. W. Vishny, 'Takeovers in the '60s and the '80s: evidence and implications', *Strategic Management Journal* 12 (1991), 51–9; G. A. Jarrell, J. A. Brickley, and J. M. Netter, 'The market for corporate control: the empirical evidence since 1980', *Journal of Economic Perspectives* 2 (1988), 49–68.

The economic model represents a perfect circle: on the one hand, the more management increases the profit of the corporation, the better it is able to prove its quality to shareholders, but also the better it serves its own interests by incentive aligned compensation; on the other hand, the higher the profit of the corporation, the more positively shareholders judge the performance of the management, but also the higher the remuneration of shareholders in the form of dividends. In this way, shareholders control not the corporation, but the controller of the corporation. The financial markets become the locus of corporate control, judging the quality of management, choosing strategies, and, in the final analysis, exercising the function of the entrepreneur. As we have shown in Chapter 5, the PEM serves as a very important intellectual and ideological point of reference for the late twentieth-century development of public governance.

3 An economic model of corporate governance in the liberal spirit

Our analysis has shown that it is necessary to differentiate between two stages in the liberal economic effort to take possession of corporate governance. At a first level of emphasis, we find the introduction of economic performance as a criterion for the legitimacy of corporate governance. This thesis gives corporate governance a new framework of evaluation, beyond the political and the ethical: efficiency matters. The more the capital base of the corporation gets diluted and ownership gets separated from control, the greater the necessity to find ways to reconcile the different interests of management and owners so that the corporation will act in a way that furthers the general interest on the basis of the conjunction of individual interests, without the intervention of a Leviathan (public or otherwise), in the spirit of liberalism. This was the challenge Berle and Means launched.

At a second stage in the liberal effort, we find the argument that economic efficiency is the *only* consideration to be taken into account in evidencing the proper functioning and justifying the legitimacy of corporate governance. This is the emphasis of the pure economic model of corporate governance, elaborated to address systematically the economic questions in corporate governance identified by Berle and Means, but resulting in the overturning of their conclusions. This model is *pure* in the sense that it seeks to base the evaluation and the regulation of corporate governance on economic performance alone: *only* efficiency matters.

With the support of developments in agency theory in the 1980s, the pure economic model (PEM) reaches completion. Summarizing the logic of the model, we can say that the PEM succeeds in resolving the dilemma identified by Berle and Means: the large, managerial corporation is *not* synonymous with economic sub-optimization, and political/institutional intervention is *not* necessary. The PEM has built a new structure for corporate governance: (1) by partitioning property rights into the separate dimensions of *usus*, *fructus*, and *abusus*; (2) by describing how shareholders, although deprived of the right of *usus* and direct control in the managerial corporation, can exercise the right of *abusus* (buying and selling shares) to achieve indirect control; and (3) by setting incentive mechanisms that motivate/force management to control the corporation in the interests of maximizing shareholder profits.

The logic of the PEM aligns the three dimensions of property rights towards a single objective: maximization of profits (*fructus*). Maximization of profits makes the link between *usus*, entrusted to management, and *abusus*, the shareholders' means of exercising pressure in their interests. The simple game of profit maximization reunites control and ownership, and the conclusion of Berle and Means is overturned. The PEM's principal contribution is to show that the couple shareholder/management reconstitutes the original figure of the owner director by the disciplinary mechanism of the financial markets. The separation of ownership and management is not inefficient; on the contrary, according to the PEM, the separation of powers between ownership and control is what makes the managerial corporation efficient. Dilution of the capital base makes it possible to allocate considerable resources to the most profitable entrepreneurial projects, to the extent that shareholders are able to use the financial markets to arbitrate between different projects. The economy does not need political or institutional intervention: its internal mechanisms permit self-regulation and the achievement of socially optimal outcomes. In effect, the shareholder is an indirect entrepreneur, a kind of larger than life alter ego of the original founder entrepreneur. In practice, when the corporation becomes too large for ownership and control to be held by the same individual or family, the financial markets perform the entrepreneurial function of ensuring profit maximization. In contrast to the

ambiguous conclusion of Berle and Means, the PEM does not comprehend the evolution of capitalism as leading to a questioning of liberalism and the liberal project; rather, the PEM sees the liberal project
confirmed.

By making private property and individual self-interest central to the
argument, the PEM takes corporate governance back to the origins of
liberal political thinking, to the questions posed in Chapter 1. While
society debates the political regulation of capitalism to overcome the
shortcomings of the modern corporation, economists of the PEM show
that the entrepreneur can in fact still exist, albeit in a different guise
(that of the shareholder), if financial markets are allowed to work
freely. In the ideal, financial markets make rational choices and take
calculated risks that recreate the original conditions for profit maximization. In this way, the financial markets take on the role of the ideal
entrepreneur of liberal thought, and capitalism is reconciled with its
ideological foundations: individual liberty (and the pursuit of private
interests) leads to collective performance (in the general interest).[21]

The PEM represents an outstanding intellectual achievement, with
admirable internal rigour and considerable formal aestheticism. The
model triumphs over academia and practice in the 1990s and spreads
beyond its American home base with remarkable speed in the wake of
financial market globalization. In Europe in particular, but also more
generally, the more the capital base of corporations has become
diluted, the more frequently reference is made to the PEM. For many
researchers in corporate governance today, it represents the *only* way
of thinking about corporate governance, indeed the very starting point
of the question. In our view, this perspective reflects a lack of historical
distance and a confusion between the current realization of liberal
thinking as it appears in the PEM and the liberal foundation of corporate governance, a foundation that can be traced to the origins of
modern society, as we have shown in Part I of this book.

---

[21] Although, strictly speaking, he was of course not a PEM economist, Hayek also
drew upon the classic liberal logic. Hayek argued that shareholders had a
political role to play in modern democracies, in the sense that profit
maximization helped individual interests to converge and thus enabled social
harmony. See F. A. Hayek, 'The corporation in a democratic society: in whose
interest ought it and will it be run?' Reprinted in M. Anshen and G. L. Bach
(eds.), *Management and Corporation*, New York: McGraw Hill, 1985.

Although the PEM is today very widely approved, both by academics and by practitioners, it does not constitute an end in itself, and we cannot accept the framework for corporate governance resulting from this model without further inquiry. Like any model, the PEM is only as good as its assumptions: at the origin of the PEM is the hypothesis that financial markets are uniform, that is to say that all operators in the financial markets are driven by the maximization of the same individual self-interest: profit. This assumption is indispensable to explaining theoretically why the separation of ownership and control can be reconciled by the linking role ascribed to profit. However, this hypothesis in fact raises its own questions, particularly if one accepts that the growth in mass and the fragmentation of property ownership are essential characteristics of the contemporary shareholding body (see Part II). Is it realistic to assume that all shareholders have the same expectations, and the same interests, and are looking for the *same level of profitability*? If such is not the case, what are the consequences for a model which ascribes to profit the critical role in aligning shareholder interests? It is to these questions that we now turn.

8 | Critique of the Pure Economic Model of corporate governance

As successful as it has been in shaping the research agenda of economics and influencing the corporate governance structure of corporations over the last twenty years, the pure economic model (PEM) has also begun to face substantial criticism, of its empirical validity and of its internal logic. Indeed, many of its predictions have not been borne out by rigorous examination, and there are several non-trivial assumptions in the model's internal construction that merit reflection. Given the model's pretension to scientific truth and our sincere desire to evaluate its reach and merit, empirical failures have to be taken seriously (1). In this chapter, we will show that the empirical failures of the PEM are closely tied to the hypothesis that all of the shareholders' interests can be subsumed under profit maximization and that the incentives of management can be aligned to this objective (2). With the partition of property rights among several economic actors and the dispersion of the shareholding body among individuals pursuing different interests, it becomes very difficult to maintain the fiction of a unity of interests. The PEM appears to underestimate the degree of fragmentation in modern society and its effect on the behaviour of economic actors (3).

It is important to note that the current state of economic research does *not* permit the conclusion that corporate profits are maximized and thus also social benefits fully realized when the different parties to corporate governance pursue their own individual self-interests according to purely economic calculations. Worse, there are important reasons to think that the pursuit of different individual self-interests can have a negative effect on corporate profits and hence reduce social welfare. The tremendous contemporary increase in the number of shareholders could lead to what one might call a Hobbesian confrontation of 'all men against all men'. In spite of its desire to return to the liberal ideal and restore the figure of the entrepreneur to the modern corporation in the form of the financial markets, the PEM appears to ignore that the modern liberal dialectic in fact has two sides – the directing force of the entrepreneur and the dividing force of social fragmentation. Paradoxically, it would appear that the PEM (and with it much of neo-liberal economics) can be faulted not for an excess of liberalism, but, rather, for a lack of rigour in the examination of liberal hypotheses.

1 Empirical failures

In general, the PEM suffers from a lack of realism. This is without a doubt the most common and most serious criticism of a model that pretends to 'purity' and the appearance of scientific truth. The examples cited below are selected from several levels of analysis to show the scope of the empirical problem. In response to this criticism, proponents of the PEM have formulated hypotheses concerning the *long-term* validity of the model: on the one hand, the hypothesis of a slow but inevitable convergence of local forms of governance towards the financial markets ideal described in the model; on the other hand, the argument for fine-tuning the model itself, as corporate governance becomes further aligned with the financial markets.

Listing on the financial markets is not a necessary condition for performance

Observation of contemporary economic reality shows that the reach of the PEM is not that extensive. Only 10,000 firms world-wide are actually publicly listed, albeit representing 60% of global economic activity by sales, but only 1% of the entire number of incorporated businesses. In other words, only very few firms satisfy the most basic requirement for consideration by the PEM: listing on the financial markets and a diluted capital base (high liquidity). These figures do not mean that the PEM is in error. However, it is worth noting that the PEM cannot be directly used as a model of reference for corporate governance in a numerical majority of cases, because it focuses on a 'special case' of contemporary capitalism, as Eisenhardt correctly notes in her review of agency theory.[1] Since the PEM advances the hypothesis that performance is improved when

---

[1] K. Eisenhardt, 'Agency theory: an assessment and review', *Academy of Management Review* 14 (1989), 57–74.

the financial markets exercise the entrepreneurial force, it is necessary to explain how corporations that are not directly exposed to the financial markets also manage to perform well.

One could argue that the corporations that are publicly listed and hence do come under the coverage of the PEM are so large that they influence the whole economy, in much the same way as we argued the influence of larger corporations on corporate governance in the historical review presented in Part II of this book. However, this remark cannot explain away the fact that the PEM does not address successful corporations that do not correspond to the theoretical ideal of ownership. Indeed, in many industries, world-leading corporations have family, state, or cooperative ownership structures and are not publicly listed: Cargill (family – agrofood), Mars (family – consumer goods), Areva (state – nuclear energy), EDF (state – power), etc. Many large, successful publicly quoted corporations have founding families or founding institutions holding large swathes of shares and hence also do not fit the model well (e.g. Wal-Mart, Microsoft, BMW, Axa, Mittal Steel, Bouygues, to name just a few). The PEM would predict that publicly quoted corporations with diluted capital bases outperform publicly quoted companies with concentrated capital bases, but this prediction is often contradicted in practice – for example, there are many examples of concentrated ownership succeeding in takeovers of diluted ownership: Daimler over Chrysler in 1998; Sanofi-Synthelabo over Aventis in 2004, Mittal Steel over Arcelor in 2006. What is more, broader research studies fail to show any relationship between ownership structure and performance.[2]

If we restrict consideration to the actual playing field of the model, namely the large corporation with a diluted capital base, many of its predictions are still difficult to corroborate. Meta-analyses, that is to say studies that collect and compare the research results obtained on a particular problem in order to evaluate whether or not these results converge or diverge, confirming or disproving theoretical expectations, are particularly instructive about the level of ambiguity and contradiction surrounding the PEM. As discussed above, incentive mechanisms are

---

[2] Cf. H. Demsetz and B. Villalonga, 'Ownership structure and corporate performance', *Journal of Corporate Finance* 7 (2001), 209–33; H. Demsetz and K. Lehn, 'The structure of corporate ownership: causes and consequences', *Journal of Political Economy* 93 (6) (1985), 1155–77.

a critical component of the PEM, as they permit the 'spontaneous' alignment of the interests of management who exercise the right of *usus* in
the corporation and shareholders who hold the right of *abusus*. By the
model, one would expect managerial incentives to maximize corporate
profits (bonus, stock options, etc.) to be accompanied by improved
performance. However, empirical results on this question do not conform
to expectations. In a meta-analysis of 137 studies drawn from the empirical literature, Tosi, Werner, Katz, and Gomez-Mejia show that 40% of
the variation in the magnitude of managerial remuneration is explained
by the size of the corporation and only 5% by the performance of the
corporation. In other words, the alignment of interests between the CEO
and shareholders by the mechanism of remunerations is not confirmed.[3]
Even worse, Deci, Koestner, and Ryan's extensive meta-analysis of sixty-
eight experiments (and ninety-seven experimental effects) published in
fifty-nine articles between 1971 and 1997 shows that remuneration plans
tend to distract executives, turning their attention towards finding ways
of enhancing their pay and away from the tasks that they are supposed
to complete.[4] Similarly, the hypothesis that independent boards would
do a better job of ensuring high performance, by maintaining strict oversight on the activities of self-interested management in the shareholders'
interest – another basic, micro-level prediction of the model – does not
hold up to empirical testing. For example, after comparing eighty-five
different empirical studies testing the link between board composition,
board leadership structure, and economic performance, Dalton, Daily,
Ellestrand, and Johnson conclude that the results are contradictory and
therefore do not definitely establish a relationship between the dimensions studied.[5] These examples of the PEM's empirical failure to live up to
its predictions could be further extended and multiplied. Although the
conclusions of this research can be read as disappointing, the work con-
forms to the scientific ambition of the model, seeking to establish results

[3] H. Tosi, S. Werner, J. Katz, and L. Gomez-Mejia, 'How much does performance
matter? A meta-analysis of CEO pay studies', *Journal of Management* 26 (2)
(2000), 301–39.

[4] E. L. Deci, R. Koestner, and R. M. Ryan, 'Meta-analytic review of experiments:
examining the effects of extrinsic rewards on intrinsic motivation', *Psychological
Bulletin* 125 (1999), 627–68.

[5] D. Dalton, C. Daily, A. Ellestrand, and J. Johnson, 'Meta-analytic reviews of
board composition, leadership structure, and financial performance', *Strategic
Management Journal* 19 (1998), 269–90.

that are robust to variations in method and context. In the final analysis, the conceptual triumph of the PEM over academia and parts of practice is not matched by the empirical record. One is left with the impression that the PEM cannot fully live up to its scientific pretensions.

To these pragmatic doubts, proponents of the PEM have responded in two ways: acknowledgement that the world was not yet fully compatible with the model, coupled with the assertion that the world was moving in the model's direction (this is the so-called convergence hypothesis); and further, more refined testing of the model (this is the fine-tuning argument).

The recourse to the (future) convergence hypothesis

Under the convergence hypothesis, globalization of financial markets and competitive rivalries are to lead to more corporations adopting diluted capital structures and corporate governance guidelines in line with the model's conditions. The so-called German, French, Japanese, and transition economy models are seen as intermediate, locally idiosyncratic stages in the general evolution towards the efficient financial markets and diluted capital bases that already characterize the United States and the United Kingdom.[6] Pushing significant criticism aside, the rhetoric of convergence reached its apogee during the late 1990s, under the impression of the very rapid appreciation of the American stock markets, apparently closest in expectations to the PEM.[7] The US stock market's superior performance seemed also to herald victory for the neoliberal model, providing (temporary) evidence that governance forms that were less closely aligned with the PEM underperformed and should be considered to be 'slow' or 'behind' in terms of economic development. The bursting of the speculative bubble in 2000/2001 hit proponents of

---

[6] R. La Porta, F. Lopez-de-Silanes, and A. Shleifer, 'Corporate ownership around the world', *Journal of Finance* 54 (2) (1999), 471–517.

[7] For an overview of this debate, see the following articles: M. Guillen, 'Corporate governance and globalization: is there convergence across countries?' *Advances in International Comparative Management* 13 (2001), 175–204; H. Hansmann and R. Kraakman, 'Toward a single model of corporate law?', in J. McCahery *et al.*, *Corporate Governance Regimes: Convergence and Diversity*, Oxford: Oxford University Press, 2002, pp. 56–82; J. Coffee, 'Convergence and its critics: what are the preconditions to the separation of ownership and control?', in McCahery *et al.*, *Corporate Governance Regimes*, pp. 83–112. See also R. Whitley (ed.), *European Business Systems: Firms and Markets in Their National Contexts*, London: Sage, 1992.

the PEM hard, necessitating a review of the optimistic but basically simplistic approach adopted to this point. What had looked like superior performance turned out, in many cases, to have been merely the out-growth of speculative fever. Rather than performing as virtuous entre-preneurs, in line with the prediction of the PEM, financial markets appeared to have been myopic, to have been incapable of analysing the information provided by corporations, and finally to have let the herd instinct take precedence over economic calculation. The spectacular failures of Enron and Worldcom, for a long time considered to be shining examples of the PEM, with all the requisite incentive mechanisms in place, put a stake in the model's claim to setting standards of corporate governance. Of course, the argument could be made that speculative fever and fraudulent corporate accounting were not compatible with the ideal of the PEM. Indeed, new approaches analysing the limitedly rational behaviour of financial intermediaries (behavioural finance[8]) leading to market exuberance[9] have begun to study the mechanism of the market's invisible hand and explore its consequences for corporate governance. As we will show, the market is no longer considered a mechanical instrument that is immune to the number of actors involved, the effects of mimetic behaviour, and the resulting potential for spec-ulative bubbles – all of these effects have become subjects for research aimed at understanding variations in market outcomes. In practice, following the neo-liberal euphoria of the 1990s, the burst of a bubble in 2000/2001 resulted in wide-spread questioning of the market's ability to regulate itself, and institutional and political intervention was called on to restore confidence in the system. The Sarbanes-Oxley Act or the IFRS accounting standards, both implemented to re-establish 'good practices' of corporate governance, can be seen as a kind of ironic, posthumous revenge of Berle and Means and the institutionalists over the partisans of a market that is entirely self-regulating. Finally, reality has demonstrated that corporate governance is a more complex subject than the PEM allows for, and that it is necessary to take this complexity into account in explaining market phenomena.

[8] D. Kahneman and A. Tversky, 'Prospect theory: an analysis of decision making under risk', *Econometrica* 47, (2) (1979), 263–92; R. Shiller, 'From efficient markets theory to behavioral finance', *Finance Journal of Economic Perspectives* 17 (1) (2003), 83–104.

[9] R. Shiller, *Irrational Exuberance* (2nd edition), Princeton: Princeton University Press, 2005.

The fine-tuning argument: working with the epistemological problems of the PEM

Proponents of the PEM are not easily discouraged. A second type of defence is often invoked to ward off criticism based on poor empirical results. This defence argues for taking a longer-term view of developments and postulates that the unsatisfactory results of the PEM are merely a consequence of imperfections. In this view, the reality of corporate governance is in a process of evolution and has not yet attained the level of maturity that the PEM describes. This is why it can be argued that particular exceptions to the model do not negate a general tendency towards the exercise of the entrepreneurial function by financial markets throughout the world. With time, so the argument goes, the PEM should achieve better proof of its analytical validity. In a manner that is entirely complementary to the convergence hypothesis, the fine-tuning argument proposes that reality will eventually come to resemble the expectations of the model. Even if this argument has an ad hoc flavour, it cannot be ignored, because it is so often invoked to predict that the future will prove the PEM right. In the second part of this book, we showed that the development of the public model of corporate governance leads to interactions between investors and shareowners, and that the exercise of the entrepreneurial force could objectively take on a variety of intermediate forms, between pure market pressure and complete ownership. The fine-tuning argument supposes that history has already been written and that corporations are generally trending towards a mode of regulation dominated by financial markets (investors). To us, this is not a fact, but a hypothesis. In posing the question in this way, we reach the epistemological limits of the neo-liberal model and confront the inherent confusion between its positive dimensions (modelling based on the existing reality) and its normative dimensions (modelling based on the desired reality).

The epistemological status of the economic model has been in doubt for a long time, even among liberal thinkers themselves:[10] is the economic model positive, or is it normative? As far as the PEM is

---

[10] See, for example, the reflections of Robbins and Von Mises: L. Robbins, *The Nature and Significance of Economic Science*, London: Macmillan, 1932; L. Von Mises, *Epistemological Problems of Economics*, Princeton, NJ: Von Norstrand, 1932; but also F. A. Hayek, *The Counterrevolution of Science*, Glencoe: The Free Press, 1955.

concerned, the question is whether it attempts to understand corporate governance as it *actually exists*, or as it *should be* for the maximization of collective utility? No clear-cut response is possible. In the case of the agency and property rights theories, for example, there exist both positive and normative approaches.[11] The first seeks to explain the behaviours of economic actors; the second seeks to create incentive alignment structures to maximize economic performance (i.e. literature on positive incentives such as bonus and stock options, see above). However, as we have discussed above, neither the positive nor the normative version shows how agency theory or property rights theory can provide a more complete explanation of the facts observed. Now, the PEM jumps from positive to normative in anticipating changes that finally correspond to the description of the world as it would exist if its positive point of view were realized. In other words, it argues that reality does *not yet* correspond to the model, but that it will eventually do so, because the results it *predicts* are superior. Clearly, this goes beyond the realm of the scientific and enters the realm of the ideological. The PEM falls prey to one of the fundamental criticisms formulated by Popper many years ago, in discussing historicism: it puts itself into a situation where it cannot be falsified by arguing that poor empirical results arise from a current weakness in reality, the very weakness that is to be corrected by the implementation of the positive model.[12]

The underlying reason for these difficulties is traceable to the epistemology of the PEM. The PEM was not constructed on the basis of observation to model reality, and in this it differs crucially from the economic approach inaugurated by Berle and Means. In the 1930s, Berle and Means observed the dilution of capital and the rise of managerialism at first hand. These were the realities that they sought to describe and model. By contrast, the PEM is based on a priori theorizing, an effort to return to the roots of individualist liberal thought, and in so doing to overcome the paradox revealed by Berle and Means. Theorists of the PEM did not base their modelling on observation of the behaviour of shareholders and data on the functioning of financial markets – shareholder behaviour and market functioning were

[11] M. Jensen, 'Organization theory and methodology', *Accounting Review* 58 (April, 1983), 319–39.

[12] K. Popper, *The Poverty of Historicism* (9th edition), London: Routledge and Kegan Paul, 1976.

assumed as a basis for theorizing (see Chapter 5). In view of its purely deductive genesis, it is not surprising that reality does not easily corroborate the model's predictions. Nonetheless, it is important not to neglect the normative effect the neo-liberal model has had on practice – through its ideological impact, as well as through teaching and research publications.[13] This normative effect has contributed to partially confirming the expectations of the model by results arising from its implementation. In this way, it has become self-confirming in certain contexts: results are confirmatory when the model has already been largely put in place, as it seemed to be in the 1990s in the United States for example. Results are disconfirmatory when the model has not yet been fully implemented, as neo-liberals argued in response to the post-Enron fall-out, again in the United States.

Although it is not satisfactory to wait until the facts do (or do not) agree with the predictions of the PEM, it is also not desirable to stop there, without explaining why the PEM appears so difficult to confirm in the reality of contemporary corporate governance, even though it stands as the dominant ideological base for today's practitioners. After all, the PEM represents a remarkable intellectual achievement in the liberal tradition, and, put into practice as it is, a strong theoretical model should yield powerful tools for analysis. Why does the PEM not provide better results? Do its failures imply the need for a more profound examination of Western society's liberal model of governance, an examination that draws an explicit link between the underlying political project and economic performance? Or is the fault to be found in the economic expression of the liberal project, as it is stated in the PEM? In order to explain the PEM's empirical failures, we must go beyond questions of research method and study the logic of the model's internal construction.

2 Internal contradictions

The fundamental hypotheses of the model are often neglected. Economists, as the proponents of the model, consider these hypotheses to be self-evident. For non-specialists, the hypotheses of the model tend to disappear behind the formal language, to the point that the latter are

---

[13] S. Ghoshal, 'Bad management theories are destroying good management practices', *Academy of Management Learning* 4 (1) (2005), 75–91.

often unable to distinguish results from assumptions. This principal critique can be advanced for the PEM's empirical failures: the fundamental hypotheses upon which the model is built – the efficient market hypothesis (1) and the shareowner as residual claimant hypothesis (2) stand in opposition to the thinking of the liberal political project, in which self-interested behaviour and potential opportunism *towards the corporation* is as likely in shareholders as in management.

Are shareholders interested in financial markets being efficient?

Market efficiency

The efficient market hypothesis states that the price of the share at any given time must perfectly translate the combined expectations of buyers and sellers on future profits. In other words, all that is known about a corporation includes information about both the present and the future. The efficient market hypothesis is absolutely essential to the PEM. Thanks to the efficient market hypothesis, it is possible to make a connection between the *fructus* and the *abusus* of one and the same property right: the shareholder buys or sells (*abusus*) shares because he/she anticipates a higher or lower future profit (*fructus*) linked to that share. Shareholders exercise pressure on the corporation through the market, buying and selling shares, knowing only the price, but not the (future) profit. In order for shareholder pressure to work (and to be acceptable) in the postulated manner and for markets to fulfil the function of the entrepreneur, it is essential that there be a rational link between share price and present and future profits, that is to say between the share price and the profitability of the corporation.

If the efficient market hypothesis were not satisfied and the shareholder bought/sold for reasons other than profit expectations (e.g. passion, ignorance, indifference, etc.), then the connection between profit and market price would be attenuated/broken, and it would not be possible to build an economic argument for corporate governance based on the logic of indirect control by the mechanisms of the market. The financial markets would merely be a form of casino or lottery and could not fulfil the function of entrepreneurial direction. Which business corporation would accept to be directed by the vagaries of chance or fantasy? If the efficient market hypothesis were not satisfied, the PEM could not pass the social legitimacy test of economic efficiency. The link between price and present and future profits is more than a hypothesis for the PEM, it is a dogma.[14]

More precisely, the dogma of the PEM consists of insisting on the unity of the three rights to property, even if these rights are held by different actors. However, empirical observation of the markets can cast doubt – even on a dogma (cf. Chapter 5): property rights are partitioned and certain actors (investors) can ignore the right of *fructus* and only pay attention to the gains to be obtained from trading in the right of *abusus*. The question of whether or not markets are in fact efficient, or only partially (semi-) efficient, has been debated for many years in economics. Thus, as early as 1980 Grossman and Stiglitz showed that, if markets were truly efficient, no one would seek additional information anymore, because it would be sufficient to observe prices as the best and cheapest access to information.[15] The demonstration of this paradox launched a much broader discussion on the significance of efficiency: the length and ardour of these debates are perhaps only comparable to the medieval scholastic disputes on the gender of angels. We will not pursue this technical argument any further here, except to emphasize that the theory itself gives rise to considering that even if each market participant behaves rationally, the resulting financial interaction may not be collectively rational. Since the early insight of Mackay and the pioneering research of Kindleberger and experimental economists, the impact of crowds and mass movements on the determination of prices must be explicitly considered in the analysis of the effects of limited rationality on imitation and speculation.[16] Beyond the relevance of these contributions, it would appear to us that the uncertainty that hangs over the rationality of the collective result where individual behaviours are highly fragmented is sufficiently high to warrant the statement that the dogma of efficient markets is not shared by market participants. Market

---

[14] See E. Fama, 'Efficient capital market: a review of theory and empirical work', *Journal of Finance* 25 (2) (1970), 383–417 and W. Sharpe, 'Efficient capital markets: a review of theory and empirical work: discussion', *Journal of Finance* 25, (2) (1970), 418–20.

[15] S. J. Grossman and J. Stiglitz, 'On the impossibility of informationally efficient markets', *American Economic Review* 70, 3 (1980), 393–408.

[16] See C. Mackay, *Extraordinary Popular Delusions and the Madness of the Crowd*, New York: Prometheus Books, 2001 [1852], and the important work of Charles Kindleberger, particularly C. Kindleberger, *Manias, Panics, and Crashes: A History of Financial Crises*, London: Wiley, 1996 [1976].

participants seem to have the same doubts as theorists, and it is not realistic to think of them as more naïve. For our purposes, we can say that market efficiency as a dogma is in doubt, a state of affairs that has important consequences for the economic analysis of corporate governance as advanced by the PEM. The critical question, therefore, is not to determine whether the markets are *truly* efficient, but rather to find out if there exist good reasons why they should not be so in consideration of the rational behaviour of the market actors themselves. For the purposes of our analysis of corporate governance, we want to direct attention to one particularly problematic but often neglected reason for market inefficiency, namely shareholder opportunism against the corporation.

Shareholder opportunism against the corporation

Is it to the advantage of shareholders for markets to be truly efficient? Market efficiency may not be an advantage in all cases. Shareholders do not necessarily want markets with perfect and transparent information on future profits, but may instead prefer to exploit imperfect information for their personal gain. Although counterintuitive in the context of the PEM, shareholder opportunism is a very good reason for market inefficiency to persist. In fact, the PEM has conditioned us to think that the interests of the shareholders and the interests of the corporation are one and the same. However, if one is true to economic reasoning, one must accept that shareholder opportunism towards the corporation is as likely as managerial opportunism. This hypothesis derives from the same precepts of individual autonomy and rational behaviour as liberal political theory, a theory that is, after all, based not on the convergence but on the divergence of individual interests.

In fact, shareholders can make more money by selling shares at a higher price than justified by *actual* future profits. The seller has an interest in letting the buyer think that profits will be higher than they actually are, and that buyer in turn has the same interest when facing a third party. The individual shareholder has no interest in maintaining perfect and transparent information, because he/she hopes to make money by *exploiting imperfect information*. We know that *highly liquid markets* are a necessary condition for the PEM to work; however, liquid markets also make it possible for shareholders to enter and exit opportunistically, taking advantage of any and all imperfections. Now, if it is more profitable *for the shareholder* to exploit information imperfections in buying and selling stocks several times a year than to wait for the annual dividend, a form of remuneration which is uncertain and depends on management's performance and good will, then the shareholder will be far less concerned with corporate profitability than postulated by the PEM and far more interested in creating or finding market inefficiencies.[17] As Shiller has convincingly demonstrated, the reality of today's stock markets is that differences in expectations and interpretations among shareholders are so great that the profitability of speculation on information imperfections is much greater than and, in some cases, also more certain than the dividend.[18] Even on large, bellwether stocks like Deutsche Telekom or Procter & Gamble it is possible to outperform the dividend on the basis of only one day of share price movement. Thus, on 10 August 2006, for example, the stock price of Deutsche Telekom dropped over 8%, following a profit warning; even more spectacularly, on 7 March 2000 Procter & Gamble lost 30% of its value in a single day of trading, with failure to meet analyst earnings expectations cited as the reason here also. Under such volatile conditions, which rational shareholder would or should prefer to be remunerated on the profit of the corporation?

Where property rights are partitioned, with managers controlling the right of *usus* and shareholders the right of *abusus*, the apportionment of *fructus* is a matter of negotiation between managers and shareholders, and managerial opportunism indeed becomes a central concern, as captured in the PEM. In the way the financial markets work, it is possible to consider the right of *abusus* to be independent of the other two property rights. However, thanks to the liquidity of stock markets, shareholders can also obtain profits by taking advantage of information imperfections. In other words, it is possible to play with shares as speculative objects, independent of the rights of *usus* and *fructus*. Thus, a fund may buy and sell shares purely in anticipation of a variation in

---

[17] The investment class that has seen the greatest growth since the 1990s – hedge funds – has always included many funds that focus explicitly on taking advantage of market inefficiencies through a variety of arbitrage techniques. According to latest estimates (2007), hedge funds hold anywhere between $1 and $1.3 trillion in assets (see J. Preiserowicz, 'The new regulatory regime for hedge funds: has the SEC gone down the wrong path?', *Fordham Journal of Corporate and Financial Law* 11 (4) (2006), 807–49, and also *Wall Street Journal*, 5 January 2007: 'No consensus on regulating hedge funds').

[18] R. J. Shiller, *Market Volatility*, Cambridge, MA: MIT Press, 1989; R. J. Shiller, 'Market volatility and investor behavior', *American Economic Review* 80 (2) (1990), 58–62.

price of the share and without consideration of the economic results of the corporation. The development of technical trading that ignores corporate profitability and mechanically focuses on price (historic and current) and volume signals is perhaps the clearest manifestation of this kind of activity.[19] When the shares of a corporation are bought and sold many times during the year by the same investor, as is common in the financial markets, it is very hard to conclude that the profits sought by the trading investor are in any meaningful way linked to the profitability of the corporation in the PEM's logic of the financial markets as entrepreneur. The PEM fails to recognize that the financial markets could primarily or even exclusively be markets for the rights of purchase and sale (*abusus*), rather than markets for property rights as an unpartitioned whole (*usus, fructus,* and *abusus*). As we will show, the dilution of capital makes it possible not only for management but also for shareholders to pursue interests that differ from those of the corporation.

As long as the shareholder and the manager are one and the same person (i.e. the founder entrepreneur), the long-term interest of both functions is profit maximization. Once the shareholder and the manager no longer coincide, liquid financial markets make it easy for shareholders to enter into and exit from the corporation's capital. It is not clear why shareholders' utility is best served by corporate profit maximization in the long term. One can argue that shareholders seek rather to maximize their profits from the financial markets, by playing with information imperfections. It seems that one cannot have it both ways: if the markets are less than liquid, the shareholder is implicated in the long-term development of the firm and must of necessity work for long-term corporate profit maximization.[20] But, from the point of view

---

[19] For a recent review of research on technical trading, see M. Qi and Y. Wu, 'Technical trading-rule profitability, data snooping, and reality check: evidence from the foreign exchange market', *Journal of Money, Credit, and Banking* 38 (8) (2006), 2135–58. The foreign exchange market is considered by many to be the most efficient of financial markets; this is why the existence of *profitable* technical-trading rules in the foreign exchange market represents such a striking finding. For examples of technical trading in the stock markets, see B. R. Marshall, J. M. Cahan, and R. H. Cahan, 'Is the CRISMA technical-trading system profitable?', *Global Finance Journal* 17 (2) (2006), 271–81.

[20] Refer to the discussion of John Pound's work in Chapter 6, and J. Pound, 'Proxy contests and the efficiency of shareholder oversight', *Journal of Financial Economics* 20 (1988), 237–65.

of the PEM, this would put us back in a pre-managerialist context. If, on the other hand, the markets are liquid (necessary condition for the PEM), then shareholders will be tempted to maximize their short-term interests, even if these interests are different from those of the corporation.

Whereas it excludes the first possibility (or only considers it as a particular case), the PEM also screens out the latter, despite the presence of a clear economic rationale for shareholder opportunism. The model posits that shareholders use the financial markets to exert pressure on management to maximize corporate profits, and concludes from this that financial markets thereby exercise the entrepreneurial force of direction. In the long term, share prices certainly do reflect corporate profits. However, effective corporate governance and economic behaviour are based on a series of short-term outcomes, and we must say that the market efficiency hypothesis tends to mask an important problem in the application of the PEM: shareholder opportunism *against the corporation*. If, moreover, management are to align their personal interests with those of shareholders, as the PEM proposes, the problem may be even further magnified. If management also focus on personal profits from financial markets over corporate profitability, then management, too, will be serving shareholder opportunism, against the interests of the corporation.

Finally, if one pursues the argument of the PEM to its logical conclusion, the partition of property rights can lead to a marked decline in the significance of the right of *fructus*. Which rational shareowner fitting the utility-maximizing description given in the PEM would be interested in waiting to get his/her remuneration out of corporate profits when the buying and selling of shares on financial markets is much more attractive? Which rational management would be interested in waiting for long-term corporate profits when the a priori determination of a return on equity objective by shareholders permits him/her to adjust the economic constraints to the results, rather than taking the more difficult traditional path of adjusting the results to the economic constraints? The partition of property rights makes it possible for the two principal actors in corporate governance, the management and the shareholders, to obtain rents from the property rights that they respectively hold and to be relatively less interested in the *fructus*. For example, management can increase their incomes by choosing strategies that tend to increase share prices: significant strategic alliances, spectacular innovations, or major strategic shifts can all have the effect of attracting speculative money and raising the share price. Shareholders accept salary increases for management as long as share prices continue to go up.[21] However, neither management nor shareholders have an incentive to stay loyal to the corporation. Both can turn their investment to gold in their own respective markets: management on the market for senior executive talent, shareholders on the financial markets, where each of them seeks to maximize personal gain.

Residual claims and the role of profit maximization

In the PEM, the attribution of the entrepreneurial function to the financial markets is closely tied to the shareholder as residual claimant hypothesis. As residual claimants, shareholders are only paid if the corporation makes a profit; hence, shareholders will do their utmost to ensure that management maximizes corporate profitability. We draw attention to the fact that the residual claims hypothesis requires that all shareholders exhibit the same behaviour, in other words that they all seek to maximize the *same* profit from the corporation and hence all demand the *same* level of performance from the corporation (different from corporation to corporation, but the same for a particular corporation). In fact, if different shareholders expected different levels of profit from a particular corporation, it would be difficult to demand any kind of control in the name of profit maximization: maximization for some would not be maximization for others. For the financial markets to fulfil the entrepreneurial function, it is necessary that *all shareholders expect the same*, maximized level of profit – what Nobel Laureate Gunnar Myrdal called the 'communist fiction' in the heart of the liberal economic thought.[22] Traceable to the liberal political project and its definition of the legitimate entrepreneur, the robustness of this hypothesis bears closer examination.

---

[21] For several recent examples of work on this relationship, see G. W. Fenn and N. Liang, 'Corporate payout policy and managerial stock incentives', *Journal of Financial Economics* 61 (1) (2001), 45–72; B. E. Hermalin and N. E. Wallace, 'Firm performance and executive compensation in the savings and loan industry', *Journal of Financial Economics* 61 (1) (2001), 139–70.

[22] G. Myrdal, *The Political Element in the Development of Economic Theory*, London: Lewiss, pp. 54 and 150.

If, in fact, shareholders are numerous and all expect the same maximum level of profits, they can be considered not the residual but the *primary* claimants on the corporation. In some cases, their power may be such that they are even able to determine the level of remuneration paid to equity capital – although this may not be in the long-term interests of the corporation.[23] Such shareholders may only stay with the corporation if they are in fact paid what they demand: *pay me to stay*. Then management must see to it that this level of remuneration is realized by adjusting the pay-out to other stakeholders in the corporation (e.g. employees; public authorities). If, for example, the total pay-out to employees is reduced through lay-offs and/or off-shoring in order to achieve a pre-determined level of remuneration to shareholders, then the employees are in fact the real residual claimants, in the sense that they receive only the variable amount that is left over, *after* shareholders have been paid. Similarly, if the corporation seeks to reduce the total pay-out to public authorities by off-shoring and/or establishing bases in tax havens in order to increase the remuneration to shareholders, according to a priori demands, the public authorities become de facto residual claimants.

The residual claimant gets paid after all the other parties to the corporation have been taken care of; if shareholders are powerful enough to fix the level of remuneration to equity capital in advance, they cannot anymore be considered residual claimants. As financial markets develop, this second view of shareholders has a distinct possibility of being realized. In this case, financial markets integrate a great number of shareholders who carry considerable economic weight, but also great social and political influence. Even if individually shareholders are weak, they can become collectively dominant when the invisible hand of the markets acts in their name. In recent years, the power of the 'markets' to fix the level of remuneration to equity capital has grown substantially, with ever higher demands being made on Return on Equity. Corporations have in fact adjusted their methods

---

[23] As Chandler has shown in his analysis of British capitalism, this effect could also be observed in family-influenced corporations that were publicly listed. In order to ensure themselves a steady revenue stream, British family owners of the early twentieth century (1900–20) preferred to pay out higher dividends than their American competitors, thus constraining capacity to invest of the corporations they controlled. See A. Chandler, *Scale and Scope: The Dynamics of Industrial Capitalism*, Cambridge, MA: Harvard University Press, 1990.

of management in order to serve these demands, adopting internal systems based on Economic Value Added and other similar measures to allow return on shareowner equity to be extracted at all levels of the organization. The corporate focus on quarterly results and the scramble to beat expectations/not to disappoint expectations help solidify the redefinition of ROE as an objective of management as opposed to a residual claim.

It is difficult to maintain the hypothesis of shareholders as residual claimants, when management is so focused on earning levels of return to equity capital that shareholders have set out in advance as objectives to be achieved. Under the conditions described here, at least, shareholders are not taking the economic risk associated with the status of residual claimant. Rather, it is employees and public authorities who are increasingly taking this risk, not knowing how much they will be paid for their contribution to the corporation until *after* shareholders have been satisfied. The inflexibility of requirements for return on equity makes it necessary for labour and the state to be flexible.

The pure economic model of corporate governance finds itself in a Catch-22 situation: either shareholders are not powerful enough to influence management and corporate profits are not maximized – this was the concern of Berle and Means – or, shareholders are too powerful and impose a pre-determined level of remuneration to equity capital. In both cases, it is difficult to maintain the shareholder as residual claimant hypothesis. However, if shareholders cannot be safely considered residual claimants, then the financial markets' entrepreneurial function is in doubt. As already pointed out by the critics of shareholder capitalism in the 1920s and 1930s, nothing is less risky than a pre-determined level of remuneration. This takes us back to the classic anti-capitalist critique (see Chapter 4) that considered shareholders to be not too passive *à la* Berle and Means, but, on the contrary, *too active to be satisfied* with *residual* claims. It is important to emphasize that some of the PEM's founders have evolved towards less radically neo-liberal positions in an attempt to address substantial criticism. For example, Jensen recently revisited the problematic question of shareholder profit maximization as the engine of economic activity and noted,

we must not confuse optimization with value creation or value seeking. To create value we need not know what maximum value is and precisely how it can be achieved. What we must do, however, is to set up our organizations so that managers and employees are clearly motivated to seek value – to institute those changes and strategies that are most likely to cause value to rise.[24]

This kind of theoretical adjustment makes it possible to overcome certain contradictions inherent in the PEM, but it also weakens the rigour and undermines the parsimony of the model, inviting new questions about conflicts of interest among multiple parties in the evaluation of value creating strategies.

In sum, the two principal hypotheses of the PEM – the efficient market hypothesis and the residual claims hypothesis – have a common objective: to ensure the unity of shareholders and, beyond that, the unity of the rights they hold. Thus, efficient markets render *fructus* (expected dividends) coherent with *abusus* (purchase of sale of share). This maintains the unity of property rights over time (*fructus* and *abusus* remain tightly linked). The residual claims hypothesis ensures the unity of shareholder behaviour – *all are supposed to seek to maximize the same profit.* Uniform shareholder behaviour, in turn, maintains the unity of property rights in space (the same kind of *fructus* is sought). Not only are the two principal hypotheses of the PEM very optimistic, they also stand in direct contradiction to the potential for opportunism in shareholders that liberal economic thought *would lead us to expect*, in keeping with the basic precepts of the liberal political project of which the PEM is an avowed descendant. This is why we must conclude that the empirical failures of the PEM are a question of internal logic and not only a question of method. The empirical failures and analytical inconsistencies described above reveal that the PEM suffers from a major flaw: it underestimates the contemporary fragmentation of property ownership and the consequences of this fragmentation for corporate governance.

3 The unseen problem: today's fragmented ownership of property

Paradoxically, the clarity of the PEM allows us to see that all of the critiques of the model have a common root: what is underestimated is the degree to which property ownership is fragmented. The partition of

---

[24] M. C. Jensen, 'Value maximization, stakeholder theory, and the corporate objective function', *Journal of Applied Corporate Finance* 14 (3) (2001), 8–21.

property rights and the fact that the different constitutive dimensions of property rights are held by different categories of economic actors makes it possible to disconnect the interests of the holders of property rights from the interests of the corporation. The rights of *usus, fructus*, and *abusus* on the same property can obey different logics and have different valuations. When the holders of the different elements of property rights can each obtain value for their right in separate markets, the ties that once linked *usus, fructus*, and *abusus* become unclear and may break down completely.

If one takes into account the fact that the number of shareholders is continuously growing and that these shareholders have different interests, one from the other, then one is led to an even more sceptical attitude towards the notion of a unity of interests. In fact, over and above the partition of property rights into their constitutive dimensions, as described above, the right of *abusus* is dispersed among a growing number of shareholders. A greater number of shareholders implies greater competition between shareholders to obtain information, and to buy and sell shares by exploiting information imperfections. As we showed in Chapter 6, the shareholding body splits into investors and shareowners, differing in terms of time horizons and objectives; moreover, investors and shareowners may also differ among themselves. These differences make it difficult to interpret the market. For the prospective shareholder, therefore, the cost of collecting and interpreting information goes up with the number of shareholders: shareholders, who may have privileged access to important information, may hide or falsify information, or may use the information they have in self-serving ways. In deciding whether or not to buy the shares of a particular corporation, the prospective shareholder must take the behaviour of other shareholders into account. In the final analysis, the shareholder is more interested in having his/her portfolio outperform the market than in having the individual corporation in which he/she owns shares perform well.

Although the PEM seeks to align the three dimensions of property rights on the same objective, that of profit maximization, partition of property rights and dispersion among the holders of property rights make it very difficult, if not impossible, to align all of the interested parties on the same objective. Contrary to the expectations of the PEM, then, a dilution of the capital base does not necessarily lead to a corporate focus on sustainable profit. Rather, capital dilution and managerialism can turn the corporation away from profit maximization and towards short-term maximization of the share price. Each shareholder, seeking to maximize the return on his portfolio rather than the profitability of a particular corporation, enters into *competition with the other shareholders*, in order to 'beat the market'. We do not assert that this redirection of effort always happens, but merely state that it is a plausible and rational outcome, consistent with the analysis of the PEM. Consistent with the logic of the PEM, this outcome raises anew a question that has been central to liberal thought since Hobbes: what prevents the pursuit of individual self-interest from degenerating into a *war of all men against all men*?

This dilemma is at the heart of the recent speculative bubble; it can also be referred to in explaining why the PEM is not able to address the associated corporate governance issues. The PEM cannot successfully distinguish between those corporations favouring long-term profit maximization and those corporations aiming for short-term share price increases. It therefore seems better suited to explaining the success of Enron than the success of General Electric; unfortunately, the reality is that, of the two, only General Electric still thrives. Our analysis of the internal contradictions of the PEM and its resulting empirical failures leads to the rather cheerless conclusion that, despite the great efforts invested to remain true to the foundations of the liberal political project, economics has not been able to show how or indeed *if* corporate governance can be regulated by purely economic means.

For many researchers and practitioners, the pure economic model of corporate governance remains the standard; indeed for some it is the only model. If we are to advance in our understanding of corporate governance, we cannot assess or build on existing models without having made a serious attempt to address their method of reasoning and the assumptions upon which they are based. The purely economic model of corporate governance stands as an important scholarly contribution. It represents a comprehensive attempt to resolve the difficult question of legitimacy in corporate governance at a time when the liberal political project was threatened by both technocratic oligarchy and state intervention. The model frames the question of corporate governance in terms of economic performance, building on the fundamental insight that individual economic successes enhance collective social justice. With performance as the ultimate yardstick, justifying governance structures chosen and conferring legitimacy to people in control, there is no reason to have recourse to politics or ethics. The world of corporate governance regulates itself in a decentralized manner, shaped only by the free interplay of individual interests. In this sense, the PEM is less a positive scientific model than a strictly economic reformulation of liberal political reasoning.

As we have seen in the previous chapter, Berle and Means did not subscribe to this view of the world. For them, political and institutional interventions were necessary responses to the dysfunctions of a strictly market-based economy, in all areas of concern to them, including corporate governance. In the liberal debate which pits Hobbes' Leviathan against Locke's conception of spontaneous self-regulation, Berle and Means seem more Hobbesian than Lockian. By contrast, the successors to Berle and Means took a *pure* Lockian approach, sanitized of all factors not directly relating to economic efficiency. The PEM's great contribution is to explain and develop the meaning of property rights in economics and its substantial contributions to understanding corporate governance and providing a framework for addressing the many calculations of economic interest that arise in the managerial corporation. The PEM asks the right questions: what is the scope of property rights and what specific privileges do they entail? What is the role of the shareholder in the managerial corporation? How does management respond to the demands of the financial markets? The PEM has provided insightful but partial answers to these questions and demonstrated how complex it is to deal with the 'variety of claims' described by Berle and Means.

The model's great failure is its inability to show how the problems created by the partition of property rights and the dispersion of shareholdings can be overcome to create a system of corporate governance that is economically efficient and socially legitimate. More generally, we can say that the PEM underestimates the importance of one of the pillars of modern liberal society, social fragmentation. In the PEM, managers and shareholders remain united in the pursuit of the single objective of corporate profit maximization; in the modern liberal reality of social fragmentation, not only do management and shareholders try to maximize the value of different dimensions of property rights that have been *partitioned*, the shareholding body itself is *dispersed*, with different shareholders pursuing their own, potentially conflicting interests. One is led to conclude that, contrary to much of the criticism that the model has received in the past, the PEM is not too liberal in overestimating the function of the markets, but not liberal enough in underestimating the degree of fragmentation in society.

Without a doubt, this is the principal reason for which the effort to create a pure economic theory of corporate governance that would exclude all non-economic considerations and base the legitimacy of governance on performance alone has foundered. Recent events – speculative bubble, stock market crash, widespread fraud and misdealing, and, finally, major regulatory reform – have demonstrated that a model of corporate governance based only on the calculations of individual interests does not maximize economic performance and may, in some cases, have a negative effect on it. Recourse to political legislation such as Sarbanes-Oxley in the United States, institutional intervention such as the codes of good governance articulated in the United Kingdom, and the legion of reports and evaluations around the world in the wake of the collapse of the bubble show that market self-regulation alone is inadequate. All of these institutional efforts to define and circumscribe corporate governance cannot be reconciled with the PEM's dream of spontaneous auto-regulation – in fact, they are the enemies of this dream. It appears as though public regulation has gained the upper hand and that Hobbes is winning out over Locke. More than seventy years after Berle and Means, we are led to conclude that efficiency matters in the legitimization of corporate governance systems, but that efficiency cannot be the sole yardstick for evaluating corporate governance. What we still do not understand exactly is in what way the efficiency of the corporation and the quality of corporate governance are related.

9 | Economic performance, corporate governance, and the fragmentation of ownership

Does the failure of the Pure Economic Model imply that it is impossible to establish a clear link between corporate governance and economic performance? Is corporate governance determined solely by political, social, and legal considerations, without any tie to corporate profitability? An economic calculation should be able to explain why, all else equal, a corporation with an inadequate model of corporate governance performs less well than an apparently well-governed corporation. Even if corporate governance does not have a *direct* effect on corporate results, the choice of governance model and its implementation must have an impact on costs, with more or less costs generated for a given level of efficiency. In this way, at least, corporate governance and economic performance are necessarily tied.

We want to stress the necessity of establishing a clear link between corporate governance and economic performance. On the one hand, as we have already shown in Chapter 1, economic performance is fundamental to the legitimacy of corporate governance. On the other hand, it is not acceptable to point out the difficulties of an existing theory (the PEM) without providing an alternative that builds on what has already been demonstrated.[1] Rather than casting off the economic approach, therefore, we should try to integrate it as a critical dimension of analysis and show how it fits in with the other dimensions of legitimate governance in modern liberal society. Without such an effort, any theory of corporate governance could not be applied to the economic subject that is the business corporation. This chapter attacks the following question: is it possible to provide a framework for thinking about corporate governance and economic performance, while

---

[1] To our mind, this is a weakness of socialist critiques: they have never been able to establish how or even if a system of governance based on collective ownership could maintain a level of performance that would permit the continued existence of the productive organization. A non-liberal *economic* theory of corporate governance is still to be written.

taking into account the gradual democratization of corporate governance structures observed over time, since the origins of capitalism? Our objective is not to propose a new economic theory, but rather, in the tradition of Berle and Means and with all modesty, to understand how a theory of economic performance can be compatible with the modern liberal context.

In the preceding chapter, we showed that, paradoxically for a model focused on the liberal ideal, the PEM fails to adequately take into account the fragmentation of property ownership among individuals with different interests – the partition of property rights (*usus, fructus, abusus*) and the dispersion of these rights among an increasingly large number of economic actors. It is this failure to appreciate fully the fragmentation of liberal society that raises questions about the descriptive validity of the PEM and weakens the model's conclusions. To us, the PEM appears to be not too liberal but, on the contrary, *not liberal enough*, because it underestimates the consequences for corporate governance arising from the fragmentation of property ownership.

This is why we think it is necessary to base the economic analysis of corporate governance upon the fragmentation of property ownership – after all, fragmentation of property ownership was an essential feature of the political and hence also the economic project of liberalism from the very earliest days. From a liberal point of view, the concentration of ownership described in the historical part of this book (particularly in Chapter 3) is only a step in the inevitable evolution towards fragmentation in a society that is founded upon the two pillars of individual property ownership and potential equality (of ownership) among all individuals. If one thinks of concentration of ownership as the 'normal' state of affairs and fragmentation of ownership as something new, one is in fact inverting the liberal mindset. On the contrary, even if it has taken many years to become established, fragmentation of ownership is the intended state of affairs in the modern liberal societies.

This conclusion leads us to the following working hypothesis: in order to evaluate the performance of a given model of corporate governance, the essential economic actor to consider is the potential or the actual holder of property rights, motivated by his/her own private interests. We will not try to prove or disprove this hypothesis, or even argue its realism; in the liberal line of thought, it is merely a necessary starting point. In the logic of modern liberalism, the person who is already or who could still become an owner of the corporation rationally discriminates (chooses) between good and bad corporate governance in making the decision to hold or buy rights in a corporation. Our task is to understand how this choice is made under conditions of fragmented ownership, that is to say when property rights are not only partitioned, but also widely dispersed in the public. How does a general pattern of behaviour and hence a common evaluation of corporate governance emerge from different individual interests?

Based upon existing research in economics including the PEM, we can say that the institutions of corporate governance represent agency costs that negatively impact profitability: a part of corporate performance is sacrificed by shareholders to pay for the information that allows them to exercise surveillance over corporate decision makers. However, under fragmented property ownership and generalized opportunism, a prospective shareholder also has to pay transaction costs for obtaining and analysing information pertinent to the corporation from market actors who are potentially better informed than he/she is. The prospective shareholder weighs agency costs against transaction costs. From an economic point of view, this problem statement allows one to deduce a model of corporate governance that positively affects the absolute level of corporate performance, in which corporate governance is understood as a system of guarantee for the shareholders of the corporation (1). Since there is competition between corporations, there is pressure to increase the relative performance of the corporation versus its competitors by finding a governance model better suited, as a system of guarantee, to the context actually faced. We will demonstrate how competition between corporations leads to the selection of models of reference in corporate governance, that is to say models of corporate governance that economically dominate others in a particular historical context (2). In so doing, we will be able to establish, from an economic point of view, what we have demonstrated in Part II from historical and political analyses, thus 're-inserting' the economic logic of corporate performance in a system that assures the legitimacy of corporate governance.

1 Corporate governance as a guarantee

If we stick to the principles of liberal thought, we must anticipate the consequences of a generalized pursuit of individual interest on the part of all of the actors involved in corporate governance. The cost of governance can then be considered as the result of an economic calculation of transaction costs and agency costs, and increases with the number of shareholders. Pursuing this line of reasoning to its logical conclusion would suggest that corporate governance has a systematically negative effect on economic performance, for it raises costs. Further, democratization of corporate governance would appear politically necessary, but economically inefficient. In order to overcome these pessimistic conclusions, we will argue that economic rationality leads actors not to seek complete information, but rather to settle for credible information on the permanence of the corporation in which they hold shares. Corporate governance can be considered as a system of guarantee for the shareholder.

Corporate governance, mistrust and the optimization of governance costs

In terms of the economics of information, the costs of corporate governance can be defined as the costs of coordination incurred by the different actors involved in the governance of the corporation. As argued above, it is necessary to consider these costs from the point of view of the shareholder. How much does the (prospective) shareholder have to pay to obtain information about the corporation (transaction costs) and how much does the corporation have to pay (and hence reduce the profit of the shareholder) to disseminate information related to corporate decision-making (agency costs)?

Transaction costs and agency costs
First, let us consider the costs of coordination from the point of view of the individual who pays for obtaining information about the corporation in relation to the decision to buy the property rights and become a shareholder. These are *transaction costs*, that is to say the 'costs necessary to gain access to the market'.[2] The individual who wishes to become shareholder needs to spend time and money in order to obtain, interpret, and evaluate information pertinent to the corporation. The fact that the prospective shareholder relies on market actors who are supposedly better informed than he/she (i.e. existing

---

[2] The work of Coase is at the origin of transaction cost theorizing. R. H. Coase, 'The nature of the firm', *Economica* 4 (16) (1937), 386–405.

shareholders, brokers) to obtain this information means that the process is fraught with the potential for opportunism.

Second, we can consider the costs of coordination paid for by the corporation to obtain and disseminate information related to corporate decision-making. These are *agency costs*, as defined by the PEM. Agency costs are incurred in ensuring that the information communicated to the different actors involved in corporate governance is sufficient for each one of them to make rational choices at their level of influence: executives, board members, auditors, shareholders, employees, and public stakeholders. As the PEM has convincingly shown, these costs include not only the direct costs of reporting and publishing information, but also the indirect costs of verification and evaluation in enforcing the accurate communication of information.

The effective or prospective shareholder faces an economic trade-off: either to pay the agency costs necessary to ensure the quality of information provided by the corporation, or to pay the transaction costs required to ensure the quality of the information obtained from market actors. Both transaction costs and agency costs are borne by the shareholder. These costs reduce the ultimate profit obtained by the shareholder, so that the *fructus* is only $I-C_g$, where I is the hypothetical profit of the corporate without corporate governance and C_g is the sum of transaction costs and agency costs. The shareholder seeks to minimize the cost of corporate governance C_g without changing the performance I. What factors determine the magnitudes of transaction costs and agency costs and what is the relationship between these two types of costs?

The argument articulated in the previous paragraph suggests that the corporation owned and directed by one and the same person, the artisan's shop for example, constitutes the economic ideal – after all, this is the model that minimizes governance costs and represents the point of departure for the liberal political project. Indeed, the entrepreneur is perfectly informed (self-informed) about the quality of the property owned and does not have to pay governance costs, neither on the market (transaction costs), nor for the corporation (agency costs). In keeping with the logic of Berle and Means' paradox, one is tempted to say that corporate governance only has a negative effect and that the main reason for improved performance is size. The evolution of corporate governance has allowed for growth in the capital base and broader access to financing. Greater accumulation of productive capital in turn helps explain increased performance. The attendant increase in the costs of governance is (more than) made up for by the increase in performance due to the effect of economies of scale. Reasoning in this manner implies that corporate governance forms are interchangeable and only have an indirect effect on economic performance – as a source of costs, but with no direct benefit of their own. In other words, as long as the increase in performance it allows is greater than the costs it generates, any model of corporate governance will do. If this were the case, why would corporations and markets have any economic interest in corporate governance?

Increasing fragmentation of the shareholding body and consequences for opportunism

In fact, the potential opportunism of the actors involved in corporate governance – that is to say the pursuit of their own private interests to the detriment of the interests of other stakeholders – is the principal explanatory variable for the costs of corporate governance. Opportunism increases both transaction costs and agency costs. The more opportunistic the individuals involved, the greater the mutual need for information before choices can be made, with the amount of information communicated and the amount of information sought increasing in proportion to the level of opportunism suspected.

In the PEM, the costs of corporate governance are a function of managerial opportunism, $C_g = f(I_u)$, where I_u is the profit accruing to managers from making decisions for the corporation that maximize their own personal gain. For the PEM, the costs of corporate governance are *entirely* attributable to the agency costs stemming from managerial opportunism. In the previous chapter, we showed that this hypothesis ignores the potential for opportunism in the other economic actors involved in corporate governance. Managers may be tempted to siphon off part of the corporate profit and maximize their personal gain, I_u; by the same token, however, opportunistic shareholders may also try to redirect corporate strategy to *their* advantage: for example, by exerting their influence to favour short-term cash payouts over long-term capital investments. If one considers shareholder opportunism as well, the costs of governance are $C_g = f(I_u; I_s)$, where I_s is the gain that some shareholders could obtain by appropriating a part of the corporate profit for themselves to the detriment of the other shareholders.

As economic actors, shareholders are just as prone to opportunistic behaviour as managers, and hence just as likely to act in a manner that is detrimental to the corporation. A shareholder may prefer to minimize

$I-C_g$ and maximize I^*_s, the part of the corporate profit that he/she can siphon off by opportunistically exploiting an advantage of information or power. Hence, the agency costs of governance, C_g, need to be calculated as a function of *both* I_u and I_s. In the interest of the viability of the corporation, the corporate governance model in place must allow for the communication of information about *all* opportunistic practices, whether manager or shareholder driven.

Clearly, the greater the number of shareholders, the greater the scope for shareholder opportunism, and hence the greater the agency costs incurred by the corporation in addressing this type of behaviour. As stated earlier, a greater number of shareholders implies greater scope for shareholder opportunism. For the prospective shareholder, therefore, the cost of collecting and interpreting information goes up with the number of shareholders: shareholders, who may have privileged access to important information, may hide information, or may use the information they have in self-serving ways. In deciding whether or not to buy the shares of a particular corporation, the prospective shareholder must take the behaviour of other shareholders into account. This means that an increase in the number of shareholders increases not only agency costs, but also transaction costs.

Putting the agency costs and transaction costs arguments advanced above together, we can say that the total costs of corporate governance (agency and transaction) increase with the number of shareholders: $C_g = f(I_u; N)$, where N is the number of shareholders. This line of argument necessarily leads to the inference that the fragmentation of property ownership that has accompanied the evolution of capitalism increases the costs of governance. Increased fragmentation of property ownership leads to higher agency and transaction costs – to the point where the increase in governance costs seems to rule out the regulatory function of private property. The economically rational solution is for owners, if they are numerous, *not to intervene in the control of the corporation.*[3] This finding contradicts one of the principal regulatory

---

[3] This line of reasoning is implicit in many business conversations today: although managers have to inform a great number of shareholders, many of whom are very small, they often take comfort in the knowledge that, 'luckily', shareholders do not seek to control the corporation. This kind of attitude undermines the legitimacy of the shareholding body: if not in controlling the corporation, then wherein lies the purpose of the shareholding body, and what distinguishes it from other sources of finance?

forces of modern society, as described in the first part of this book: diversity of interests of the many as a limitation on the power of direction of the individual. How to overcome this apparent inconsistency in the capitalist system? It is necessary to understand why governance costs *do not increase indefinitely*, despite the ever increasing fragmentation of property ownership.

Starting from liberal principles and taking into account the fragmentation of private property, we are led to conclude (1) that corporate governance systems have no effect on economic performance, as long as they allow the corporation to grow to the right size; and (2) that corporate governance systems, under fragmented property ownership, are increasingly expensive, a finding that suggests that although democratization may be politically necessary (see Part II), it is economically inefficient. We will now proceed to show how these results can be reconsidered by reformulating the implicit hypotheses upon which they are based.

Markets, risks, and the role of a guarantee

It seems to us that the error in this line of reasoning consists of presuming that each shareholder (in a fragmented shareholding body) seeks complete control over information related to the corporation and therefore pays transaction costs (or agency costs) that are totally disproportionate to the personal benefits expected. In other words, the reasoning is built on the presumption that each shareholder acts as if he/she represented the entire shareholding body.

The economic rationality of the shareholder and systems of guarantee

Our discussion of agency costs demonstrated that the fragmentation of property ownership in the hands of many economic actors leads to a considerable increase in the amount of information communicated by the corporation and hence to higher necessary costs of corporate governance. The resulting, apparently unsolvable dilemma only remains unsolvable if one insists that shareholders require *complete* information on the corporation, because of the risks posed by generalized opportunism. If shareholders do require complete control over information, they will indeed have to pay extremely high transaction costs (or agency costs), costs that rise with the number of shareholders, N.

When opportunism is generalized, there is a very large amount of information to treat, and markets may not work. With prospective shareholders unwilling to pay for complete information, and unable in any case to process such information, we have to ask why the market for shares works at all. What do prospective shareholders require in order to participate in the market for shares? Or, put another way, what does the prospective shareholder expect from corporate governance (defined as the total of agency costs and transaction costs) and how much is he/she willing to pay for it?

Since the pioneering work of Akerlof,[4] it is understood that the functioning of markets under generalized opportunism and disproportionately high transaction costs requires a system of guarantee. When a seller and a buyer enter into a business transaction, the chances are very small that one gives the other complete information spontaneously. Akerlof used the example of the used car markets to show that a seller has no interest in showing a potential buyer all the faults of the car for sale (*lemon*). The buyer has every reason to be suspicious, because, by definition, the seller knows more about the real qualities of the car: there is an information asymmetry, because withholding information can yield better terms of exchange for the seller. Akerlof concluded that this type of market should not exist or should quickly come to a halt, because of generalized, economically rational distrust – this is *Akerlof's paradox*.

Why do markets such as these nevertheless exist? Their existence is not due to the capacity to communicate *complete* information, because, Akerlof argued, the transaction costs of obtaining complete information would strangle them. Markets for used cars and others like them exist and work reasonably well, because there are systems of guarantee in place limiting the risk of the buyer in view of the potential opportunism of the seller (and other buyers). For example, the buyer may have the possibility to return the used car within a certain period after purchase if not satisfied, and this limits the risk perceived by the buyer. The great virtue of systems of guarantee is to avoid the economically inefficient costs arising from an excess of information and effectively to put a cap on transaction costs. This insight has been largely incorporated into modern economic theory, particularly in the

---

[4] George A. Akerlof, 'The market for "lemons": quality uncertainty and the market mechanism', *Quarterly Journal of Economics* 84 (3) (1970), 488–500.

study of contracts and markets.[5] In his major work, *Uncertainty, Risk and Profit* (1921), Knight showed that the entrepreneur's principal role was to serve as a wedge or obstruction to other actors' uncertainty about the future, by himself (herself), through actions and dynamic behaviour, *incarnating* the future. Self-confidence and the confidence that other stakeholders have in him/her create a *guarantee* that suffices to keep uncertainty at bay and enable economic calculations. This theory is a very important addition, from a liberal point of view, to our understanding of the entrepreneur, for it provides a foundation for conceptualizing the economic function (to allow economic calculation in spite of generalized social mistrust) of the entrepreneur as a political figure (who incarnates the general interest). Building on the contributions of Knight, the role played by the entrepreneur can be extended to that of corporate governance, as founder entrepreneurs disappear and are replaced by systems of governance.[6] Although they do not refer directly to Knight, contemporary observers of corporate governance such as C. K. Prahalad or Mary O'Sullivan argue along the same lines.[7]

If one considers the corporation as an object of property, it is clear that shareholders have neither the interest nor the competence to obtain and analyse complete information on the corporation – the governance costs (transaction and agency costs) are too high. In other words, the market for shares closely resembles the context of uncertainty described by Knight and Akerlof. The rational shareholder n, a fraction of the total population of shareholders, N, wants to be sure that his/her stake has a *fair chance*, within his/her time horizon, to earn a return according to his/her expectations. When one argues that the individual shareholder seeks to have complete information on the corporation and control the management, one is in effect proposing

---

[5] See Coase, 'The nature of the firm'; O. E. Williamson, *Markets and Hierarchies*, New York: The Free Press, 1975.

[6] Based on the work of Knight and Keynes (see below), the economics of uncertainty have developed as an important line of thought, focused on understanding how economic rationality and calculation remain possible under uncertainty. See, especially, P.-Y. Gomez and B. Jones, 'Conventions: an interpretation of deep structures in organizations', *Organization Science* 11 (6) (2000), 696–708.

[7] See C. K. Prahalad, 'Corporate governance or corporate value added? Rethinking the primacy of shareholder value', *Journal of Applied Corporate Finance* 6 (4) (1994), 40–50; M. O'Sullivan, 'The innovative enterprise and corporate governance', *Cambridge Journal of Economics* 24 (4) (2000), 393–416.

that the shareholder will *personally ensure the guarantee*. This implies not only an overestimation of the shareholder's cognitive capacities, but also a misunderstanding of the shareholder's economic interest. As an economically rational actor, the shareholder would prefer to *buy a guarantee*. By buying a guarantee, the shareholder can ensure not the actual level of the return, but the fair chance to achieve that return, without major risks stemming from the lack of a guarantee concerning the future state of affairs. The transaction costs the shareholder is willing to pay are limited by the costs of the guarantee. *It is our hypothesis that the shareholder seeks not to know the 'true' value of the corporation, but rather to obtain a guarantee on the continued existence of the property rights he/she buys.* As we will show in the following pages, this reformulation of the problem permits a resolution of the paradoxes presented above and provides the key to explaining the role played by corporate governance in the performance of the corporation, both in absolute terms and relative to the competition.

What kind of guarantee is needed to ensure that the market for shares works?

The work of a contemporary of Berle and Means and Knight, J. M. Keynes, offers the decisive distinction between normal economic risks and systemic risks due to the absence of a guarantee concerning the future state of affairs. Keynes writes:

> The state of long-term expectation, upon which our decisions are based, does not solely depend, therefore, on the most probable forecast we can make. It also depends on the *confidence* with which we make this forecast or how highly we rate the likelihood of our best forecast turning out quite wrong. If we expect large changes but are very uncertain as to what precise form these changes will take, then our confidence will be weak.[8]

In Keynes' view, the shareholder is subject to two kinds of risk: a risk of position, deriving from the shareholder's choices and personal calculations; and a risk of failure due to the disappearance of the corporation invested in or the disappearance of the market itself. In the consideration of the first type of risk, the shareholder can make mistakes of evaluation or portfolio allocation – the risk is tied to his/her cognitive

---

[8] J. M. Keynes, *The General Theory of Employment, Interest and Money*, London: Macmillan and Cambridge University Press, 1936, Ch. 12, II.

limitations. In the second type of risk, the corporation or the market may simply disappear, for reasons that the shareholder *could not suspect*. How to evaluate this second type of risk?

In practice we have tacitly agreed, as a rule, to fall back on what is, in truth, a convention. The essence of this convention though it does not, of course, work out quite so simply lies in assuming that the existing state of affairs will continue indefinitely, except in so far as we have specific reasons to expect a change. This does not mean that we really believe that the existing state of affairs will continue indefinitely ... We are assuming, in effect, that the existing market valuation, however arrived at, is uniquely correct in relation to our existing knowledge of the facts which will influence the yield of the investment, and that it will only change in proportion to changes in this knowledge ... Nevertheless the above conventional method of calculation will be compatible with a considerable measure of continuity and stability in our affairs, so long as we can rely on the maintenance *of the convention*.[9]

Applying these remarks directly to the ownership of shares in a corporation, we can say that shareholders in a large, fragmented share-holding body do not necessarily seek complete information. However, in order to accept to become shareholders and hold property rights that earn a return over time, they have to have Keynes' confidence that 'the existing state of affairs will continue indefinitely, except in so far as we have specific reasons to expect a change' (citation as above). As Keynes shows, this confidence is a necessary condition for interpreting the information provided and making rational choices.

For, assuming that the convention holds good, it is only these changes which can affect the value of his investment, and he need not lose his sleep merely because he has not any notion what his investment will be worth ten years hence. Thus investment becomes reasonably 'safe' for the individual investor over short periods, and hence over a succession of short periods however

---

[9] Keynes, *General Theory of Employment*, Ch. 12, IV. Note that these results do not contradict the reasoning of liberalism's original thinkers: Montesquieu, Hume, Tocqueville, and Mill all insisted on the important roles played by opinion and custom in reaching stable equilibrium in societies founded on the basis of individual liberty. For example, in *On Liberty*, Mill writes: 'The effect of custom, in preventing any misgiving respecting the rules of conduct which mankind impose on one another, is all the more complete because the subject is one on which it is not generally considered necessary that reasons should be given, either by one person to others, or by each to himself.' J. S. Mill, *On Liberty*, London: Penguin Books, 1982 [1869], Ch. I: Introductory.

many, if he can fairly rely on there being no breakdown in the convention and on his therefore having an opportunity to revise his judgment and change his investment, before there has been time for much to happen.[10]

In summary, we can say that *not all* shareholders seek to obtain complete information on the corporation: the amount of information obtained depends on the governance costs the individual shareholder is willing to pay. By contrast, *all* shareholders need to obtain such information as allows them to be sure that the corporation has a fair chance to continue to exist. What can offer such a guarantee?

The corporate governance system as a factor of confidence

It is our contention that the corporate governance system fulfils this role, namely to ensure for the shareholder a level of confidence that the corporation does not run the risk of disappearance. Our contention is based on an objective analysis of corporate governance codes and laws: across all four of the countries that serve as the sample for this book, as well as in many other countries, the functions of corporate governance and the role of the guardians of corporate governance – the board of directors – are associated by code and/or law with the longer-term success or 'permanence' of the corporation. Thus, in France, the Board of Directors 'defines the company's strategy, appoints the corporate officers responsible for managing the company, oversees management and ensures the quality of information provided' and is 'required to act at all times in the interests of the company'.[11] The German supervisory board 'appoints, supervises, and advises the members of the management board and is directly involved in decisions of fundamental importance to the enterprise'; it is 'obliged to act in the best interests of the enterprise'.[12] In the United Kingdom, the Board of Directors 'should lead and control the company, being collectively responsible for success'; moreover, 'all directors must take decisions objectively in the interests of the company'.[13] In the United States, finally, the Board of Directors 'has the important role of overseeing

---

[10] Keynes, *General Theory of Employment*, Ch. 12, IV.

[11] The Corporate Governance of Listed Corporations in France, October 2003, AFEP and MEDEF (summary based on the Vienot and Bouton Reports of 1995, 1999, and 2002, respectively): Article 1.

[12] German Corporate Governance Code, June 2006, also known as the Cromme Code: Foreword and Article 3.

[13] The Combined Code on Corporate Governance, June 2006: Section 1.

management performance on behalf of stockholders; primary duties are to select and oversee management and monitor its performance and adherence to corporate standards'.[14]

Economically speaking, the requirement that corporate governance must ensure the success or permanence of the corporation is ambiguous, because board members or managers cannot be forced to guarantee personally the permanence of the corporation. However, the law does expect that board members act with all *diligence* in matters pertaining to corporate governance so that market and business confidence is maintained. In effect, code and/or law cast the convention that Keynes described into the constitutions of corporations. The corporate governance system has to guarantee that the conditions to ensure the permanence of the corporation are fulfilled and that the economic risk run by the corporation is 'normal', that is to say limited to the swings of markets and competition.

We now see that corporate governance has a direct and essential economic function: thanks to corporate governance, a shareholder can take 'normal' economic risks and *'need not lose his sleep merely because he has not any notion what his investment will be worth ten years hence'* (Keynes, as cited above, our italics). Thus corporate governance puts a defined cap on the governance costs that a shareholder has to pay. Conversely, the absence of confidence in the governance of a corporation can lead shareholders to consider the risks of disappearance associated with the corporation to be so great that no economic calculation is possible – the governance costs are too high.

Corporate governance's economic function is to provide a signal to the market about the quality of the corporation. This function is not purely abstract; it translates into very clear mandates of control and evaluation of the corporation, and the economic actors can verify whether or not these mandates are being *responsibly carried out*. One can distinguish three types of signals, from corporate governance to the market: First, the corporate governance system defines the nature of corporate performance. Corporate governance is concerned not only with the level of profit, but also with the manner in which the profit is achieved: through short-term adjustment or long-term measures; to the detriment of employment and the environment; by opening the capital

[14] European Corporate Governance Network, www.ecgi.de/codes/all_codes.php: exact responsibilities differ by state of incorporation.

of the corporation or by engaging in partnership agreements that weaken control; and so forth. The manner in which profit is realized differs from corporation to corporation, depending on the interests of the actors involved in corporate governance. The essential point is that the shareholder can have confidence that the decisions taken are coherent with how the actors involved in the corporate governance have defined the performance of the corporation.[15]

Second, the corporate governance system controls the major risks incurred by the corporation and ensures that managerial decisions minimize these risks. By major risks, we mean those risks that could lead to the disappearance of the corporation, or to a change in the nature of performance as defined in the preceding point. In fact, the sustainability of performance depends not only on the basic conditions for performance being fulfilled, but also on the level of risk incurred in achieving the performance – whether or not achieving the performance incurs any risk of the corporation disappearing.[16] In other words, performance stability presupposes that all potential risks of failure are taken into account.

Finally the corporate governance system chooses the managers who are likely to produce the required level of performance. This means that the actors involved in corporate governance are responsible for ensuring the coherence of the strategies put in place and the performance expected. In doing so, the corporate governance system legitimates the managers and stabilizes their capacity for long-term economic action.

These three signals – definition of the nature of expected performance, control of the major risks incurred, and selection of the appropriate managers – constitute the objective content of the guarantee provided

---

[15] This signalling function of corporate governance helps explain why the financial markets are so strongly influenced by missed earnings expectations, whether the miss is negative or positive. The apparent irrationality of the markets' reactions is completely understandable in the context of analysing whether or not the corporation's governance 'controls' the situation and can hence make good on its guarantee for the future state of affairs. Even a positive miss can lead to doubts about the quality of this guarantee.

[16] This discussion would apply to a corporation that earns a profit from operating in a very unstable political context. The existence of profit should not mask the risk of a political change and the subsequent disappearance of the corporation, unless the corporate governance system has explicitly defined performance in terms of short-term profit from political risk (definition of performance – the first of the three signals of corporate governance).

by the corporate governance system. These signals guarantee that the corporation can be an object of exchange of property rights (*usus, fructus,* or *abusus*); normal business risks are not covered by the guarantee – what is covered is the question of whether or not the corporation is capable of confronting these risks. Thus, corporate governance provides markets with the confidence they need to work, the confidence to evaluate the corporation without the uncertainty that the future state of affairs has not been considered with due diligence.[17] On the basis of the argument developed to this point, we are now ready to examine how the confidence of the markets affects the performance of the corporation.

Why and when does the shareholder have confidence in a corporate governance system?

Quite clearly, the shareholder's evaluation of a corporate governance system's adequacy as a guarantee contains both subjective and objective elements. Subjective elements include the good reputation of the corporation and the capacity of the actors involved in corporate governance to convince the markets of the quality of their work to ensure the permanence of the corporation. These subjective elements are perceptions that can be erroneous, subject to fashion or market manipulation; this is why there also need to be objective elements in the shareholder's evaluation of a corporate governance system's adequacy as a guarantee. What shape might these objective elements take?

It stands to reason that the more complex the environment faced by the corporation, the greater the number and magnitude of major risks in Keynes' terms, and the greater the need for the shareholder to receive the reassurance that the corporate governance system in place is capable of

---

[17] There exist, of course, public institutions with the purpose of preventing the intentional communication of erroneous information to the markets (the SEC in the United States; the FSA in the United Kingdom; the AMF in France; and the Boersenaufsicht in Germany). These institutions do contribute to the establishment of a certain level of confidence in the markets. However, even if the public authorities work to prevent information *fraud*, their role cannot be extended to ensure the economic permanence of the corporation; in a liberal society, public institutions cannot take on such an extended role, and the kind of guarantee offered by the SEC and its counterparts in other countries is in no way comparable to the guarantee offered by the state on its bonds. It is not the vocation of the state to certify that a corporation is not a *lemon*, and that it will continue to exist in the future.

integrating and dealing with complex information. If the shareholder wants to make sure that the corporate governance system performs its function of signalling to the market with all due diligence, then the system has to be coherent with the characteristics of the business environment of the corporation. What is the probability that a major risk will lead to the disappearance of the corporation? One can say that this probability rises with the complexity of the environment of the corporation. The greater the complexity C, the higher the risk that some information will be missing, that some elements will escape consideration or be subject to fraud, and that a mistaken estimation will be made, with increased consequences for the corporation and, ultimately, a higher probability of disappearance. This is a basic result of information theory: the probability p of disappearance or total loss tends towards 1, as the complexity of the business context tends towards infinity.

We have posited that the corporate governance system can guarantee that major risks are considered and incorporated in the strategy of the corporation. Such a system's capacity to evaluate these risks has to be a function of its own complexity, c_G. The more complex the system of corporate governance the better its ability to interpret complex information – this is Ashby's Law of requisite variety applied to corporate governance. Ultimately, then, the probability of total loss depends on C *and* c_G, or the complexity of the corporate governance system relative to the complexity of the business context. The closer the complexity of the corporate governance system to the complexity of the business context, the lower is the probability of disappearance p. We can say that $p = f^{-1}(C/c_G)$ with $p \to 0$ if $C/c_G \to 1$ and $p \to 1$ if $C/c_G \to \infty$. In the case of disappearance, the shareholder loses all of the capital, K, put in. If the shareholder includes the risk of disappearance in the calculation and Π is the performance of the corporation, the shareholder's expected profit is $\Pi - (K * p)$ or $\Pi - [K * f^{-1}(C/c_G)]$.

For the guarantee provided by the corporate governance system to be credible, the shareholder has to perceive that the complexity of this system is adapted to the complexity of the business context in which the corporation operates. On the basis of the guarantee argument articulated to this point, we can resolve two dilemmas which the introduction of fragmentation of ownership posed to the PEM (see above). First, we are now able to affirm that the choice of corporate governance system has a direct economic effect – it is not merely one way among others of enabling capital expansion (size effect). The shareholder's perceived risk of total loss depends on the corporate governance system's credibility as a guarantee. Second, the historical evolution of corporate governance systems towards increased complexity described in the second part of the book finds its support in economic reasoning: even if the single owner is a great entrepreneur, his/her cognitive capacity is constrained by the limited rationality of the single human being (or entity). Let us call this upper bound c_G^{ent}. If the owner takes the risk of capital loss into account, his/her expected profit is $\Pi - (K * p)$ or $\Pi - [K * f^{-1} (C / c_G^{ent})]$. In other words, the higher the complexity of the business context, the more the expected profit of the owner is reduced by the risk of total loss due to the owner's limited rationality. This is why, above a certain threshold of complexity in the business context (for which size is a proxy), the corporate governance system has to change towards a greater capacity to deal with complexity. Finally, the inclusion of democratic procedures in corporate governance is a consequence of the fragmentation of the shareholding body – democratic procedures such as the separation of powers and representation with public debate imply a greater complexity of the corporate governance system, well suited to the increasingly complex business context of today's corporation. In sum, the confidence shareholders have in a corporate governance system represents a solution to the mistrust engendered by generalized opportunism: this confidence or trust is the resultant of the evaluations made of the corporation's institutions and can be comprehended as a function of the system's capacity to address complex information, a capacity that is all the more important if the corporation itself faces a complex business context.

2 The economic function of corporate governance as a system of guarantee

Building our argument upon the notion of guarantee, we can now respond to the question underlying the entire economic development presented in this chapter: from the point of view of the owner, in what way does the corporate governance system directly impact the performance of the corporation? In order to answer this question, it is necessary to define the concept of economic performance more precisely. We can speak of *absolute* performance (the level of profit observed at the end of one period) and of *relative* performance (the level of profit compared to the focal corporation's competitors at the end of one period).

Minimization of governance costs and absolute performance of the corporation

Let us assume a rational actor who wishes to acquire a property right of a corporation. Let us further assume that there is no system of corporate governance in place. The prospective shareholder would have to pay transaction costs (costs of information, of contracting, etc.)[18] that diminish the profit expected from acquiring the property right. The more complex the business context of the corporation, the larger the amount of information our prospective shareholder would have to treat. In other words, transaction costs for the prospective shareholder increase with the rising complexity of the corporation (greater size, greater diversity of markets, larger number of processes, etc.).

If the corporate governance system *guarantees* the permanence of the corporation by the control it has over major risks and by the adequate complexity of its governance procedures then the transaction costs that the prospective shareholder has to pay are reduced. Thus, the more confidence the prospective shareholder can have in the corporation's governance, the greater the gain in reduced transaction costs that he/ she will expect from the acquisition, but the more the guarantee will cost (the higher the shareholder's willingness to pay for the guarantee). Instead of controlling by himself (and paying for this), the shareholder relies on corporate governance to do the job (its job). For example, shareholders can gain confidence from observing active boards, serious auditors, thorough accounting publications, transparent information policies, etc. Thanks to these signals, shareholders do not have to interpret all of the information on the corporation themselves – they simply verify that the controls exist and are performing as expected. Such a guarantee is not free: it has the price of the agency costs required to communicate the necessary information on controls, verifications, and evaluations. In effect, the corporation has to prove that due diligence is done in corporate governance to provide a credible guarantee. There again, however, the amount of information needed is limited by a credibility threshold at which the signals are considered believable by the shareholders. As we have said, this credibility threshold is a function of the complexity of the corporation's business context and hence of the necessary complexity of its governance system.

---

[18] Williamson, 'The nature of the firm'.

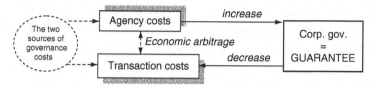

Figure 4 Dynamic of corporate governance as a guarantee

The shareholder is placed in a position of arbitrage: either to pay transaction costs or to pay agency costs. An equilibrium is reached when the guarantee provided by the corporate governance system is considered credible and the transaction costs that would have to be paid are decreased (see Figure 4).

The objective of a shareholder n, in a fragmented shareholding body, is not to control the corporation and hence pay a cost of control out of all proportion with his/her potential gain; rather the shareholder's objective is to minimize governance costs to maximize return, while being assured of the permanence of the corporation. The governance costs are minimized when the marginal governance costs are zero, that is to say when an increase in agency costs of 1$ leads to a decrease in transaction costs of 1$. If the increase in agency costs is 2$ for a saving (gain) in transaction costs of 1$, one can clearly see that the shareholder can have no interest whatsoever in raising controls that diminish his/her return. There exists an optimal level of guarantee at which agency costs are lower than the savings (gain) in transaction costs. At this level of guarantee, the corporation offers the maximum return for the shareholder while *minimizing governance costs.*

Our analysis has shown that corporate governance has a direct positive effect on the performance of the corporation. A governance system that is judged to be poorly adapted to the treatment of information necessary to ensure the permanence of the corporation will have a negative effect on its value, because buyers of property rights in the corporation will have to bear more of the transaction costs. Conversely, a credible (well-adapted) governance system fulfils the function of guaranteeing the corporation's capacity to sustain its performance and hence decreases the transaction costs associated with the exchange of property rights.

The costs of governance rise with the complexity of the business context faced by the corporation, such that the complexity of the governance system is directly proportional. Trust plays the key role here: economic actors do not calculate the costs of governance and then conclude on the sufficiency or insufficiency of the guarantee offered by the corporate governance system; rather, because they accept the guarantee, *they do not calculate all the costs of corporate governance*. In other words, the guarantee provided by the corporate governance system 'blocks' economic calculations at a certain level and hence makes the system economically acceptable.

Under the familial governance model, George Westinghouse could say: 'The *Name* of Westinghouse is a guarantee.'[19] As the size of the corporation increases, corporate governance tends to become more complex and to include greater use of democratic procedures, as our historical review showed. The fragmentation of property ownership and the democratization of corporate governance have had the economic consequence of allowing the corporation to navigate successfully a world of increasing complexity without the necessity of irrationally complex controls and purely passive shareholders, as the paradox of Berle and Means supposed. Democratization of corporate governance has allowed for an increase in the level of guarantee provided to shareholders without an exponential increase in the costs of control. This, then, is the link between the economic function of corporate governance as developed in this chapter and the confidence of the business system in corporate governance, the political dimension we discussed in the first and second parts of the book. The economic analysis corroborates the political and historical analyses. What remains to be shown is how the economic analysis helps explain the selection of corporate governance systems and the emergence of models of reference as presented in the description of the historical evolution of governance forms.

Relative performance and the evolution of corporate governance

How does arbitrage between agency costs and transaction costs take place?

At this stage of the analysis, we can state that a corporation is free to choose its model of corporate governance; there is no single best model – a corporation's choice of governance model depends upon the expected economic performance of that choice. Who makes the choice of

---

[19] See Ch. 3.

corporate governance model? Ultimately, the choice is a result of the reasoned preferences of the shareholding body, whether unified or fragmented.

Up to this point, we have argued on the basis of one corporation, without considering its position in the competitive system. This has allowed us to define the effect of corporate governance on the absolute performance of the corporation. We will now extend the analysis to include the question of competition for resources. Under competition, the choice of corporate governance model depends not only on the minimization of a corporation's own governance costs, but also on the focal corporation's chosen corporate governance model's capacity to do a better job of minimizing governance costs than the corporate governance form opted for by competitors, while at the same time providing the same level of guarantee, that is to say the same level of trust. *Ceteris paribus*, this will lead to higher relative performance in the focal corporation. By introducing the notion of competition between corporate governance forms, we hope to be able to explain, on the basis of economic reasoning, why certain forms of corporate governance come to dominate others and become models of reference. In this way, we want to show how the historical description of Part II and the economic analysis of Part III can be tied together.

Competition over resources

Corporations are in competition with each other over economic resources. The competitive productive process we refer to is a direct consequence of the liberal economic order and the fragmentation of property ownership, as described in Part I. The process of capturing resources under competition appeals to the free, economically rational choices of the individuals holding these resources. In other words, resources are allocated by market forces, not by the planning of a Leviathan. Two types of economic resources are fundamental to the development of the corporation: capital resources that allow corporations to increase productive investment – these resources are provided by shareholders and bankers who have the choice of which corporation to invest in, depending upon the relative expected return; and labour resources that allow corporations to make use of human capital – these resources are provided by employees who have the choice of which corporation to work for, depending also upon the relative expected return on their productive capacities.

Each individual with resources to offer seeks to maximize his/her personal benefit. Therefore, according to our reasoning, the individual will seek out the corporation that optimizes governance costs – *ceteris paribus*, this is the corporation that returns a higher level of profits. In other words, the individual will prefer to offer resources to the corporation whose model of corporate governance provides a better guarantee than competing corporations. Thus, if their choice is perfectly rational, economic individuals offering resources to a corporation will first consider how much confidence they can place in the corporation, based on the signals of corporate governance. If they can be very confident of the corporation, they will not seek to obtain additional information and therefore do not have to pay the associated transaction costs. The *perceived* costs of governance are small. Conversely, if confidence in the corporation is low, individuals will be more likely to pay transaction costs to find out more about the corporation to reassure themselves and to evaluate the agency costs necessary to provide a credible guarantee.

If we take the point of view of the corporation and reason in symmetric fashion, we can conclude that the corporation which offers a better guarantee (by its governance) has better chances of capturing capital and labour resources: compared to its competitors, it offers better economic performance. All else equal, the economic profit expected is higher the lower the perceived governance costs. By capturing these resources at a lower price, the better-governed corporation confirms its advantage over its competitors. If one applies the rules of rational economic calculation, one can state that those corporations offering a lower level of guarantee because their corporate governance inspires less confidence have only two possible solutions: either they raise the level of profits paid out, thereby paying more for their resources, a kind of risk premium that equals the difference in governance costs perceived by the resource holders; or, they change strategic fields so as to escape the resource competition of corporations perceived to be better governed.

Alignment of optimal guarantees and convergence towards governance models of reference

It is rational to think that the owners of property rights *compare* the corporate governance forms of corporations that are in competition over productive resources. As stated earlier in this chapter, the confidence carried by a corporation's guarantee can be ascribed to both subjective and objective elements. Since the holders of resources have the choice, the more fragmented ownership becomes, the more the evaluation of the guarantee is based on a comparison among corporations. As a result, confidence in a corporation depends upon the level of competition among corporations in signalling the quality of their corporate governance. Competition for resources leads to competition for confidence in a corporation's governance.

This finding is of great importance in understanding the economics of the historical evolution of corporate governance, and more particularly in understanding why models of reference for corporate governance first emerge and are subsequently replaced. According to economic theory, every competitive system tends towards profit minimization. If a corporation profits by capturing resources more cheaply thanks to the more credible guarantee its corporate governance represents in the eyes of resource providers, that corporation will face imitation from its competitors. In order to capture resources as well, the competing corporations will have an interest in reproducing the corporate governance model that apparently represents the best guarantee. In a given competitive space, governance costs will have the tendency to equalize, and the advantage gained from better governance to disappear. The excess profit (or the relative performance) due to 'good governance' tends towards zero. This explains the diffusion and standardization of good governance practices, throughout the history of capitalism, and finally, the generalization, at each major stage of this history, of a model of reference for corporate governance. In each era, those corporations undergoing rapid development and seeking to capture the maximum amount of resources adapt to each other in a game of competitive interaction aimed at presenting a model of corporate governance that represents a credible guarantee to resource holders.[20]

The model of corporate governance that best captures resources and is adopted by the leading corporations becomes the model of reference for an era. History has seen a succession of models of

[20] In effect, the reasoning outlined here echoes that of Chandler, see
A. D. Chandler, *Strategy and Structure*, Cambridge, MA: MIT Press, 1962.
Like organizational structure, corporate governance can be considered a factor in the effectiveness of corporations; by the process of competitive adaptation, then, the governance model that better fits the environment of the time drives out the model that fits less well.

reference emerge this way: familial governance, managerial governance, and then public governance. In their time, each of these governance forms was considered by resource holders to be the most credible,
because they offered an optimal guarantee (that is to say the guarantee
that minimizes governance costs, as demonstrated above).

Our economic analysis is compatible with the historical observations
made in Part II: the transition from one model of reference to another
has always been accompanied by an economic crisis. Whether it was
the industrial revolution that saw the emergence of familial governance
or the vast increase in the size and complexity of economic activity that
accompanied the rise to pre-eminence of managerial governance, or the
demise of national borders (globalization) and the technological
changes that led to public governance's ascent, each historical transition
has called for great new contributions in terms of financial and human
resources in order for corporations to face up to the challenge of bigger
and more complex markets. The economic crises decisively alter the
complexity of the corporation and hence call into question the credibility of the guarantee of permanence offered by existing forms of
governance. Shaken by economic crisis, resource holders move to
corporations that offer a better guarantee. As a result, certain models
of governance become obsolete and wither: this is how first familial
governance and then managerial governance lost their dominant positions and were eventually replaced as the models of reference. The crisis
of confidence they faced went hand in hand with an economic crisis of
historical proportions and eventually led to a reallocation of resources
and a redefinition of the level of the guarantee represented by corporate
governance.

Barriers to entry and the maintenance of locally divergent forms of governance

In spite of the force of the self-fulfilling process described above,
clearly not all corporations conform to a single model of governance.
In every historical stage of capitalism, multiple governance forms
co-exist. Even if, as we noted at the end of Part II, a model of reference
has a strong influence on the governance of the period in general, in
some cases ownership and certain informal practices do refer to a form
other than that of the model of reference. How to explain this apparent
exception to the general pattern within the framework set forth in
this book?

In two particular cases, we can observe strong differentiation, with governance forms that differ markedly from the general trend and the model of reference for the particular stage of capitalist evolution: first the case of the charismatic entrepreneur (charismatic differentiation), and second the case of corporations operating in sectors or strategic groups that are isolated from the rest of the market (differentiation by niche).

The first case represents that of a corporation in which the leader incarnates the entrepreneurial force of direction. Be it as the founder or as the transformer, the charismatic leader's personality and the performance of the corporation are inseparably linked. It is entirely consistent with the results of our analysis to this point to argue that, in some cases, resource holders can consider the personal guarantee that the entrepreneur represents to be sufficient and even better than other possible forms of governance. The resource holders' allegiance is owed to the personal energy and the specific projects of the charismatic entrepreneur: in terms of economic rationality, resource holders are all the more satisfied that the confidence they can have reduces and indeed minimizes the costs of governance. In other words, economic calculation is favourable to this model of governance that reduces, at least for a given time, the considerable agency and transaction costs associated with fragmentation and democratization (as pointed out earlier in this chapter). However, charismatic differentiation is transitory; as was also made clear above, the case of governance by the entrepreneur reaches its upper bound when the economic environment of the corporation becomes too complex and outgrows the necessarily limited rationality of the entrepreneur. There is a threshold above which the charismatic guarantee becomes doubtful. Nevertheless, below this threshold of complexity, one can conceive of a model of governance centred upon the entrepreneur that offers a sufficient guarantee to be preferred to all other, more expensive forms of governance.

The second case of maintaining a model of governance that differs from the model of reference of the era refers to corporations operating in isolated strategic groups. In the foregoing argument, we reasoned as if the markets for capturing resources were perfectly homogeneous, that is to say that all corporations (within an industry, broadly conceived) were in competition for the same resources. Of course, this is not a realistic assumption. Each industry is divided into several strategic groups, a set of corporations that base their strategies on similar competitive advantages and hence require identical resources.[21] Owing to the presence of strategic groups, we can say that competition for resources is primarily played out not in the economy or the industry as a whole, but rather among corporations belonging to the same strategic group.

It is therefore possible that some strategic groups come to be aligned on a governance model that is not the same as the model of reference. If the group is sufficiently isolated, that is to say based on very specific competitive advantages and a narrow set of resources, then corporations in the group can maintain similar forms of governance. Resource holders will compare the guarantees offered by corporate governance *within* the strategic group. At a given level of environmental complexity, the group may then come to adhere generally to a model of governance that is different from the model of reference, but that is shared by the corporations in the group. In certain industries, one can observe strategic groups in which the familial, managerial, or even other models are overrepresented. For example, within banking, where public governance is the norm today, private banks have preserved the professional partnership (typically with unlimited liability) as the preferred model of governance for over two hundred years. The differentiation of governance by niche is only possible if the strategic group stays homogeneous: if, on the other hand, one or several corporations modify their model of governance in the search for new resources (especially financial resources), it is highly probable that this modification, should it increase the level of guarantee perceived by the resource holders, generalizes to the strategic group as a whole.

The concepts of charismatic differentiation and differentiation by niche allow us to explain why and how local specificities function as a barrier to entry: in some cases, the characteristics of the corporation and its environment offer an acceptable guarantee to resource holders, even if the model of governance is different from the model of reference of the era. This situation does not represent a paradox, from an economic point of view. One can speak of a general tendency towards

---

[21] M. S. Hunt, 'Competition in the major home appliance industry 1960–1970', PhD dissertation, Harvard University; H. H. Newman, 'Strategic groups and the structure–performance relationship', *Review of Economics and Statistics* 60 (August, 1978), 417–27; R. E. Caves and M. E. Porter, 'From entry barriers to mobility barriers: conjectural decisions and contrived deterrence to new competition', *Quarterly Journal of Economics* 91 (May, 1977), 241–62.

democratization in corporate governance without neglecting idio-syncratic local differentiation.

3 An economic interpretation for models of governance

The objective of this chapter was to show that the economic dimension of corporate governance could be articulated in a manner that is consistent with the fundamental expectations of liberal ideology. The extent of fragmentation of property ownership among individuals with different interests – a corollary of the liberal fragmentation of society – plays a critical role in the relative efficiency of different models of corporate governance and hence also in the evolution of corporate governance systems.

In fine, our argument is based on the distinction we draw between two sources of governance costs: agency costs, as stressed by the PEM, but also transaction costs. The dilemma faced by the holders of property rights is not whether or not to pay agency costs. Rather, the dilemma is whether to pay agency costs or transaction costs. We have shown that if one considers corporate governance as a system for guaranteeing the permanence of the corporation, then one can say that corporate governance increases agency costs and decreases transaction costs. This means that there exists a point of equilibrium at which the marginal agency cost is greater than the marginal saving in terms of transaction costs: it is at this point that governance costs are minimized and the optimal guarantee stands. Simply by applying classical economic reasoning, we have been able to provide an explanation for why corporations converge towards a model of reference for corporate governance; by the same reasoning, we have been able to show why corporate governance forms diverge locally and may differ from the model of reference by exploiting the need for idiosyncratic resources.

Thus, the fragmentation of property rights can be integrated in the economic analysis of the liberal project. For the PEM, the investor-dominated form is the general case towards which the corporation trends. In this view, it is the invisible hand of the market that allows private interests to coalesce into the general interest, in a context where the shareholding body is very fragmented. In the preceding chapter, we showed that this result is only obtained if one accepts very restrictive hypotheses about the convergence of shareholder interests towards profit maximization. However, neither observation nor the internal logic of the liberal model would suggest that these hypotheses have general validity. On the contrary, divergence of private interests would appear to be the general case, and convergence towards a common interest the particular case. This is why it seems important to us to place the fragmentation of interests at the centre of our economic reasoning, in keeping with the principles of liberalism.

Our model shows that it is possible to think of public governance taking on either investor dominated or shareowner dominated forms. In both cases, the financial markets play an important role, but not to the same degree. In particular, domination by shareowners is possible when the complexity of the economic environment is such that the guarantee provided by corporate governance cannot be based only on the free transfer of information. More formal owner control is necessary in this case, even if it takes the form of representation and sometimes public debate. For the shareholding body as a whole, this may be a necessary condition for the establishment of confidence. Economically, the increase in agency costs associated with shareowner involvement is less than the increase in transactions costs would be if mistrust became generalized. It is therefore wrong to argue for an inexorable trend towards investor domination on the basis that such a form minimizes the governance costs incurred by shareholders. In some cases, shareowner domination can reduce transaction costs and hence be economically more efficient. The argument presented here reconciles economic analysis with our observations of the last thirty years' developments in the corporate governance of the publicly listed corporation.

Conclusion to Part III

The defining challenge of the economic approach to corporate governance consists of integrating the question of performance in the analysis of legitimate governance forms. This is a challenge that goes to the heart of corporate governance, because economic performance and the legitimacy of the corporation are inextricably linked. Since the business corporation is a productive organization, it follows that corporate governance becomes established and grows stronger in line with its capacity to ensure the economic prosperity of the organization.

This line of questioning emerges and develops at precise moments of crisis in the history of the corporation: initially in the work of Berle and Means, as the separation between ownership and control materializing at the time signified the end of the genetic legitimacy of the founder entrepreneur. Berle and Means, and with them the institutionalists who dominated the technocratic period, argued that state intervention was necessary to ensure the performance of the corporation no longer controlled by its owners. In the 1970s, the time of a second crisis in corporate governance, a different line of thinking emerged to challenge the institutionalists and propose a return to the basic principles of the liberal political project. In a society of fragmented property ownership, it was suggested, the financial markets were the appropriate locus of entrepreneurial power. The evolution of corporate governance over the last quarter of the twentieth century has gone in this direction, a development that has contributed to the impression that corporate governance was now based on economic science. This impression is mistaken; in fact, economics has only recently translated the implications of the liberal political project for the corporation into its own terms. As we have described, the neoliberal approach has developed into a Pure Economic Model of corporate governance (PEM), a model with its own logic and its own limitations. By giving a fresh articulation to the economic dimension of the legitimacy of the entrepreneur, and by showing that the financial markets could play the entrepreneur's role, the PEM has made an important contribution; it provides one avenue for reconciling performance and legitimate governance in a context of social fragmentation. In this sense, the Pure Economic Model opened the door, but it has remained an incomplete opening. We have shown that the PEM, in postulating a convergence of interests among owners, fails to account for the diversity of interests that is an extreme but defining consequence of liberal society.

This is why we have sought (a) to embed the economic analysis in a comprehensive framework, compatible with the conditions of modern liberal society, that is to say a society fragmented among countless individual interests that do not converge *a priori*, and (b) to understand how corporate governance forms stabilize and become legitimate, in the *name of the level of economic performance* they can sustain. It seems to us that approaching the problem in terms of a guarantee that balances the costs of transaction and control provides a promising response to this challenge. Such an approach allows us to understand how a generalized lack of trust, the inevitable consequence of liberty and the autonomous pursuit of individual interests, as Hobbes pointed out in the earliest liberal debates, can be avoided by confidence in a structure of governance that all shareholders subjectively consider to be the most efficient (least costly) of all possible structures. Emphasizing the theme of confidence focuses autonomous individuals on acceptable governance forms and represents the other side of the coin to the mistrust which is a natural corollary of their autonomy. We have shown that this reasoning is economic, inasmuch as it permits the minimization of costs under uncertainty and hence improves the performance of the corporation. The conversion of public mistrust into institutional confidence helps explain the role played by the different forms of external counterweight in the evolution of corporate governance: the family, the unions, and public opinion have each participated in the establishment of a collective perception of confidence in corporate governance. Overall, as we have presented it, the economic approach to corporate governance reinforces the political approach. Going even further, one can say that, in order to understand fully the consequences of social fragmentation on corporate governance and its long-term evolution, it is imperative to consider economic performance as a necessary dimension of the legitimacy of corporate

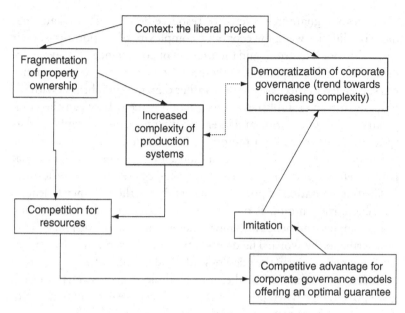

Figure 5 Process of democratization of corporate governance

governance. This is why we have insisted on articulating an economic approach.

From an economic point of view, we have pointed out that the risks of failure rise with the size of the corporation: therefore there exists a threshold of credibility for each model of corporate governance. Beyond this threshold, the guarantee offered is no longer credible; the owners of property rights are in doubt, transaction costs go up, and the value of capital invested declines. Consequently, corporations are led to modify their corporate governance. The capacity to deal with complexity grows with the number of actors involved: by integrating a greater number of individuals and viewpoints, corporate governance increases its ability to guarantee the permanence of the corporation faced with a more complex environment. In the sense of the term defined in Part I of this book, corporate governance adopts democratic procedures. Since the increase in the level of guarantee obtained in this manner leads to the payment of increased agency costs, there exists a point of equilibrium, such that a marginal increase in agency costs leads to a less than proportionate decrease in transaction costs; this is the point at which democratization stops, a level of complexity that optimizes the guarantee offered to resource holders. This means that there is a link between the economic complexity of corporations, their level of democratization, and their model of governance. The existence of this link helps explain why the evolution of corporate governance has succeeded in successive stages, rather than in brutal breaks with the past. Each stage establishes a credible adjustment between the complexity of the corporation and its environment, on the one hand, and its system of governance, on the other. Each stage represents an equilibrium of power and counterweights and a level of democratization that is sufficient to render the model of governance credible and efficient.

The fragmentation of property ownership has the tendency to lead to the generalization models of corporate governance that are more and more complex and hence also more "democratic" in the technical sense we ascribe to the word. The democratization of corporate governance is in alignment with the ideology of modern liberal society which considers democracy to be the most credible system of guaranteeing good governance when power is divided. Thus, we can say that democratization in corporate governance represents a self-fulfilling process, reinforced by economic rationality, as pictorially described in the Figure 5.

Reasoning from an economic point of view, we arrive at the same conclusion as the political and historical analyses presented in the first two parts of the book. Democratization is not a political constraint that seeks to impose itself in opposition to economic performance; on the contrary, democratization accompanies increasing complexity in the corporation and contributes to performance.

Epilogue

Our contemporaries are incessantly racked by two inimical passions: they feel the need to be led and the wish to remain free. Not being able to destroy either one of these contrary instincts, they strive to satisfy both at the same time. They imagine a unique power, tutelary, all powerful, but elected by citizens.[1]

Corporate governance is too often reduced to arcane technical questions and discussed in a way that focuses on particulars but lacks perspective. Our objective, in this book, has been to describe the fundamental drivers of corporate governance, so as to permit a broader appreciation of its roots and thereby contribute to a more nuanced debate in the field. Without pretending to do all the work of political scientists, historians, and economists, we wanted to show how political philosophy, history, and economics could be combined to present a coherent explanation of both the significance and the evolution of corporate governance. The point of departure for our reflections was provided by the understanding that corporate governance is but a particular case of the much more general subject area of modern governance. Corporate governance represents to us an application to the productive organization of the same questions that have pervaded the debates and the political practices of modern liberal societies for over two centuries, namely: when the governed are defined as free and equal before the law, *what* gives a person (or a group of people) the right to direct a unit of social organization, whether it be a country, a town, or a corporation? More specifically, how can shareholders, numerous and motivated by different interests, collectively exercise sovereignty, and how can decision makers maintain (economic) efficiency without impairing collective sovereignty? In response to these contradictory demands, over the last two centuries a set of

[1] Tocqueville, *DA* II, 4, 6, p. 664.

307

institutions, rules, and practices has evolved to define the framework for corporate governance in modern Western societies. Because the business corporation does not function in isolation from society, but, on the contrary, plays an integral part in the development of economic and social modernity, the men and women of business have had to find answers to the same questions posed by modern governance. Like their counterparts in political governance, they have had to make governance acceptable to the governed, both as a means of directing economic activity and as a guarantee for the continued pursuit of that activity.

Our analysis has shown that, in the corporation, the tension between the individual and the collective can be articulated in terms of two opposing forces: that of the entrepreneur, a force essential to the process of directing, canalizing, and organizing the energies of individuals in modern society, and that of social fragmentation, a force that, over time, tends to divide interests, balance those of some against those of others, and introduce an ever greater number of actors to the exercise of authority and/or control. The entrepreneurial force ensures a focus or concentration of power that social fragmentation continuously undermines. Democracy is a technique of government that, through the use of appropriate institutions and processes, permits the establishment of equilibrium between these two forces – an equilibrium that always remains precarious and open to reconsideration, subject to the powerful tension between entrepreneurial direction and social fragmentation. Under democratic governance, the governed consider the form of governance exercised over them to be just and acceptable, even necessary, as long as it maintains a balance between the directing force of the entrepreneur and the contrary force of social fragmentation.

The shaping of corporate governance

The political logic we have described sheds light on both the substance and the evolution of corporate governance since the origins of capitalism. The interplay of the forces of entrepreneurial direction and social fragmentation defines corporate governance and determines how it changes over time. Consider how social fragmentation has manifested itself in the ownership of the corporation: with the partition of property rights into *usus*, *fructus*, and *abusus*, in the modern corporation described by Berle and Means, we see the emergence of a variety of independent expectations, each of which represents a separate force in the exercise of power over the corporation. However, social fragmentation does not stop there: over time, the different dimensions of property rights spread among an increasing number of individuals. Thus, the shareholders' power of oversight is diluted by the advent of mass capitalism and the broad dispersion of share ownership, while managerial power becomes vested in an increasingly sophisticated technocratic system. In corporate governance, social fragmentation is manifest in the changing nature of ownership and has led to a multiplication of different sources of power – each with the potential to counteract the other.

The force of entrepreneurial direction adapts to the multiple forces of social fragmentation: the stronger the forces of fragmentation, the harder, in turn, the entrepreneurial force works to harness the diversity of interests so represented in the direction of the corporation. Historically, the entrepreneur was a single person, owning the entirety of the property rights and hence complete sovereignty over the corporation. Absent fragmentation of property ownership, the original entrepreneur was not constrained by any other powers and could fully exercise the right of direction. The family of the entrepreneur already represents a first stage in social fragmentation as played out in the ownership of the corporation: by inheritance and transmission, property rights are dispersed, further with each generation. As a consequence, already under familial governance, the entrepreneur has to work with a counterweight to absolute power and be attentive to the consideration of different opinions in decision making, the respect of family traditions, the defence of family and religious values, etc. In this way, the family deprives the entrepreneur of a part of his/her power. With the advent of the modern corporation, the fragmentation of family capital (dispersion of *abusus*) is accompanied by the partition of property rights and the emergence of professional management, with the right to direct the corporation (*usus*). Now, management collectively holds the entrepreneurial force, but they have to reach agreement over different interests, not only with respect to shareholders, but also among themselves. From the effort to render this diversity of interests coherent emerge the techniques of modern administration developed with the large corporation: *reporting, control, strategic planning*, etc. These techniques allow for the entrepreneurial force to be transformed

Table 2 *Corporate governance evolves between the entrepreneurial force and the fragmentation of property ownership*

Fragmentation of property ownership	Model of governance	Entrepreneurial force and possible Leviathan
Property divided within and/or between families	Familial	General interest realized by the family head
Property rights partitioned between management and shareholders; management itself divided into functions	Managerial	General interest realized by the managerial technocracy
Partition and large-scale dispersion of property rights	Public	General interest realized by the financial markets and/ or by shareowner groups

into a routine that can be exercised by a managerial technocracy.[2] Finally, the great growth in mass of the shareholding body and the attendant dispersion of ownership rights (*abusus*) leads to a new stage in the interplay between fragmentation and entrepreneurial direction. With ownership now dispersed among millions of rights holders, the financial markets and/or specific shareowner groups come to constitute the new locus for exercising the entrepreneurial force of direction. Here again, we see the emergence of techniques of administration especially adapted to ensuring coherence among divergent interests: concentration on shareholder value, management by EVA or ROE, increased emphasis on public information and disclosure, etc. Whereas the original entrepreneur was a single person who exercised the entrepreneurial force of direction alone, the development of capitalism has seen the fragmentation of property ownership, but has also brought about new ways of ensuring that fragmentation does not block the entrepreneurial force of direction. On the contrary, the entrepreneurial force feeds on fragmentation to provide orientation to economic activity, up to the point at which further fragmentation of property ownership undermines the entrepreneurial force and gives rise to a new, better-suited model of corporate governance, as depicted in Table 2.

[2] Schumpeter, *CSD*.

The implosive process described in this book can be observed at multiple levels of analysis: both in the historical evolution of corporate governance as portrayed in Part II, and in the development of the specific corporation, with successive stages of growth typically accompanied by transformations in the model of corporate governance in use – transformations that are driven by the need to adapt to and integrate the increasing number of economic actors concerned. As we have noted at various points in the argument, this does not mean that *all* corporations follow the same model of corporate governance at any given time. Today, for example, even as the public model of governance becomes dominant, there are still many corporations that adhere to certain aspects (but not all) of the familial and managerial models. Nonetheless, it is not possible to govern any corporation, no matter what its size or ownership form, without taking into consideration society's views on what constitutes a legitimate exercise of power on the part of the directors. Even if the entrepreneurial force of direction is held by one person, with fully concentrated ownership, and even if that person has only a single employee, he/she cannot exercise power and hence govern the corporation in opposition to the values of the society in which it is implanted. With increased size and the fragmentation of property ownership as it is common today, the influence of society on corporate governance is that much stronger. As our historical review has shown, corporate governance has democratized over time, with the successive incorporation of economic enfranchisement, separation of powers, and finally representation with public debate in the media and the markets. The observed tendency towards democratization of corporate governance should not be read as a value statement, positive or negative: our approach is not ideologically driven. Rather, our analysis simply demonstrates what Tocqueville or Schumpeter already pointed out long before us: democracy is the technique of government that is compatible with social fragmentation, one of the defining forces of the modern liberal world – this is what makes it so well suited to the political governance of capitalism. Corporate governance has democratized over time, because the corporation has become an integral part of modern society.

Democratization as a dialectic synthesis of opposing forces

Economic enfranchisement, separation of powers, and representation of different interests with public debate, these are the democratic procedures that allow the fragmentation of property ownership to work with the entrepreneurial force of direction. More than that, they provide the means for the entrepreneurial force to *build on* fragmentation as a *new engine of governance*. A good way to understand this process is to analyse how the institutions of corporate governance have evolved with the increasing fragmentation of property ownership in the corporation. The board of directors, for example, marks a formal line of separation between direction and accountability; under managerial governance, the board is composed of managers and operates as a round table of technocrats whose legitimacy is based on the special competences of its members; under public governance, on the other hand, the same institution of the board is opened to outside directors, to shareholder interest groups, and to stakeholders more broadly conceived, and links the corporation to the markets and society. In this way, the same institution has adapted over time to recreate a synthesis between the fragmentation of property ownership and the entrepreneurial force of direction. Similarly, the redefinitions of the role of the annual general meeting, of the functioning of the board and its committees, of the status of auditors and regulators, such as they appear in contemporary codes of best practice, permit a rebalancing of the equilibrium between the entrepreneurial force exercised by investors in the financial markets and shareowners and the increasing fragmentation of the private interests of the corporation's stakeholders.

In the last part of the book, we observed that this evolution has led to a model of corporate governance that is increasingly complex, adapted to the need continuously to integrate more people, more information, and better controls. Of course, this level of complexity increases the costs of corporate governance, but it also allows for the legitimization of corporations that are themselves increasingly complex, operating in a highly diverse environment of countries, products, and technologies. The democratization of the Western societies has been accompanied by more complexity in their economies, a level of complexity that democracy is particularly well suited to govern. Indeed, with increasing complexity in the economy, the diversity of private interests also increases, in turn providing a broader base for the democratic technique of governance. This is a positive dimension of governance by democratic procedure, a positive dimension one should not forget when evaluating the evolution of corporate governance towards ever more refinement of control. Contrary to what many pundits may think, the democratization of corporate governance may well increase the strength of the guarantee the corporation is able to offer, relative to its long-term prospects for survival.

If our hypothesis is correct, it is likely that the democratization of corporate governance will go hand in hand with increasing complexity, independent of the corporation's country of origin or the legal regime it operates under. Thus, we can expect emerging economies to follow through the same process of democratization of corporate governance, from familial to managerial to public, just as we have seen it in the Western countries, but much faster under the pressure of globalization and the concomitant effect of imitation. Again, we do not wish to engage in political or ideological debates – we merely want to point out the economic necessity underlying the democratization of corporate governance. To us, democracy represents a technique of governance that is particularly well suited to responding to the fragmentation of property ownership (but also of society more generally, as already stated) and the increasing complexity of the economic environment. Capitalist economic development can be read as a story of intensifying fragmentation of property ownership and of increasing complexity – this is why the democratic technique of governance is so important to its functioning.

The market as a Leviathan?

These last remarks should not be misconstrued: the long-term viability of the liberal democratic model is not a given. In order for the model to continue to work, it is important that individuals maintain confidence in the system – without confidence, any guarantee provided by corporate governance would be far too costly. The strength of the democratic technique of governance is traceable in no small part to the fact that it can be presented as the 'ideal of good modern governance', benefiting from the convention of general acceptance and by that very fact particularly cost effective. Absent this shared belief about the legitimacy of democratic governance, or if doubt becomes pervasive, the costs of governance (sharing of information, audit, control, etc.) would rise considerably, in proportion to the degree to which property is dispersed and ownership interests are fragmented. In such a context, corporate governance would be both economically and socially inefficient.

Therein lie both the force and the fragility of a system such as ours: force, as long as public acceptance is maintained and the directing role of the entrepreneur is assured either by an individual, the management, or the markets; but fragility, as soon as public confidence wanes. A generalized lack of confidence quickly blocks the system and stymies the entrepreneurial force of direction. In the past, public mistrust struck first the individual entrepreneur and then the management of the modern corporation. In our time, the financial markets may well be struck with self-doubt: can the markets trust themselves with the entrepreneurial force? To economists and finance theorists, these variations of confidence are well known as the driving force behind speculative bubbles.[3] As individuals become more and more confident in the financial markets, so confident that they suspend judgement, these markets tend to overheat. Individuals, participants in the markets, may attain an excessive level of confidence in the capacities of the real economy, leading on the one hand to higher and higher share prices, but on the other hand, and more profoundly, to the conviction that business can only get better with corporate governance guaranteeing this happy future, *as long as corporate governance sticks strictly to the principles of the financial markets turned entrepreneur.* As we know, an overdose of confidence can suddenly turn, leading individuals to doubt the information they receive, to question the competences of the corporations and the qualities of their management, with the corollary of falling share prices and a more generalized suspicion towards the legitimacy of the system of governance in place. In such a situation, the body politic has to intervene, even vigorously if necessary, to re-establish confidence in corporate governance. This is why the United States moved swiftly to enact the Sarbanes-Oxley legislation in 2002, primarily in response to the collapse of the new economy stock market bubble and secondarily in the Enron and Worldcom 'scandals' that the collapse of the bubble brought out into the open. By attracting attention to these scandals and by overreacting with legislation that is extremely constraining, it is clear that the federal government could

[3] Cf. R. P. Flood and P. Garber, 'Market fundamentals versus price level bubbles: the first tests', *Journal of Political Economy* 88 (1980), 745–70; R. J. Shiller, 'Do stock prices move too much to be justified by subsequent changes in dividends', *American Economic Review* 71 (1981), 421–36; and the major works of Kindleberger discussed in Chapter 8: C. P. Kindleberger, *Manias, Panics, and Crashes: A History of Financial Crises*, London: Macmillan, 1978.

not hope to prevent the possibility of fraud or illegal future behaviour – by definition, criminal activity will always attempt to defy the law. The principal driver of the enactment of this legislation was the need to restore public confidence in the corporate governance system, in other words to strengthen the legal, institutional, and practical bases for individual confidence in the long-term viability of publicly quoted corporations. Senators Sarbanes and Oxley reproduced what Congress realized back in 1934, when they voted on the Securities and Exchange Act: the necessity to intervene forcefully to re-establish public confidence. With local variations, the majority of the large markets have followed the lead of Sarbanes-Oxley, either by adopting new standards for audit and accounting (including attempts at international harmonization), or at least by confirming that existing rules were adequate. In this way, by 2003, confidence was re-established, and the markets could start a new ascent, at least until the next, predictable crash.

The succession of speculative bubbles on the way up, followed by bursts, and new bubbles on the way down has become a characteristic of the economic landscape. This succession of boom and bust is related to the evolution of corporate governance towards increasing fragmentation of property ownership. With more and more different individual interests concerned, each with its own point of view – managers, shareholders, financial intermediaries, members of society at large – the amount and the cost of information necessary to ensure adequate corporate governance become very high. Under such conditions, the financial markets' role of effecting strategic choices and acting as the entrepreneurial force becomes a process driven not by deliberation, but, increasingly, by *opinion*. Tocqueville emphasized the increasing reliance on opinion as an inexorable tendency of democratization, not as an inherent fault of the democratic technique of governance, but as an inevitable by-product of democracy's extension to ever larger circles of individuals. Market and public opinion can thus become a new Leviathan.

But, it is not possible to *have your cake and eat it too*, in other words, to have property rights partitioned and widely dispersed with ever more actors involved, and, at the same time, to have a deliberative process based on the structures that were adequate for corporations with a handful of shareholders sitting around the same table. Thus, annual general meetings have an antiquated, obsolete feel (who could realistically pretend to assemble millions of shareholders in the same room for a few hours once a year, to deliberate collectively over the future of the corporation?) and the legitimacy of corporate boards is questioned (when capital is so widely dispersed, whose interests do board members represent?). On the other hand, the opinion of the financial markets, relayed and amplified by the media, increasingly plays the role of the voice of the public: phrases such as 'the markets think', or 'the markets expect', or 'the markets welcome a decision', or 'the markets are disappointed', are all part of contemporary business vocabulary. To some degree, the markets express public opinion, just like surveys; this is what conveys to them the mantle of legitimacy of the entrepreneur under public governance. The financial markets exercise the force of the entrepreneur by representing the 'general opinion', in a manner that is as powerful and often as capricious as the movement of crowds. A crowd or mass of people is driven by imitation, and this amplifies the movements of opinion. Hence, we can conclude that the more widely dispersed the shareholding structure, the more likely we are to see a succession of speculative bubbles, on the way up and on the way down. This is state of the world that researchers and policy makers in corporate governance will henceforth have to take into consideration: the opinion of the entrepreneur is no longer carried by a single individual, or even a group of managers, but rather by public opinion, as expressed through the financial markets and the media. The democratization of corporate governance has allowed corporations to become very large and very complex, but it has also weakened corporations by making them increasingly dependent on the vagaries of public opinion. If one is not to be ideological about it, one cannot deny that corporations have become more fragile. Our focus has not been to comment on the economic rationality of increasing social fragmentation, but rather to describe the changes these developments imply for corporate governance. Still, our reading of the present, however strongly anchored in the analysis of the past, naturally begs questions about the future of corporate governance. The final remarks in this book therefore focus on the perspectives that can be derived from our approach.

Foreseeable changes in corporate governance: an evolution without end?

It is quite clear that the traditional institutions of corporate governance are not particularly well suited to a large, widely dispersed shareholding body. As we have pointed out, the annual general meeting and the board of directors, such as these institutions are currently implemented, are not adapted to the processes of democratic deliberation in an age of very widespread fragmentation of property ownership. This means that one can expect a number of reforms over the coming years. This process has already started with the generalized introduction of independent directors, a modification that marks a major step in the decline of the power of the managerial technocracy. With independents in leading positions, the board is opened up to a broader variety of interests and can hence provide a stronger guarantee for good corporate governance in a context of partitioned and widely dispersed property rights. Nonetheless, this naming of independent directors is only a first step, and the coming years will probably see increased measures of education, professionalization, and control, aimed at ensuring that board members fulfil their fiduciary role; in addition, the process of selecting board members is likely to evolve away from designation by management and towards selection by shareholders. Driven by the same logic of democratization, the annual general meeting is in for even more radical change. The size of the AGM has become absurd and untenable, given the wide dispersion of the shareholding body. In line with earlier developments in political governance, we would expect that the general meeting will be complemented by a smaller, more select assembly, composed of a limited number of representative shareholders, who will be elected by the entire shareholding body and will provide a counterweight to the management throughout the year, in the manner of a parliament. This development is already visible, with the emergence of 'shareholder associations' and 'minority associations' in a number of large corporations or even stakeholder panels in companies like Lafarge or Kodak.

The outline of the institutional future of corporate governance we have sketched here is based not on mere intuition, but rather on our observation of similar developments in the practice of political governance; if our hypothesis of democratization holds true, it is hard to accept that the same causes will not produce comparable effects in corporate governance. Social fragmentation gives rise to intermediary institutions whose role is to ensure adequate representation of diverging interests – even if that representation is more theatre than fact. The more this kind of representative institution develops, the less it is necessary to rely on public opinion as a measure of the general interest. The dilemma facing the corporation is the following: either to put in place more and stronger representative institutions that permit serious deliberation, with the effect of making corporate governance and strategy matters of public discussion and forcing management, after lengthy discussion, to live with decisions imposed upon them in areas that they had heretofore regarded as their exclusive domain, or to restrict the practice of deliberation, with the consequence of yielding power to public opinion, as expressed by the financial markets and the media. In the latter case, the entrepreneurial force of direction which guides and shapes the corporation would be left largely to the mercy of changes in opinion, bubbles, and crashes, as described earlier. With the high level of fragmentation of property ownership we know today and even more pronounced fragmentation likely in the future, the choice is between deliberation and hence more economic inertia or more 'laissez-faire', with long-term corporate policies subject to short-term vagaries of opinion.

Valuing and retaining human capital: a new challenge to the sovereignty of property

Can ownership of property be fragmented even further? The more the pressure of markets and public opinion can be considered as a new Leviathan, the more this question is worth asking in the very logic of liberal thought. As we have seen, property rights were partitioned into *usus*, *fructus*, and *abusus*, and then the ownership of these rights was first separated and then widely dispersed. Today, thousands, even millions of people will hold a fraction of the rights of *usus*, *fructus*, or *abusus* of a publicly listed corporation. Even if one admits that the number of owners of these property rights will continue to go up, one could think that fragmentation has reached qualitative limits – dispersion to 10 million is qualitatively little different from dispersion to 100 million people. And yet, a new type of fragmentation of property ownership of the corporation is already in process. With the development of the knowledge economy, the value of the corporation depends more and more on human capital and the creative activity of employees. It is to be expected that the notion of ownership in the corporation will undergo change in response to this development. Indeed, as long as the corporation creates value by the accumulation of machines and technologies that it allows employees to work on, the financial capital of the corporation corresponds quite closely to these assets and hence reflects true ownership of the corporation – property ownership means ownership of the means of production without which the employees would be incapable of creating value. Now, this is the traditional view introduced by Smith in analysing the manufacture of pins, and also of Marx, even if Marx described ownership in this way in order to debunk it.

Clearly, property ownership cannot be understood in the same way, when an increasing share of the value created by the corporation does not depend on technology or if it is essentially the product of the specialist expertise of certain employees. 'The capital of my corporation goes down every evening – when it takes the elevator and walks out the door' is the ironic but lucid way the director of one of the biggest French investment banks described this issue, implying that several hundred employees were largely responsible for the value added by the bank. If they were to leave and not come back, the value of the corporation would also disappear. Similarly, a pharmaceutical company, even if it uses the most sophisticated technologies in its laboratories, is dependent on a handful of leading researchers whose genius will lead to the discovery of the next blockbuster drug that ensures the survival of the corporation. In other words, these researchers own the corporation's essential means of value creation. What does ownership in the corporation then mean, if shareholders, by definition, cannot own the people who create value and who can *freely* leave and enter into contracts with competitors? With the increasing importance of knowledge in the production processes of so many industries, such examples are multiplying rapidly, providing evidence of a new kind of fragmentation: to the extent that human capital plays a part in the corporation, property ownership continues to fragment.

The challenge, in the coming years, will be to recognize and properly attribute the contribution of human capital, much as one has been able to recognize technological capital by new methods of financial evaluation. Pioneering research is already underway in this area, and this will no doubt change the way we look at property and corporate governance.[4] In addition to the fragmentation of material property as represented by financial capital, we will have to consider the fragmentation

---

[4] We are thinking of the works of Margaret Blair: M. Blair, *Ownership and Control: Re-Thinking Corporate Governance for the Twenty-First Century*, Washington, DC: Brookings Institute, 1995; M. Blair, 'Closing the theory gap: how the economic theory of property rights can help bring "stakeholders" back into theories of the firm', *Journal of Management and Governance* 9 (2005),

of human capital. In the modern liberal system, human capital is the inalienable right of the individual. It is therefore to be expected that the increased importance of human capital will lead to significant new questions about the exercise of direction over the corporation. If our hypothesis is correct, the recognition of human capital will result in further democratization in corporate governance, making the structures of representation more complex and the exercise of authority more difficult. Since human capital has not yet been intellectually theorized or practically organized in as thorough a manner as financial capital, we are only at the beginning of these changes.

Between global and deeply rooted: the place of the individual under public governance

In looking out over the future of corporate governance in the world, a third question presents itself: is it possible that corporate governance will become global, that is to say no longer rooted in any particular country or economic space? The fragmentation of property ownership in the largest corporations points in this direction – shareholders are not only more and more numerous, they are also multinational and, what's more, increasingly indifferent about the economic or political environment they operate in. A fund manager who is mandated by a pension fund typically does not define his overall portfolio in terms of the nationality of the pension fund or the corporation. He/she will only look at the numbers, the perspectives, the value he/she can obtain from his/her investment strategy. Whether the fund manager is American, French, or German does not enter the calculation per se, except when the risks and opportunities associated

33–9; or the new theory of property rights articulated by Rajan and Zingales: G. Rajan and L. Zingales, 'The influence of the financial revolution on the nature of firms', *American Economic Review* 91 (2) (2001), 203–11; G. Rajan and L. Zingales, *Saving Capitalism from the Capitalists*, New York: Crown Business, 2003. Of course, stakeholder theory has also explored these perspectives, starting with the early contributions of E. Freeman (*Strategic Management: A Stakeholder Approach*, Marshfield, MA: Pitman Press, 1983). What we have wanted to show in this book is that democratization and corporate governance are closely linked, *even if* one restricts consideration to shareholder theory; this is why we demonstrate democratization of corporate governance not in reference to opening up the corporation to stakeholders, but rather in reference to the fragmentation of property rights that of itself necessitates the opening of the corporation.

with each country are considered. Indeed, the fund manager may even prefer that all the corporations he/she invests in are country-less, since this would avoid any kind of political imbroglios, when factory closures, restructurings, or mergers are considered. In this way, fragmentation of property ownership contributes to separate the corporation to some degree from its home country, as well as from the nationality of the bulk of its shareholders.

The same thing can be said about the executives: the spread of business across borders implies that managers have themselves become persons without countries, that is to say indifferent about whether or not the corporation is locally rooted. For such executives, but also for many managers operating locally for multinational corporations around the world, any notion of local roots for the corporation is becoming harder to define and harder to defend. Thus, from the points of view of both the shareholders and the managers, the corporation tends to lose its ties to the 'home' country. In this sense, perhaps, corporate governance may be able to realize the age-old dream of 'global governance', as sceptically discussed by Immanuel Kant at the beginning of the modern liberal era.[5] Multinational corporations are organizations that overcome local idiosyncrasies and allow business to benefit to the maximum from the opportunities offered by different competence and employment zones.[6]

The positive vision of global governance also has a negative side: whereas capital and management may be global, the *governed* (the employee, the individual shareholder) are commonly strongly rooted in a particular locale. They live and work in a country, start a family and build a house there. Whatever the future brings in terms of reduced international constraints to the movement of people or improved travel conditions, the flexibility of labour will always be much smaller than the flexibility of capital. One can transfer 10 million dollars from one side of the world to the other with a simple click of the mouse, but one can never move people as simply. Human beings become enrooted in social and cultural environments and need these to live and to grow. Not only do these environments protect the human being, they also permit the individual to develop his/her human and social capital.

---

[5] See I. Kant, *Zum ewigen Frieden*, 1791.
[6] Cf. M. Porter, *The Competitive Advantage of Nations*, New York: Free Press, 1990.

If one ties these considerations together, it is possible to detect a growing risk of divorce: large corporations risk becoming further and further removed from their own employees, their suppliers, and their clients. Whereas from the point of view of the *governing* the corporation is global, without a home, from the point of view of the *governed* the corporation is local, situated in its social, cultural, and economic environment. As a consequence, corporate governance in a world without borders turns out to be more complicated than it would appear at first glance. The global legitimacy earned by the executives and financial capital may be contradicted and even fought by the local legitimacy arising from the fact that the corporation is enrooted in particular environments that the governed will do their utmost to conserve. The strategy of the globally operating corporation may have no link whatsoever anymore with the strategy of the local environment in which the corporation plays a part. If this vision of the future takes hold in practice, the democratization of corporate governance is likely to be confronted with the same difficulties that more and more political democracies are encountering: a separation or divorce between the legitimacy of those who govern at higher, global levels (Europe, the United States, the United Nations) and those who are governed and seek their points of reference at local levels such as their town or their region. In the same way, the unity of corporate governance could be defied by the multiplication of social and cultural environments that may come to hold the primary allegiance of the governed: employee groupings, supplier associations, communities. This could have serious consequences for the formulation and implementation of global strategies. The emergence of local interests and identities is also a result of social fragmentation: large, globally active corporations may increasingly have to combat communitarian economic challenges and new entrepreneurial forces that are locally anchored.

The questions we have posed here help us understand how the tendencies described in this book may play out over time, but they do not exhaust the subject. The democratization of corporate governance is underway, because the corporation is but another form of organization of modern liberal society, and democracy is the model of reference for governance in that society. We will therefore see democratization of corporate governance continue, more rapidly in some environments than in others according to the economic conditions, but, we believe, *inexorably*. In adopting this point of view, we echo Tocqueville's well-known democracy hypothesis. To Tocqueville, all of history could be read as the slow but inexorable struggle of the collective values underlying democracy, namely the values of fairness and equality of condition, to assert themselves. It was Tocqueville's central hypothesis that democracy constitutes the sole model of acceptable governance in modern society and will eventually prevail in all spheres of organized activity.

When one runs through the pages of our [European] history, one finds so to speak no great event in seven hundred years that has not turned to the profit of equality.... In whichever direction we cast a glance we perceive the same revolution continuing in all the Christian universe. Everywhere the various incidents in the lives of peoples are seen to turn to the profit of democracy ... The gradual development of equality of conditions is, therefore, a providential fact and it has all the principal characteristics of one: it is universal, enduring, each day escapes human power; all events, like all men serve its development ... To wish to stop democracy would then appear to be to struggle against God itself and it would only remain for nations to accommodate themselves to the social state that Providence imposes on them. ... It appears to me beyond doubt that sooner or later we shall arrive, like the Americans, at an almost complete equality.[7]

In subscribing to Tocqueville's democracy hypothesis, we do not, for a moment, wish to imply that democratization of corporate governance does not present considerable challenges – to the contrary, these challenges are of great concern, and we hope to have given some idea of their magnitude. A clear tendency can be determined, for better or for worse: this tendency towards democratization does not end history or close the future, but rather it opens up the door for major changes in the governance of corporations, changes that are likely to be as significant and as unexpected as those corporate governance has already undergone, over the last two centuries.

[7] *DA*, Introduction, pp. 6–12.

Index